BUSINESS WRITING TODAY

A Practical Guide

Second Edition

*This book is dedicated to
Greg, my personal gold standard.*

BUSINESS WRITING TODAY

A PRACTICAL GUIDE

Second Edition

Natalie Canavor

New York University

Los Angeles | London | New Delhi
Singapore | Washington DC | Boston

Los Angeles | London | New Delhi
Singapore | Washington DC | Boston

FOR INFORMATION:

SAGE Publications, Inc.
2455 Teller Road
Thousand Oaks, California 91320
E-mail: order@sagepub.com

SAGE Publications Ltd.
1 Oliver's Yard
55 City Road
London EC1Y 1SP
United Kingdom

SAGE Publications India Pvt. Ltd.
B 1/I 1 Mohan Cooperative Industrial Area
Mathura Road, New Delhi 110 044
India

SAGE Publications Asia-Pacific Pte. Ltd.
3 Church Street
#10-04 Samsung Hub
Singapore 049483

Printed in the United States of America

Cataloging-in-publication data is available from the Library of Congress.

ISBN 978-1-4833-5866-6

This book is printed on acid-free paper.

SFI Certified Sourcing
www.sfiprogram.org
SFI-00453

Acquisitions Editor: Maggie Stanley
Editorial Assistant: Nicole Mangona
Production Editor: Olivia Weber-Stenis
Copy Editor: Megan Markanich
Typesetter: C&M Digitals (P) Ltd.
Proofreader: Victoria Reed-Castro
Indexer: Jeanne R. Busemeyer
Cover Designer: Gail Buschman
Marketing Manager: Liz Thornton

15 16 17 18 19 10 9 8 7 6 5 4 3 2

Brief Table of Contents

TABLE OF CONTENTS

PREFACE

This book is for you if

- ✓ you're preparing to begin your career in business, communications or a profession;
- ✓ you're already engaged in a career but want a competitive advantage to help you advance;
- ✓ you're a technology, science or other specialist and want to brush up your contemporary writing skills; or
- ✓ you're an entrepreneur who writes proposals, websites, marketing materials and blogs and wants to make them better.

Today, everybody writes. From everyday e-mails to customer communications, reports to tweets, business writing is a make-or-break skill for just about every career path. Digital technology keeps expanding the possible: It enables us to reach people anywhere in the world and find opportunities. It levels the playing field so small and new businesses can compete with giants. It empowers us to communicate what we can do and who we are to huge audiences and draw selected people to us.

The price of admission is writing—*good* writing, to be more specific.

This book's goal is to show you how to stand out, whatever your endeavor and aspirations. It may differ from other books on writing you've worked with. Rather than focusing on theory or grammar, *Business Writing Today* is based on the author's practical experience as a magazine editor, corporate communicator, journalist and public relations consultant.

It's also based on a history of helping professional communicators and businesspeople write better and more recently, teaching advanced writing seminars for M.S. students in NYU's Public Relations and Corporate Communications program.

Business Writing Today equips you to dramatically improve your writing in two ways.

First, it shows you how to strategize everything you write to achieve your goals, both immediate and long-range. You'll emerge with a structured process for thinking through the content, style and tone of everything you write with confidence.

Second, it gives you professional tips and practical techniques to identify your own writing problems and fix them. The ideas are all demonstrated with examples that relate to the messages and documents you'll need to write e-mails, memos, letters, executive summaries, reports, proposals, profiles, networking messages, websites, blogs, presentations, news releases and more.

Complete with assignments, discussion ideas and projects, the book is designed for the classroom. It is also written as a friendly and accessible self-help tool for independent use. Readers will find many ways to make their writing more immediately successful plus tools to sustain their own progress.

If you're familiar with the predecessor edition—*Business Writing in the Digital Age*—you'll find a substantial reorganization, new material and examples, more resources and activities, and many updates. A new chapter provides a toolbox of journalism and PR techniques—how to write news releases, talking points and headlines, and tips for research and interviewing. An expanded chapter on writing for the job hunt brings together guidelines for successful résumés, cover letters and networking. Internal memo writing is covered in its own right, and an expanded presentation skills chapter shows you how to tell your own story and plan presentations.

New View from the Field sidebars, contributed by specialists, offer additional ways to think about effective messages and documents. And more Success Tip features show you how to use communication skills to achieve your personal goals.

This new edition draws on thoughtful input from teachers who use the book and reviewers who generously offered guidance on how to make *Business Writing Today* more useful and valuable.

I'm happy to hear *your* ideas, comments, and questions about the book or any aspect of business writing. Find me at natalie@canavorcommunications.com.

ACKNOWLEDGMENTS

This new edition was gracefully supported by editor Maggie Stanley, whose enthusiasm for the project was so sustaining, and Megan Markanich, whose careful copyediting improved the presentation—thank you! As more SAGE people stepped in to supply their expertise, I've appreciated the high level of professionalism and caring shown by all, including Catherine Forrest, Olivia Weber-Stenis and Nicole Mangona.

Appreciation also goes to my agent, Stacey Czarnowski of Studio B, always responsive and helpful. And I am more than grateful to all my colleagues who generously shared their professional insights and techniques in the three dozen-plus View from the Field features that amplify my own experience. I feel privileged to know every one of you.

And special thanks to the reviewers who provided thoughtful critiques, ideas and suggestions to make *Business Writing Today* a yet-more effective tool for teaching and learning: Allen Mogol, New York University; Antoinette Larkin, University of Cincinnati; Brenda Nevidjon, Duke University; Tim Green, University of Michigan; Steve Thompson, New York University; and Kimberly Laux, University of Michigan-Flint.

Part I

A Structured Planning System for All Your Communication

Chapter 1

BUSINESS WRITING IN THE DIGITAL AGE—AND YOU

LEARN . . .

- Why good writing matters
- How employers view writing
- The value of writing to you
- How to use this book

When I give workshops for businesspeople, I often ask them to describe the writing they like to read. Invariably, they offer a list of attributes that include:

Clear	To the point
Concise	Obvious purpose
Easy to understand	Reader oriented
Conversational	Jargon free

These characteristics add up to a pretty good definition of contemporary, reader-friendly business writing that achieves its goals.

So if everyone intuitively knows how to describe good writing, why do so few people write that way?

Common experience tells us that most business writing is exactly the opposite: unclear, wordy, stilted, unfocused, full of jargon and not oriented to the reader.

Here are a few reasons why we're surrounded by so much terrible business writing.

First, practical writing is rarely taught in school. Typically we learn academic writing, which aims to demonstrate what we know and please the teacher. It values erudite language, abstract thought and precise grammar. Most of this is contrary to good business writing.

Second, because most people don't learn to write well during their school years, they conclude that they lack natural talent and can't learn. This book is here to tell you that's not true: I promise you can write infinitely better, once you understand what good business writing looks like and sounds like and absorb some easy step-by-step processes to guide decisions on content, style and language.

A third reason so many people don't develop their abilities is because they think learning to write isn't much fun. But that's based on the school model. In the business world, it's not about rules. Good writing is about understanding other people and what motivates them, clarifying your own goals and strategizing your messages to achieve those goals.

Good writing is not "a way with words"—ultimately, it's good thinking. This book gives you techniques and tools that help you think more clearly and therefore write better.

That's not to say that basic correctness doesn't count: We need other people to understand our messages and not get bogged down by annoying mistakes. But grammar and punctuation are the servants of ideas, not the masters. And the good news is that you can improve the technical side of your writing with some commonsense ways to spot problems and fix them.

The time you invest in improving how you write will reward you well.

WHY EMPLOYERS VALUE WRITING

Once upon a time, few people needed to write. They did business in person or worked in places where professional specialists were responsible for most communication. Managers typically depended on support staff to correct and improve their documents.

The digital revolution came and all this changed. Soon after, computers replaced typewriters, and people found themselves writing everyday messages on their own. As communication channels grew from e-mail to websites and more recently, blogs and social media, more and more people were called on to write. Plus, there seems to be an ever-increasing mountain of material that needs writing. Today's media offer organizations and individuals infinite ways to be heard and known—but all require writing.

It's taken the business world a while to catch up to this reality. But the realization is dawning.

Good business writing saves time and money. It prevents mistakes and helps solve problems. It bridges time zones and culture gaps, connecting people. It empowers individuals and helps organizations succeed.

Unfortunately, the general quality of writing in the business, government and not-for-profit worlds is dismal. The evidence for this is not just anecdotal. Recent research studies demonstrate that bad writing is a significant challenge to American industry. Writing that comes from government agencies, for its part, is considered so bad that a federal law was passed—the Plain Writing Act of 2010—which mandates that all documents aimed at the public be clearly written.

In business circles, far more attention has been given to face-to-face communication than writing. In-person skills are, of course, critical. But there's no way around the fact that writing is the key communication tool of the 21st century. Everything we do from planning to marketing to interacting with other people depends at pivotal stages on what we write. Even media we think of as visual or oral need to be written—for example, websites, speeches, PowerPoint presentations, video. From everyday e-mails and social media posts to websites, proposals and business plans, the written word makes or breaks us.

Why do so many people seem oblivious to the new importance of writing? It can be hard to view the big picture when we're living in it. The past 10 years have seen major shifts in how we work and behave. Technology empowers us to communicate quickly and globally. By enabling us to reach people anywhere, bring them to us and directly interact, it's reversing centuries of one-way, top-down communication.

We haven't even begun to realize how this shift affects us. To begin with, we now live in an opt-in world. Possibly excepting political despots or rulers of multibillion-dollar empires, no one any longer owns a captive audience. People are not obliged to read what you write—they must choose to. Readers' attention must be earned.

Further, the digital revolution affects how we relate to one another in basic ways. It enables a growing number of people to work at home or in remote locations and rely on virtual teaming. Through online media, we can collaborate with people we may never see across national boundaries—and across the corridor. In many an office, people come to work each day and text or e-mail each other instead of talking.

Across the generations we're using the telephone less, too, and moving steadily toward written, voice-free exchanges.

The bottom line: The new range of communication options doesn't just supplement the traditional varieties or speed up delivery. It is transforming how we relate. We talk less and meet less. The channels we rely on all demand one thing—writing. But just as this huge need to write well becomes understood, the skill proves hard to come by.

BAD WRITERS LOSE OPPORTUNITIES

The most significant report on the importance of writing in business remains *Writing: A Ticket to Work . . . or a Ticket Out,* issued in 2004 by the National Commission on Writing for America's Families, Schools, and Colleges. A year earlier, the same group issued *The Neglected "R": The Need for a Writing Revolution,* a benchmark study. Both reports were hard on the schools for failing to teach adequate writing skills. Here are a few findings:

- People who cannot write and communicate clearly will not be hired and are unlikely to be employed long enough to be considered for promotion.
- Half of all companies take writing ability into account when making promotion decisions.
- Eighty percent or more of companies in the finance and service, insurance, and real estate (FIRE) sectors—the corporations with the greatest employment growth potential—assess writing during hiring.

About one third of respondents said that one third or fewer of their current and new employees possess writing skills that companies value. As far back as 2004, companies were spending more than $3 billion annually on writing remediation.

HOW EMPLOYERS SEE WRITING

Smart leaders know that poor proposals don't win projects, indifferent reports don't provide useful platforms for decision making and stale websites don't accomplish their goals.

Fuzzy communication can capsize the most expensive efforts to keep customers, employees, stockholders and donors happy. It also prevents organizations from demonstrating transparency and building trust, both essential to today's corporations, nonprofits and government agencies alike.

Moreover, most businesses and government offices must maintain expensive customer support functions to handle consumer complaints resulting from poor instructions—the primary reason people contact organizations. And some industries, such as aerospace and automotive, find that a high percentage of accidents and disasters trace to inadequate records, muddy cross-departmental memos and poor descriptions of problems.

On a day-to-day basis, poor communication impairs overall organizational efficiency. When everyday messages are unclear, incomplete or even irrelevant—as many are—untallied fortunes must be invested to rectify errors and remedy bad feelings.

And all well-run organizations share an imperative: to engage and motivate employees. In large part this is accomplished by good communication practices. Writing-based information systems encourage the staff on all levels to understand the company mission, stay informed, learn new ways of working and contribute their best efforts to the community all are part of.

Leaders "listen" to employees and respond most often in writing, too. Change management—the art of adapting organizations to function better in a shifting environment—is wholly tied to good communication.

For a long time writing has been devalued in the private sector—it was the redheaded stepchild in the communications food chain. But the shift to a knowledge based economy meant it was only a matter of time before people recognized that writing matters a lot, that strong clear compelling content affects the bottom line. But now they do. The realization is dawning at a time when even in communication firms, the number of people who can write is actually dwindling. As the millennials rise, their skills are very poor.

—Dan Gerstein, president/ founder of Gotham Ghostwriters and political consultant, analyst and commentator

There's even more: In addition to transforming how most messages are written and delivered, the digital revolution has given most organizations an ever-hungry set of channels via the Internet. Every business, nonprofit and government office alike is faced with an endless demand for new material to draw people to online sites, maintain their interest and bring them back.

Even the art of selling, traditionally a face-to-face endeavor, depends on producing the right written message somewhere along the way. Most organizations today center their marketing, customer relations and publicity efforts on their Internet presence. As a result, more and more employees are called on to contribute to this enterprise.

No wonder so many employers cite writing as one of the top requirements for hiring and promoting. And no wonder a growing number of them give their job candidates a writing test—no matter what level job they're competing for.

GOOD WRITING—AND YOU

If you are currently preparing for your career, expect that you need writing to win opportunities and communicate who you are. Your résumé, cover letters and social media presence must be outstanding. And you may well have to pass that writing test.

Once employed, you'll find writing at the core of everyday life wherever you work. Your immediate or future jobs may require letters, memos, e-mails and reports; blogging and social media posting; PowerPoint presentations; and an elevator speech to introduce yourself to colleagues and others in your industry.

Professionals and specialists of every kind, too, find that they must regularly write most of this material and perhaps articles and funding applications. Do you dream of owning your own business some day? As an entrepreneur, you'll have everything to gain from good writing because digital media levels the playing field. Virtually anyone can compete with long-established enterprises and directly connect with customers, the media, investors and collaborators—if their writing works well.

In sum, whatever your immediate and future career aspirations, writing gives you a unique opportunity to outmatch your competition.

Develop your writing skills and you are more likely to be hired, better able to build the positive image you want and better prepared to prove your value. You will, in fact, be more valuable. If you question this premise, think about people you've worked with who were identified as early rising stars. Good writing is often one of the abilities that distinguishes them. Consider, too, all the people hired off the Internet because they write good tweets, blogs or comments.

Writing well on the job makes you more efficient because people who get your messages understand them.

You succeed more often because you're more likely to get the response you want.

You're able to showcase your competence, capabilities, professionalism and resourcefulness with good everyday messages and major documents when called for.

And, online media open up new vistas for you, just as for organizations: The Internet gives you amazing access to people you want to reach. You can't show up in a CEO's office, but you can deliver a well-thought-out comment or idea through an in-house channel or the web.

One more incentive to develop your writing is this: It is an indispensable—if generally unheralded—leadership asset. Good communication skills are always cited as an essential tool of good leaders. But we often ignore the role of writing, despite the fact that it is one of only two basic ways human beings communicate. We tend to forget that writing is our memory—the foundation upon which civilization and knowledge have been built.

We've made writing a much bigger part of our focus and our screening process, because if people can't learn to write they're relegated to a lesser role. We give a writing test asking candidates to distill down the ideas from a batch of documents as if they were writing a quick policy brief with a limited number of words. We assess the clarity of their communication and also how they were able to take in, understand and express various ideas.

—Erin Mathews, director of Iraq Programs, National Democratic Institute (an international development agency)

BUSINESS WRITING REDEFINED FOR THE DIGITAL AGE

All this doesn't mean that writing skills must be mastered in the traditional way. While many principles of good writing hold steady—and give you a foundation to depend on—the academic, literary style most of us learn in school doesn't work in business.

Here are some of the essentials of how to write for the digital age:

- Write to engage and be clear, simple and conversational.
- Write strategically, using every piece of writing as a tool for accomplishing immediate and long-range goals—both your own and your organization's.
- Frame every message and document in terms of *you,* not *I,* and make it instantly clear why the reader should care.
- Plan messages to take better account of our opt-in world by understanding your readers and their viewpoints.
- Employ the proven techniques of persuasion and advocacy to state your case and represent your interests.
- Write for an overscheduled, information-loaded, low attention span, impatient and skeptical audience—which is all of them.
- Write in ways that foster dialogue and interaction.
- Write for a globalized world with many nonnative English speakers and many who don't speak English at all and will read translations.
- Write, consciously, in ways that build and maintain relationships.

The last point is an especially important takeaway. An environment that leads us to interact through writing rather than face-to-face is depersonalizing, even dehumanizing. It starves us for warmth and authenticity. We need to purposely counter this drift by writing more caringly. The curt, abrupt style that texting and instant messaging foster does not contribute to relationship building.

Especially with ever-faster delivery speed, we've become careless of how our messages make other people feel. The fact that we communicate without hearing tone of voice or seeing visual cues leads us to chilly exchanges where we not only lack the in-person advantage but also miss the cues that a written message can contain.

Digital media benefit from personalization in a different way. Even though we're writing for unknown and unseen

---

A nonprofit's messaging is critical to success. You need support from the community, donors, funders—and the only way you can get that word out is through writing: websites, brochures, appeal letters, reports to funders. Writing is even more important today because everyone is seeking the same amount of money from a more limited pool. Someone who can communicate powerfully and effectively will always go straight to the top. When we do executive searches we don't even pass a letter with an error on to the next level.

—Ann Marie Thigpen,
director of the Center for
Nonprofit Leadership at
Adelphi University

---

audiences when we blog or contribute to an online conversation, individual voice is an asset. Readers respond to the sense of warmth, spontaneity and authenticity that the best bloggers generate.

The bottom line: If you want to inspire trust, build teams, motivate subordinates, cultivate relationships with colleagues or clients, influence people, keep customers, be someone other people want to know better, or just want to get things done, then use the tools of thoughtful writing. Aim not just to be clear but also warm and empathetic. You'll be repaid hundreds of times over for this investment of energy.

This book will help you with all these needs. They are all a part of better writing.

The goal is to make you a more confident, capable, and resourceful writer able to approach any writing need with confidence. You'll find, too, that building this skill will help you clarify your thinking process—something that always comes in handy.

THE PLAIN LANGUAGE MOVEMENT ADVANCES

Two Washington, D.C.–based groups are advocates for clarity in all government communications. Both work to promote awareness of clear writing and provide training. The government group Plain Language Action and Information Network (www.plainlanguage .gov) was founded in the mid-1900s. The private-sector, nonprofit Center for Plain Language (www.centerforplainlanguage.org) was established in 2003. The movement's biggest achievement to date is passage of the Plain Writing Act signed by the President in October 2010 (P.L. 111-274). The act requires government agencies to use plain language in documents directed to the public and to train their employees to apply guidelines such as simplicity, brevity, plain words and clear organization. How compliance will be enforced is not yet clear. The full Plain Writing Act is posted at www.plainlanguage.gov.

The Plain Language movement is also international—check out the Plain Language Association International at plainlanguagenetwork.org and www.clarity-international.net.

VIEW FROM THE FIELD: GOVERNMENT-SPEAK MEETS THE PLAIN LANGUAGE MOVEMENT

We define plain language as something your intended readers can understand and use the first time they read it. Given that, I don't believe there's any material that cannot be put in plain language. In fact, if it's very technical there's an even greater responsibility to put it into plain language.

We understand the Plain Language Act is not a silver bullet, but its passage has brought the writing problem more to the forefront and hopefully agencies will really start to take notice. It's important that Congress made a statement that this is important. It will affect what the

(Continued)

(Continued)

government produces that goes out to the public, and we believe that if government writes better, it will leak into the business world.

We believe that communicating clearly improves an organization's bottom line and helps it give better customer service. A lot of people think that using all those big words leads people to respect them more—but studies show this is just not true. People who write clearly are thought to be better educated or smarter.

Why don't people complain more? I think they take it for granted that the government puts out stuff they can't understand and that's the way the world is. It's very frustrating.

—Annetta Cheek, board chair, Center for Plain Language
(check out the annual awards program for the best and
worst writing at www.centerforplainlanguage.org/awards)

HOW TO USE THIS BOOK

Preferably, work with this book in the sequence presented. The chapters lead you through a natural learning progression. After considering the strategic nature of writing, you'll develop the practical skills of clear expression. Subsequent chapters cover the various major areas of writing with a focus on how to apply the basic process you're mastering and the differences involved in producing each kind of document.

The premise is that you can build the capacity to handle more complex documents by starting with everyday messages. When you know how to write an e-mail that achieves its goal, you're a long way toward writing a powerful proposal. The strategies are basically the same.

View From the Field insets offer practical tips and guidance from a wide range of specialists including professional communicators, psychologists, negotiators, businesspeople, graphic designers and experts on specific kinds of writing.

Success Tip features offer practical, useful ideas to help you stand out from the crowd.

You'll find that sometimes one contributor's insights somewhat contradict another's—or don't completely align with my viewpoint. Writing is not a science. There are many ways to successfully write the same message, and there are many different legitimate ideas of what works. Plus, we differ from one another. A technique that's successful for one person may not help someone else.

So read with an open mind and absorb all the ideas and strategies. Adopt those that resonate for you. Engage in the **Practice Opportunities** at each chapter's end. Many of the examples and activities are drawn from "real-world" situations like those you will encounter on the job.

I hope that in addition to assembling your own repertoire of concepts, techniques and tricks of the trade to make you a better writer, you will emerge from this book with a new energy for writing and find it more enjoyable. And that beyond improving your ability to express yourself more clearly and forcefully, you'll absorb the central idea this book is built on—that writing is a strategic tool and that everything you write matters.

Business writing is part craft, part psychology, part negotiation, part management strategy and part detective work. Build your practical skills, but also exercise your imagination. You'll find yourself well compensated, because when your writing succeeds, you succeed.

PRACTICE OPPORTUNITIES

I. Write a Memo to Yourself

Think about the career path you're preparing for. What written materials do you anticipate being called on to write? List them, including both the everyday kinds of communication (perhaps e-mails, tweets and social media posts) and formal business documents such as various kinds of reports, proposals, website material and so on. For each entry on your list, write down what a well-written message might gain you.

II. Start a Personal Reference Resource of Strong Writing

This week, collect at least three examples of writing you like from any arena such as newspapers, magazines, online articles, blogs, and book excerpts. For each one, write a paragraph explaining why you chose it. Start a file, organized however you like, to keep the examples in. Plan to add at least one example per week on an ongoing basis.

III. Group Discussion

In a group of four or five, share one or more of the examples you collected for Activity II. Discuss: Does everyone agree on the quality of each example? If not, what are the reasons for disagreement? What generalizations can you make as a group about the characteristics of good writing? Does this give you any ideas about the ways you'd like to improve your own writing and what you want to learn from this book?

Chapter 2

WRITING TO ACCOMPLISH GOALS

Build the Foundation for Every Message

LEARN HOW TO . . .

- View writing as a strategic tool
- Plan messages based on goals
- Frame messages for your audiences
- Maneuver generation gaps
- Write to groups, gatekeepers, and the universe

How do I know what I think until I see what I write.

—E. M. Forster, British novelist

Yes, it's how to get things done, open doors, and connect with people and immediate opportunities. But effective writing does far more than accomplish the goal of the moment: It's a powerful tool for achieving your long-range ambitions, a tool to use consciously.

From e-mails to proposals to blogs to résumés, every message offers a chance to build toward your future. The better your writing, the more you'll succeed. Writing gives you one of the best ways to showcase your strengths and demonstrate your value.

This chapter gives you a framework for planning all your documents and making the right decisions about content, structure, and style.

WHY PLANNING IS ESSENTIAL

Effective writers don't just plunge into any written communication—first, they plan. And always, they begin with two questions that guide them through every necessary decision.

Question 1: What's my goal? What do I want?

Question 2: Who—exactly—is the audience, the person I'm writing to?

When you define your goal and consider audience characteristics, it becomes much easier to figure out the content, your key messages—the facts, ideas, or arguments that will make your document successful. And once you've systematically determined content, organizing it becomes a more natural process. You'll also be able to decide what tone the message should take.

Whether writing a letter, a report or a tweet, professional writers base everything on how the factors of goal and audience intersect. Thinking this through may mean spending more time up front than you're used to. But having a plan saves time on the writing itself, and your results will be so much better—immediately—that you'll feel well rewarded.

But why does even a "simple" e-mail merit such thought?

Perhaps you've clicked Send for one or more of the following:

- A carelessly written message to a superior or colleague that ends up forwarded right up the company hierarchy
- An embarrassing e-mail to a friend that you assumed was private but instead was widely circulated
- A badly executed cover letter for a job application that showed up on the Internet as a laughable example
- A message meant for one person that instead went to a whole group or someone who in particular should not have seen it, like a competitor

Remember the long run, too. E-mails never go away. As we see in scandal after scandal in the corporate and political worlds, they can always be retrieved to embarrass or, in a worst-case scenario, indict you. All these possible mistakes apply to social media and other digital channels, too.

Building a great reputation in any setting is a step-by-step, long-range process. *Use every message to present yourself in the way you want to be seen.* In fact, because e-mail is so important to the everyday business flow in nearly every organization, it's a stellar chance to continuously showcase yourself and impress others.

Let's look at our two basic questions in more depth.

Before everything else, getting ready is the secret of success.

—Henry Ford

STEP 1: IDENTIFYING YOUR SHORT- AND LONG-RANGE GOALS

First, Look Past the Obvious

In our early education, most of us had the same goal when assigned to write something, whether a term paper, book review, report or essay: Please the teacher and get a good grade. But in the business world, you need to know your goal for every piece of writing. What do you want to accomplish with the document? What's the desired outcome? What do you want the person to do as a result of your message?

This can be trickier than it looks at first glance. Suppose, for example, you're inviting a group of people to a meeting. Your immediate or primary purpose is to get people together at the right time and place. If that's all you want, you just need to say

Attend a meeting to plan the White Proposal, Thursday 2:00 p.m., Room 123.

But if you're running the meeting, you must make it productive. This may mean motivating attendees to feel enthusiastic. You may want them to think about the subject beforehand and come prepared with thoughtful contributions, which demands that you supply an agenda.

So your message might better say:

This Thursday at 2:00 p.m., we'll hold the kickoff meeting to plan the White Proposal. This is a terrific opportunity to land a project that will stretch our capabilities and establish our niche. Please think about the role your unit can play in developing the proposal, and come with ideas for our brainstorming. The agenda is attached.

This version frames the meeting enthusiastically—enthusiasm is contagious!—and also energizes the readers: You've told them that the opportunity is big, and their role might be significant. You've also promoted a team feeling, always more engaging than a directive.

But if you're addressing people on distinctly different levels, there's more to consider. Whether the readers are project teammates or supervisors, every message is a tool for building relationships—or damaging them. So it must take account of how you relate to the recipients: their status in the organization, stake in the subject, expected contribution to the meeting and so on.

A message to your subordinate might begin:

Jerry: Please plan on attending Thursday's meeting on the White Proposal.

If you're inviting your supervisor, you'd do well to say something like this:

Dear Joan: I've set up the meeting on the White Proposal for Thursday at 2:00 p.m., in line with your schedule. Every unit will be represented and I've put your intro first on the agenda, which is attached.

Certainly when you're on the job, even a simple message must reinforce your professional image with superiors, colleagues, collaborators, suppliers and everyone else you're writing to. It should contribute to your relationships in a positive way. And in addition to representing your organization's multilevel interests well, it should ideally contribute to your own long-range goals.

If that sounds like a lot of weight for a simple e-mail to carry, then how much thought should go into a complex document like a proposal or report?

Often, quite a lot. But fortunately, the process I'm demonstrating applies to every kind of document, both digital and print, and after a while can be applied intuitively. Practice with everyday materials pays off with the "important" documents. At heart, good writing is good thinking, so developing your writing skills also helps you in general. You'll be better able to define and solve problems, engage others, manage their perceptions and influence their actions.

Define Goals to Shift Your Vision

Closely identifying a document's purpose—or the role it plays to accomplish a purpose—can be surprisingly helpful. The cover letter you write for a proposal, for example, need not bear the burden of selling your product or service. It just needs to set the stage for the reader to view the proposal itself in a favorable light and demonstrate that you've read the specs very carefully and understand the problem.

Cover letters for résumés similarly need not summarize your credentials. They should promote interest in reading the résumé by highlighting what a good match you are with the job (and by showing that you write well). The résumé's job, in turn, is to get you an interview.

Being clear on goals gives you important guidelines, whatever the medium. And it can save you from falling into a lot of common traps and unnecessary mistakes.

Put Your Goals Analysis to Work

Here's how to begin your new systematic writing strategy: Practice writing down and defining as closely as you can the "goal" of every message you send on as many levels that apply.

Goals for the meeting invitation may include:

1. The basic action or response you want (planning to show up)

2. The below-surface response you want to achieve (enthusiasm and commitment to being prepared)

3. Your organization's goals for the meeting (e.g., a productive event that produces useful input and can be referred to in a progress report)

4. Your personal long-range goals

Goal 4 is important because when you're conscious of your personal goals, you automatically act in line with them.

You recognize opportunities you might otherwise overlook for a productive contact or an extra assignment. And you see ways to build toward your goals in almost every message you write, whether an e-mail or a report or a presentation.

For example:

Bill has been elected a board member of his professional association. No one ran against him, so he doesn't take it seriously at first. He dashes off a memo to his boss:

Mark, guess what, I'm now on the WBEL board. LOL?

Then, he thinks some more and realizes he has an opportunity to

1. raise his profile in the department,

2. strengthen his relationship with the person he reports to, and

3. perhaps bring himself to the attention of higher-ups in a positive light.

He rewrites it this way:

Mark, I'm happy to report that I am now a WBEL board member. I was elected last night. As of June, I'll be involved in all the decision making about programs and venues and, of course, look forward to contributing our company perspective and making new contacts for us.

The inauguration lunch is on May 1, and I'd like to invite you as my personal guest. Can you come?

This message is likely to accomplish all three of Bill's goals.

Note, of course, that the goals you make evident in a piece of writing should never be at odds with those of your employer—unless you're aiming to lose your job. Let's assume for now that your goals and those of your employer are basically aligned (though the more aware you are of your own long-term goals, the more selective you'll feel about where you want to work).

Aim in all your messages to pursue your employer's goals and also your own. That doesn't mean working in self-promotional statements. It means, in all your communications, take the trouble to write as you want to be perceived. Write thoughtfully, using processes demonstrated in this book, and you have the power to build your image over time as someone who's valuable, resourceful, reliable, creative, responsive . . . whatever—you fill in the blanks.

So far, it's been all about "you." Now let's move on to "the other"—the person or group you're writing to.

STEP 2: UNDERSTANDING YOUR AUDIENCE AND HOW TO ANALYZE IT

> *Always try to lift yourself out of your parochial mind-set and find out how other people think and feel. It may not make you a better person in all spheres of life, but it will be a source of continuing kindness to your readers.*
>
> —Steven Pinker, Harvard Professor of Psychology
> and chair of the *American Heritage Dictionary* Usage Panel

Why Audience Analysis Is the Key

When it comes down to it, most messages ask for something. The request may be basic:

Please send me price points for your new product line.

A request may be implicit rather than stated:

Please read this message and absorb the information in it.

And requests can be more overt:

Can we get together next Tuesday to talk about your budget?

or

Can we agree to move the project ahead on this basis?

If you're asking anyone for something—even if it's only to pay attention to the content—you want your message to be properly received. So you must communicate in terms the reader can hear, understand and relate to. Moreover, you must usually give the reader something he or she wants, or considers desirable, for your request to succeed.

If, for example, you want your supervisor to buy you a new computer, you need to match your message to who she is and what argument will make sense to her. Is she a technology buff? Efficiency freak? A must-keep-up-with-other-departments type? Does she have a new computer herself, or is she making do with an outdated one? How does she make decisions—based on data or on impulse? Does she show concern with staff members' well-being and desires? To succeed, you must take account of such factors and a whole lot more.

People are different—in how they perceive, what they value, what they care about and how they make decisions. But there is one universal to count on: self-interest. We react to things and make decisions based on "what's in it for me" (WIIFM). This doesn't mean people are selfish and ungenerous; they may be motivated by a charitable cause, an ideal or belief, or a commitment to what's good for other people above everything else.

But in the business world, if your department head cares about the quarterly profit and loss statement, you can't suggest a workplace improvement because it would make people happy and expect to succeed (unless you could prove that happy people are more productive). If you want to persuade employees that a new benefit is better than one it replaced, telling them how much the company saves will get you nowhere. They want to know how their lives will improve—or at least not suffer—in real-world terms.

The bottom line is that at the same time you define "what I want to achieve" for the message you're writing, you need to systematically analyze "who is the person I want it from"—your audience. It's the only way to determine your best content: what will achieve your goal with the individual or group you're addressing; what to emphasize; and what language, structure and tone will make this message succeed.

GET OUT THERE AND GET REAL

Especially if you're starting a new job or playing a new role in the organization, build a person-to-person pattern of interaction. Send fewer e-mails and digital messages. Instead, walk down the hall, introduce yourself, and look for chances to hold one-on-one conversations. You'll gain a reputation as a "people" person. Colleagues will react more positively to your ideas and requests and you'll find it easier to write good materials and messages. You'll know your readers better and can draw on this knowledge to frame your writing.

Understanding your audience also tells you what communication channel to use. If your boss doesn't like texting, obviously don't make a request that way. But you probably would if you want advice on the best computer from your 16-year-old cousin.

While we instinctively make such decisions all the time, you'll succeed more often in the work environment when you approach a writing challenge methodically.

SOME FACTORS THAT DETERMINE WHO WE ARE

Innumerable factors influence how individuals receive and react to messages. Only some will be relevant to each situation, but take the trouble to develop your awareness of what can matter. Here are some general considerations:

- Age and generation
- Economic status
- Cultural, ethnic, or religious background
- Gender
- Educational level (high school, college, or more)
- Where they grew up and now live
- Role or status in the organization
- Political views
- Values
- What they care about
- What they're interested in

If the person is above you in the organization's hierarchy, it can also be important to know or figure out:

- Problems and challenges: What keeps him up at night?
- Leadership style: Top-down, collaborative, or somewhere in between?
- Management style: Fair, consistent?
- How he or she makes decisions: Slowly or quickly? Based on what?
- Open to new ideas? Willing to take risks?

(Continued)

(Continued)

- Likes confrontation or avoids it?
- Sensitive to people's concerns?
- What makes him happy? Angry?
- Does he or she have a sense of humor? (Assume not)
- Is he or she comfortable with emotions? (Assume not)
- Any apparent pro or con feelings toward people your age? Either gender?

Think also about factors that affect how to communicate with the specific individual.

- What is the person's relationship to you, both by position and inclination?
- How does she prefer to receive information: e-mail, in person, letter, phone, text, social media channel? PowerPoint? Formal or informal reports?
- What kind of explanations does he prefer: Big-picture? Detailed? Logical? Statistical?
- What is the best time of day to approach this particular person? (Salesmen often aim for after lunch.)
- What are his hot buttons?

The nature of your subject may suggest that you also pay attention to factors such as:

- What the supervisor already knows about the subject. And what more might she need to know? Any prior experience with the subject?
- How does she feel about the subject?
- The person's comfort level with technology or the applicable subject matter
- Attitude toward innovation and change
- Whether he prefers ideas that he originates (or thinks he originates)

Communicate Through Personal Filters

If audience analysis sounds like a lot of trouble, consider that a primary purpose of every message is to maintain or establish good relationships. You can't do that without taking account of the individual you're writing to. Further, to achieve your goal, you must choose the right strategy for your document. Putting yourself in someone's mind empowers you to answer this all-important question: What's in it for me? You can't give people what they need if you don't know who they are.

We don't see things as they are; we see them as we are.

—Anais Nin, writer and diarist

Everyone sees the world through an individual "filter" that evolves through a combination of genetics and life history—family background and interaction patterns; temperament; physical appearance; culture, school, and work experience—everything we were born with and that we've experienced. We interpret everything we encounter and that happens to us through this filter, which also determines our expectations, reactions, assumptions and fears.

Don't ever doubt that you see the world through your own filter. The more conscious you become of your filter's characteristics, as well as those of people with whom you need to communicate, the better you'll succeed. *See communication as a bridge between different worldviews and you'll be way ahead in your personal life as well as business life.*

The good news is that once you start thinking about your audience analytically, it becomes second nature. Of course, the higher the stakes, the more thought it's worth. An e-mail or text message asking a friend to meet for lunch won't require a review of his comfort level with new ideas. But if you want to get project approvals from your supervisor or convince a client prospect that you're worth 20 minutes of her time, use audience analysis.

You need to know different things about people according to the nature of your request. If you want the recipient to understand and follow your instructions on how to file for reimbursement, then education level is important. If you need to know how formal to make your message to a client, then her position, age and management style are relevant.

There's another very important reason why knowing your audience pays off: Written communication lacks all the cues we depend on in face-to-face interaction. When we can see other people, we unconsciously adapt what we say—and how we say it—based on their reaction. If we move the conversation in the wrong direction, their facial expression or body language alone signals us to switch focus. Or else they may interrupt us or stop listening.

With written communication, we can't gauge the reader's response. Therefore, provided you want more than a random hit-or-miss success ratio, you need to target the message properly and anticipate response. In a way, you can hold the conversation in your head and write on that basis.

I tell subordinates, don't give me your mediocre material to try out. We need you to produce your best work before you give it to us so we know we can trust you. Otherwise we can't let you deal with the client directly.

—Arik Ben-Zvi, managing director of The Glover Park Group (www.gloverparkgroup .com), a strategic communications firm

Figure Out People You've Never Met

As a trial attorney will tell you, the clues about who someone "is" are everywhere: in what the person says and does, his voice, what he wears and how he wears it, what he reads, how he walks, what he laughs at, how he shakes hands, what his office looks like. If you spend time with people or have access to their work environments, observe. And always listen. Active listening with your whole attention is the best way to understand someone else.

But in a great many instances, you're writing to people you haven't met yet and may never meet. How do you analyze them?

A phone conversation can tell you a lot if you have that opportunity. Listen for the individual's conversational pace—what provokes enthusiasm, any repeated words or phrases that indicate a focus or concern or a way of thinking. One individual may cite numbers often and another may show an interest in people. And, of course, ask direct questions if the context allows, such as "What kind of data would you like to see and at what level of detail?"

VIEW FROM THE FIELD: A PSYCHOLOGIST ON COMMUNICATION

To build rapport and communicate effectively, look past your own perspective and try to understand how someone else sees things. Remember, people are more open to your viewpoint when you make the effort to understand theirs. People have genuinely different ways of looking at things and interacting and you need to respect this right.

Read their cues. Pay attention to how they talk about things and talk in frames of reference they will understand. This helps them make sense of what you're saying and opens up your own capacity for real rapport.

When you write, draw on what you know about the person. See them in your mind's eye and use your intuition to reverse roles with them. This will help you better understand how they see things and, if they are not getting your point, can show you in what way you are not attuned to how they see things and what they need.

If you're writing to someone you haven't met, do some research: Talk to colleagues, gather information. The more you understand a person's frames of reference, language, values and priorities, the more you can develop the rapport for a working relationship. Review their written communications. Look for clues in how they respond to written messages, too. Notice whether the person uses personal language, technical terms, generalizations. Consider what kind of data they need to make decisions and whether they decide fast or slowly. Take serious account of that in deciding how to proceed next.

—Susan H. Dowell, psychotherapist

Practice Reading Between the Lines

It's amazing how much "attitude" may be revealed in even a short, simple e-mail or post. In a large communications department I managed, I set a rule that at least one other person review every significant piece of writing that went out of the office, even internal memos. The feedback rarely concerned technical issues like grammar. What did emerge often were comments such as "I see you don't like this person" or "You're recommending this course of action but it doesn't sound like you believe in it."

It can be extremely hard to keep your own feelings out of your writing, so be aware of that challenge (and have a friend check out your message when it matters). On the other hand, keep your antennae up for clues when you're on the receiving end.

Reading between the lines is a particularly useful technique when you're applying for a job or responding to an RFP (request for proposals). Read the ad, posting or RFP a dozen times or more and pick up its language, hot buttons and rhythm.

You can also pick up the subtext of a message by close attention to what is *not* said as well as what's included and general "atmosphere." A good way to do this is to ask questions and imagine the answers. For example, why did this job ad specify "attention to detail," "detail oriented" and "meticulous follow-through" so many times? Perhaps the last person in the job fell through in this area, so I need to marshal my evidence that I'm strong here.

Learn How to Invent an Audience

Another useful strategy when you're writing to someone you don't know is to invent a construct of what that person is most probably like. If it's a human resources (HR) director, for example, visualize others you've known who held that job and consider what would interest and impress them. Or just take a few minutes to see through their eyes and figure out what—if your positions were reversed—the HR director would care about and want to know. Ask yourself, what's in the other person's self-interest in this situation? Assume the other person's role for a few minutes and you'll have helpful answers.

It's always easier to write to an individual than to an anonymous abstract person. But if you can't conjure one up appropriate to the situation, then write to a Standard Modern Businessperson (SMB). You can safely assume your SMB wants your written message to be:

- Respectful but friendly
- Clear in its goals (your reason for writing)
- Well planned and written
- Logical in its progression of facts or ideas
- Targeted to his or her self-interest, the what's-in-it-for-me factor
- Self-contained—no need to look up other documents or do research to understand it
- As brief as possible to get the message across
- Objective, non-emotional and positive in spirit
- Oriented to solving a problem rather than posing one
- Good for the bottom line (you score lots of points when you can show this, even in a minor way)

You can also assume that your SMB is a human being and put the old Golden Rule to work on your behalf. All (or nearly all) of us want to feel:

- Liked
- Valued

- Treated with courtesy and respect
- Part of the team

When a message doesn't convey these things implicitly, our reaction is negative, whether the message itself has merit or not. And we especially do not like anything that actively makes us feel:

- Overlooked or left out
- Disrespected
- Disliked
- Uncomfortable

- Depressed
- Inadequate
- Laughable or ridiculous

Never criticize anyone in writing, whatever his or her relationship to you. This applies to informal situations and most formal ones, with the exception of performance reviews and documentation. A careless written remark can easily torpedo a relationship and create an enemy. Similarly, irony and sarcasm are dangerous ingredients in business writing. When you criticize someone in person, you can establish a supportive atmosphere and be a responsive listener. And when you say something sarcastically or ironically, your tone of voice conveys, "I don't really mean it."

But the critical or sarcastic memo is delivered without face-to-face cues and can devastate your audience—and boomerang badly. This applies 110% to online media. If you don't want a viral reputation as a nasty human being, refrain from posting negative personal comments anywhere.

Here is the flip side: It is a rare individual who doesn't want to look good to colleagues and staff—and especially superiors. And we relish good news, including any about a staff member or the department. So make the most of every opportunity to bring good tidings, and craft those messages well. These are the documents most likely to ascend the corporate ladder and help pave your own way.

SUCCESS TIP

PROFILE YOUR ORGANIZATION

You do your best work, and are most valued, when you understand a company and the industry it's part of. Observe, ask, determine:

- How does it frame its mission? Express its values?

- What does it reward?
- What are the organization's immediate and long-range goals?
- What challenges does it face? Who are the competitors?

- What are your company's strengths and competitive advantages?
- What is its communication style, and what channels are preferred?

A newcomer will not be asked to comment on corporate strategy. But whatever your job level, a solid grasp of the big picture enables you to recognize opportunities and contribute to company priorities. You'll interact more effectively and write better messages, too. Build the profile through observation and research. Ask intelligent questions. Nearly all supervisors are glad to encourage your interest in becoming a useful member of the team.

CROSSING THE GENERATIONAL DIVIDE

If you're reading this book, you probably started working after the year 2000 and identify most closely with the Millennial generation. Your supervisors are probably Baby Boomers and Generation X. What does this differentiation mean to how you communicate?

To begin with, it may explain a lot of the experiences you've already had, both good and bad, in dealing with bosses and colleagues. When you grew up and what was happening is a big factor in shaping our personal filters. Plus, people care about different things at different times in their lives. These facts give you some strong suggestions for how to communicate more successfully.

Right off, paying attention to generational sensitivities can save you a lot of pain. It's a fact that while Baby Boomers are retiring in droves, they still maintain seats of power in almost every industry. Many will stay as long as they can because they're workaholics and because economic conditions make it necessary.

So even if your immediate supervisor and the person she reports to are from Generation X or maybe even Generation Y, ultimately Boomers often run the show. The higher you go up the chain of command, the truer this is—it's an unusual board of directors that doesn't include plenty of Boomers.

KNOW YOUR GENERATIONS

Different age groups have different characteristics. Understanding the differences can be remarkably useful. Here are the broad outlines of the basic groups you'll encounter in the workplace, starting with the youngest.

(Continued)

(Continued)

Millennial Generation (Generation Y)

Born 1981 to Early 2000s

Brought up with devoted support from Boomers, these young people are strong "natives" of digital technologies and instant communication media: Facebook, YouTube, and online gaming are natural environments. They are culturally tolerant and liberal in views as well as civic minded. They come to the workplace with high expectations and desire to shape their jobs to fit their lives. They dislike following orders blindly and do not automatically grant respect to the more experienced. Millennials like to know "why" and want to work on their own without being micromanaged. Millennials have short attention spans, like challenge and change, hate repetitive work, and want the workplace to be fun. They are usually creative and optimistic but not company loyal. They like to participate rather than watch. They prefer text messaging and social media networking to face-to-face communication. This is a big generation.

Generation X

Born 1965 to 1980

This is a relatively small generation. Many now occupy middle-management jobs. Brought up in the first period of two-income households, rising divorce rate and latchkey environment, Gen Xers value independence, self-sufficiency, freedom, responsibility, and resourcefulness. They adapted to and are comfortable with computers and technology. While ambitious and hardworking, they want work–life balance. Gen Xers possess entrepreneurial spirit, like flexible hours and a chance to work at home. They favor diversity, challenge, creative input, autonomy, and may prefer working alone rather than in teams.

Baby Boomers

Born 1946 to 1964

This is a very large group whose members are often the power holders in corporations, law firms, consultancies, and most other organizations (except dot-coms). Baby Boomers are loyal, work-centric and cynical; value office face time; and are motivated by perks, prestige, position, high levels of responsibility, praise and challenges. Boomers define themselves by professional accomplishment and tend to be workaholics. They are very competitive, confident, and comfortable with confrontation; believe in hierarchical structure; and do not like change but will challenge established practice. Many are of retirement age but holding on and believe that Generations X and Y should "pay their dues"—like they did.

To learn more about this illuminating subject, enter "generation gaps" or "generational differences" in your search engine, and thousands of references will come up written from various angles: general business management, HR, marketing and more, plus numerous major articles in established publications.

Note that Boomers tend to like face-to-face meetings. They've adjusted to e-mail and smartphones, but it's usually not effective to text important messages to them or use texting abbreviations in your e-mails. And don't friend them! Even if they're simpatico with social networking, Boomers tend to prefer keeping their personal and business lives separate. And they much prefer that you do, too: If you post an unduly revealing page, comment, photo, or video, prepare to face negative consequences from your company executives and those at other companies where you want to work.

VIEW FROM THE FIELD: INTERACTING SUCCESSFULLY ACROSS GENERATIONS

As a business development and organizational effectiveness consultant for professional firms, I realized that sustainable success largely depends on people interacting well with each other. Since 1997, I've been conducting intergenerational programs to help organizations bridge the gaps. The issues are big: client and employee attraction and retention; succession planning and knowledge transfer as people retire or leave for other employment or roles; working relationships in multigenerational teams; shifting roles to make room for younger people, and cross-generational communication in all these and other situations.

Ongoing dialogue is necessary. People need to figure out common goals and how to reach them so people can collaborate productively. Some of the tips and strategies I recommend to all generations are:

- Don't make assumptions. Listen, watch, ask questions and get to know people.
- Be as respectful of other generations as you would like to be respected.
- Be flexible in your communication style and media.
- Know how others want to be communicated with: in person, phone, voice mail, memos, texting, social media—use the platform that will be received best rather than what you prefer.
- Find out other people's interests beyond specific work tasks so you can relate to them as human beings. Everyone wants to be liked and feel important.
- Look for things to learn from each other so you can share something that's valued.

If you are a Generation Y/Millennial working with Boomers or Gen Xers, develop rapport by showing initiative. Convey confidence but don't let it come across as arrogance. Ask questions about how you can best contribute to serving the client better and help the organization. Recognize older people's achievements, which they tend to be proud of, and don't instantly dismiss their ideas even if you think you have a new and better way. You might tactfully suggest reciprocal or mutual learning so you both benefit, remembering that some boomers may not be happy to be told they must learn from younger people.

(Continued)

(Continued)

Know that older people may find your text-influenced communication style abrupt and short and impersonal. Slow down, think about what you're saying, proof the message. Missing words and bad grammar and typos don't impress others and may hold you back from promotions. Learn good writing skills and practice them.

—Phyllis Weiss Haserot, president of Practice Development Counsel (pdcounsel.com); author of *The Rainmaking Machine*, owner–manager of the LinkedIn Cross-Generational Conversation group, and founder of Cross-Generational Conversation Day

Keep in mind that people in the Boomer generation are more formal in their business relationships, and this affects what they expect, and like, in written materials. Well-written, well-thought-out and proofed messages work with this audience. Careless, sloppy, spontaneous messages are apt to insult them and instantly undermine your credibility and professional image.

Most important of all is what the differences suggest about the harder-to-define quality called "tone," the voice built into a message. When business executives are asked to identify the biggest problem with employee writing, "wrong tone" is usually complaint #1 when they talk about younger staff members.

We can see on the generation chart why this happens. People born after 1980 or so tend to be antihierarchical and skeptical of authority. In their view, age does not automatically make someone worthy of respect. But Boomers, who typically feel that they worked their tails off to get where they are, demand respect with a capital *R*.

The intergenerational writing problem is further complicated by Millennials' immersion in a digital world where communication is telegraphic. Thus, a careless 25-year-old might e-mail a client this way:

Jack—here's the info you wanted. Still waiting for the new numbers— let me know when you'll send ASAP.

—Mel

He should have written something more like this:

Dear Jack:

To follow up on our phone conversation, I'm attaching a report on the Black acquisition. I've marked the relevant areas. If this doesn't provide all the information you need, please let me know and I'll dig further.

As soon as we have the new numbers, we'll move ahead on preparing the agreement. Thanks.

Best regards, Mel

If you think the second version is a bootlicking waste of time, think again. Mel's credibility and professional image are very much at stake here. Jack may not visibly react to what he perceives as rudeness, but he's likely to register it, remember it, and even talk to Mel's higher-up about it.

VIEW FROM THE FIELD: AN "OLDER FOLKS" WARNING

One of my gripes with younger people is that with e-mail and all the other business communication tools we have today, they don't get back to you in a timely manner. That's a subliminal message and makes you think, wasn't my message important? Aren't I important? It's so appalling that anyone who does respond within 24 hours, or a business that does so, has a real point of differentiation. And be aware of generational nuances. People who text shouldn't use that jargon in e-mail—us older folks don't understand it.

—Paul Facella, president and CEO of Inside Management Ltd.
(www.insidemanagement.com), a business consultancy;
former corporate vice president at McDonald's

Look at it as necessary business protocol to write in a respectful—no, not obsequious—tone. And do so whenever you're in doubt about the relative status of your audience or where your e-mail might end up.

The guidelines equally apply when you report to a young boss or client. He or she may in fact be especially sensitive to signs of respect and disrespect. And so are clients and customers, by definition. They do not want to be addressed as a peer or feel ordered around by a junior associate.

If you're a Millennial, take comfort in knowing that adapting to the intergenerational gap isn't a one-way street. The Boomers who run law firms, accounting practices, corporations and all the rest try sometimes desperately to understand the younger generation, because they know very well that the future (and maybe their retirement incomes) depends on it. They need to attract the best talent and retain it—a real challenge because they are well aware that younger people lack the long-term loyalty of their own age group. Also, few companies are structured to meet Millennial priorities. Perks like flexible hours, lots of time off and a fun workplace are hard to graft onto an old organizational stalk.

Marketing people spend a huge amount of time analyzing generational characteristics to better calculate how to sell to each group, especially Generation X on up. And not-for-profits are very stressed about finding ways to appeal to younger donors and how to use venues that reach them. If they fail, their revenue streams will literally age out.

So you need to take this divide seriously, too.

WRITING TO GROUPS

Writing to groups is harder and more complicated than writing to individuals, to different degrees, depending on the group's size and diversity. Professionals who design communications for really big groups, like mass markets, customarily segment the audience and tailor different messages because the same one will not succeed with all. Similarly, a large company sends different information to employee groups about subjects like a change in benefits, because their concerns are different.

There are times when you should do this, too. If you're sending a résumé or inquiry to prospective employers, for example, you'll need to take a different tack for consulting firms and marketing departments.

Often, however, one message must be effective for a wide range of people with different educational levels and interests. Good presenters often pick one person at a time to focus on while speaking. Similarly, many good writers think about one individual, or imagine one, and write to that person.

VIEW FROM THE FIELD: THE WORD FROM SUPER PRO WARREN BUFFETT

Here's how the financier, known for his remarkably clear writing on complex financial subjects, pulls it off:

Write with a specific person in mind. When writing Berkshire Hathaway's annual report, I pretend that I'm talking to my sisters. I have no trouble picturing them: Though highly intelligent, they are not experts in accounting or finance. They will understand plain English, but jargon may puzzle them. My goal is simply to give them the information I would wish them to supply me if our positions were reversed. To succeed, I don't need to be Shakespeare; I must, though, have a sincere desire to inform.

No siblings to write to? Borrow mine: Just begin with "Dear Doris and Bertie."

—Warren Buffett, from *A Plain English Handbook:*
How to Create Clear SEC Disclosure Documents

Rather than writing to a faceless group, then, try picking a "typical" representative of the audience to think about, and assemble a list of characteristics from the audience analysis outlined earlier in this chapter. Different factors count depending on your subject and goal. If you're presenting a new companywide data entry program, for example, it's important to consider education, probable degree of knowledge, possible resistance, and the audience's view of what's in it for me (which encompasses "how much trouble will this cause me").

Address Gatekeepers and "Serial Audiences"

Often a document needs to be read by different people or groups in succession. There may be a gatekeeper—for example, a manager's assistant—who vets incoming messages and may choose not to pass some of them on to the boss. And with nearly every job application you send, there's probably an entire staff of people with the power to short-circuit you.

In other situations, you can anticipate that a message is likely to ascend the company ladder. You deliver a project report to your boss, for example, and see a good possibility that she'll send it to her boss, and the chain might continue to some unknown point. Or you submit your consulting proposal to the HR executive who invited it, and you count on his passing it on to the relevant department head.

Here are ways to handle this:

1. Be very conscious that you're writing to a serial audience when preparing the message.

2. Avoid anything that could annoy the immediate recipient and anything not suitable to the audience that may lie beyond.

3. Use all the principles of good writing and proof carefully.

4. Err on the side of formality when unsure of the tone to take.

5. Keep your eye on the ultimate target—what communicators call the primary audience—the person or group that will ultimately make the decision to hire you or deliver whatever you're asking for.

6. Make friends with gatekeepers. It's best to have your supervisor's personal assistant regard you favorably, for example. Public relations people and politicians court editors and reporters for the same reason: They're gatekeepers, or mediators, whose approval is essential if they are to reach their audiences.

Remember that today gatekeepers also include machines. A résumé that lacks industry keywords has a good chance of being screened out. A blog or website that doesn't incorporate the right search terms may be ignored by search engines, and won't bring them to your audience's attention. Don't write for algorithms—always write for people—but don't ignore their gatekeeper function.

Send Messages to the Universe With Digital Media

Digital media give us something that never existed before: a way for just about anyone to reach millions, even billions, of people across the country and around the world, with a click, every day, any hour. All the rules of marketing and advertising are morphing into new "truths" as a result.

Anyone can now get his message out via a website, blog, or social media post, for example. But when an audience is so vast and indefinable, how can you understand it to shape a better message?

The premise of goal and audience now works this way: Instead of knowing to whom you're writing and tailoring the message, you can create a message that your ideal audience will want to find. Through search engine optimization and global networking, this potential audience has the means to find you, rather than the other way around. And if you give it something it wants or needs, and leverage that interest intelligently and stay persistent, your audience will come.

So it's even more important to think about your goals and intended recipients in depth and figure out their age range, education, interests, values, worries, hot buttons and all the rest.

Here's the takeaway: Don't throw out the basics of good communication because the technology is new and the media channels behave differently. The principles are as important as ever, and I promise they won't change. But they do need to be interpreted in new ways.

In the next chapter, we'll explore how the groundwork of goals and audience pays off and shows you what to say, how to say it, what *not* to say, and options for organizing your message or document.

PRACTICE OPPORTUNITIES

I. Chart Your Own "Goals"

Based on this chapter's discussion of goals and the idea of the personal agenda, write down your own essential goals for:

1. This year of study

2. The entire degree program you'll be completing

3. The first year of the job you hope to get after completing your program

Write in as much detail as you can. Consider whether this effort gives you a different perspective on what you want to achieve—and what difference that might make in what you do, how you spend your time and how you prioritize.

II. Review Your Own Message

Select a substantial e-mail or letter you wrote recently and review it from the perspective of this chapter. If it yielded disappointing results, all the better. Analyze: Did you make your goals clear? Did you pitch the message well to the specific audience? Was there a clear what's-in-it-for-me element? Did it serve your personal goals? How might you write the document differently now? Try it.

III. Group Project: Define Your Generation

In class or as an assignment:

Work with others in your general age group (preferably in a group of three to five) to review the description of the "generation" you belong to by virtue of when you were born.

A. Discuss

Which described qualities do you agree with?

Which do you disagree with?

What else should have been included?

If you come from different countries and cultures, can you find differences? Similarities?

B. Write

Collaborate on writing a better description of your generation, in at least 250 words. Include cultural comparisons. Share with class and talk about results.

IV. Discuss

Contribute to a class discussion one personal experience that demonstrates a difference between your generation and another. As a group, come up with additional factors to take into account that can improve cross-generational communication.

V. Read Between the Lines

Identify a job posting in your field that you'd like to apply for someday—if not now. Clip it or print it out. In writing, analyze:

1. How would you describe the person they're looking for? Be as specific as you can.

2. What are the most important qualifications? Personal qualities?

3. What kind of problems do you think the hired person is likely to face?

4. What can you tell about the company—is it formal and highly structured? Does it value innovation and new thinking? What kind of "personality" does it have?

5. What clues does this give you about how to present yourself in a résumé in terms of:
   - Qualifications and experience
   - Personal qualities
   - Any less obvious factors you can cite to suggest you're a great match

6. Any qualifications or qualities you don't have? Can you think of ways to cover for these missing attributes, or bridge to proven capabilities you do have?

7. Can you figure out who will read your application initially?

8. And who will probably make the actual hiring decision?

9. How can you accommodate the need to address at least two different audiences?

10. What keywords and terms should you build into your response?

VI. Analyze Your Supervisor

If you're currently working, your supervisor is your best candidate for this. If not, choose someone you've reported to in the past—at any kind of job.

1. Build a written profile of the person, considering the various factors described in this chapter. Take into account age and generation, communication style, personality, status in the organization, office appearance, and as many of the other factors as possible. (If this sounds challenging, think about what you'd tell your younger sister who would take over the job when you leave or are promoted.) Write up the profile (should be at least 500 words).

2. Review the profile and write down everything your analysis tells you about how to best communicate with this individual and get what you want. Include clues and intuitions, as well as clear indicators.

3. Write an e-mail to the person requesting something you anticipate will be a hard sell: for example, approval to pay for a professional development course you'll take on company time, buy a costly new piece of technology, give you a new office or a special assignment you covet.

VII. Write an Answer

Your colleague writes this to you: "We are surrounded by awful writing. Our supervisors' communications are terrible, the people we work with write even worse, and our clients and vendors seem almost illiterate. Why should we take a lot of trouble to write better?"

What message would you send back? Write 350 words or more.

Chapter 3

PUTTING THE PLANNING STRUCTURE TO WORK

Always Know What to Say

LEARN HOW TO . . .

- Decide on best content
- Organize effectively
- Adopt the right tone
- Work out challenging messages

Good writing is not a natural gift. You have to learn to write well.

—David Ogilvy, known
as the "father of advertising"

Recently, I presented a business writing workshop to a group of successful accounting professionals in their 30s. We talked about how to apply goal and audience concepts to everyday documents like e-mail and began discussing "tone"—the emotional feel that messages convey. A participant interrupted. I'll call her "Amy."

"Wait a minute," Amy said. "I'm a very direct person and a very busy one. If I want something from a subordinate, I write, 'I need you to have the Green report on my desk tomorrow by 2:00.' You're telling me I have to take the time to personalize what I write and care about their feelings? You're saying I have to . . . *sugarcoat* it?"

My answer: "Well, we don't call it sugarcoating—we'd call it being courteous and considerate—but basically, yes."

I found that quite a few people in the group felt like Amy. But Amy and others should know this: Many executives have shared with us that tone is the biggest problem they face with employee writing. One CEO, head of an investment firm serving multimillionaires in their 50s and up, relayed that clients regularly complain about receiving abrupt, even rude messages from staff members.

True, Amy was writing to people who report to her, not a client. That actually makes no difference. In both cases, relationship building is an important underlying goal, though an unstated one. As observed in Chapter 1, we depend on writing to build bridges between people in a business environment that steadily grows more impersonal. How your subordinates feel about you, and your messages, can be just as critical to success as how your clients feel.

Takeaway: Remember the magic of *why*. Amy's message didn't include a *reason* for her demand. Whatever assignment she's giving, she loses a virtually free opportunity to foster a team spirit and make her assistant feel good about contributing to something important. Her approach creates a negative impact instead of a positive one.

Following is some practice putting the ideas of goal and audience to work. We'll use the e-mail format, needed on a daily basis, but the ideas apply to all business communication from social media to long-form documents like proposals and reports.

Suppose you are the new president of the Entrepreneur Group and responsible for planning 10 guest appearances by prominent local businesspeople. Here is how the structure explained in Chapter 2 helps you determine what to say and how to say it.

DEFINING YOUR GOALS

1. Immediate: Draw good speakers to the program.

2. Longer range: Establish contact with business leaders who could prove valuable for your future job hunt.

3. Accomplish these things without killing yourself. This means recruiting enough people to share the burden.

Clearly, the start point is to get help. The folder you received from the outgoing president includes this recruitment e-mail from last year:

To: All Entrepreneur Group Members

From: Bunnie White

Subject: Need help—important!

As incoming president, I'm taking on responsibility for assembling the next 10-month roster of speakers. Please help! Participate in the planning, organizing the logistics, taking care of speaker needs and general follow-up. This is the most important aspect of our club's work and we should all want to get good results. ***If enough people volunteer, the shared workload will be a lot easier.*** Our first meeting will be on April 10 at 7:00 p.m. in Room A.

—Bunnie

Does this make participating sound like much fun? Satisfying? No. Nor does it help to know that the writer will probably take all the credit for good outcomes. The benefits are all hers. Even worse, volunteering sounds like a risky business that could sop up an open-ended amount of time. The message is unlikely to succeed.

APPLYING THE AUDIENCE CONCEPT

Let's see how considering "audience" can help. What do you know about the people to whom you're writing?

That's easy—despite differences in gender, background, national origins and so on, they're much like you. They want to

- Look good, get a good résumé credit, be recognized and appreciated
- Establish good contacts for finding jobs
- Achieve all this by doing as little as possible
- Contribute within a collegial atmosphere (which doesn't characterize many initiatives run by inexperienced managers)

Takeaway: Always look through your readers' eyes and ask, "What's in it for me?" (WIIFM).

In this case, it means figuring out an offer that will appeal to the audience and overcome resistance to a time commitment. Some simple, private brainstorming, or conversation with a friend, can provide a set of sales points in line with the list of audience needs or characteristics.

Take a minute to think about how you would approach this e-mail. Good thinking always precedes good writing, but there is *always* more than one way to achieve what you want.

Here's a version that capitalizes on the factors I spelled out.

To: Entrepreneur Group

From: Jane Green, president, Speaker's Taskforce

Subject: Meet successful businesspeople and contribute

Dear Colleague:

I invite you to join this year's Speaker's Program Taskforce.

As this year's president, I plan to appoint up to 10 members who are ready to capitalize on a chance to become personally acquainted with the region's leading businesspeople in a range of industries.

If you become part of the team, your commitment will involve:

- A brainstorming session to come up with a short list of the people we'd most like to meet and hear speak
- Telephone and e-mail contact as needed and a checkpoint meeting or two
- Direct contact with one or more people on the A list to recruit them and plan logistics (we'll try to match you up with people you'd most like to meet)
- Welcoming "your" speaker to campus and introducing him or her

This year, all members of the task force will be listed in every program.

If you're interested in being part of the best-ever Speaker's Program, drop me a return e-mail by this Friday telling me about yourself in a paragraph. I'll pick the best candidates by the end of next week and set the most convenient meeting time possible.

—Jane

Will this message succeed? The opportunity seems a lot more tempting and the responsibilities less onerous. There's more incentive to participate. This version uses a little reverse psychology, too—remember how Tom Sawyer got Huck Finn to paint the fence? Jane presents the work as a privilege rather than a burden—and a chance to be part of a winning team, which everyone likes.

Notice that because Jane was able to structure the project as she wished, she was able to shape it to be more appealing. Often, the writing process—whether you're using it for a memo or invitation or press release or promotion—reveals the weaknesses of the event itself. If you don't have enough to construct a good message, think about what you wish you had and see if you can recast the event or project. As in Jane's case, it may cost nothing to do this.

Moreover, writing a well-planned message oriented to reader perspective instantly brands Jane as a good leader. The recipients may not consciously say that to themselves, but they do notice that she's made an attractive offer, spelled out the benefits and limited the time commitment. They accordingly assume she will run a smart operation that succeeds. *That's why good writing is a leadership asset and another reason to practice it.*

If you thought that Jane's original e-mail basically delivered the same message and that recipients would work out the reasons to participate on their own, that's a mistake to avoid. It leads us to consider this guiding principle . . .

When someone is interviewing for a job, representing another organization or coming from a consulting firm, I judge them on their writing because it will affect me. It's one of the biggest things—I care less about people's interpersonal skills, I don't need to be friends with them. But if they can't write well I'm stuck. In my job and others I work with, writing is so much of what you do that if you can't do it well you can't do your job well.

—Alicia Phillips
Mandaville, director of
development policy at
Millennium Challenge
Corporation (a U.S. foreign
aid agency)

Takeaway: Never assume your reader will make a deductive leap—especially one that helps your cause. It's always up to you, the writer, to spell things out and draw the "right" conclusions.

It's the writer's job to do the reasoning, and it always pays off.

Observe also that when Jane made the effort to see the invitation from her audience's perspective, the message's general spirit—its tone—shifted. It conveys more positive energy, frames the work as a team effort and suggests that the person in charge is nice as well as effective. This is not trivial: Beyond enticing people to join the team, the message sets a good atmosphere for the project from the start.

When you thoroughly consider what you want from your readers' viewpoint, WIIFM, you're guided to choose the right content and to naturally adopt the right tone. This contributes to achieving your immediate goal and to building relationships for the long term.

LEADING WITH STRENGTH

With her content list for the recruiting message in hand, it's easy for Jane to review it and identify the best beginning. The "lead" (or "lede" in journalistic terms), the first sentence or paragraph, focuses on the strongest argument for volunteering.

Many writers find that investing time to crystallize the lead enables them to organize and write the rest of the message easily.

Since this is an e-mail, the lead is incorporated into the subject line. It immediately brings home how the reader can benefit. This is an ideal way to start most documents. People trained in the army are taught, "Bottom line on top." Once you figure out what your reader cares about and how you can relate to that, flaunt it immediately.

Aim to accomplish several critical things:

- Tell readers why they should care, instantly, to draw them in.
- Capsulize the message's content.
- Set the audience up to read the message with the "right attitude."
- Ask clearly for what you want—generally, this is your "call to action."

The lead of a business message should function pretty much like a reporter's lead does for a newspaper, magazine or online article.

Day by day, it becomes harder to attract and keep readers' attention. This is especially true with online material and anything you read off a screen, big or mini scale. You often have only a few seconds to engage your audience: Don't waste them.

Takeaway: Assume every reader is impatient, time-stressed, and eager *not* to read your message. Prove in your lead that they need to.

VIEW FROM THE FIELD: HOW TO START A DOCUMENT

The most important thing in a letter or business document is to get to the point right away so the reader knows who you are and what you want. For example, "I'm writing at the recommendation of A who thought you might be helpful in giving me a reference to XYZ company." Or you might need to get across a client's key message points.

It's also very important that in the first paragraph you put yourself in the readers' shoes. What are they worried about? Why do they need the product or service? You have to engage people immediately by appealing to their self-interest. And you must understand what the appeal is before writing—the "what's-in-it-for-me" factor.

How do I start? Sometimes I sit and stare at the screen and think, if I were the recipient of this letter, what's going on in my life that I would respond to? It can help to get a little background on the industry if it's one that's unfamiliar to you. You might read about trends, or talk to someone in the business and ask, what are the big things these people are dealing with? Doing some market research can help put you in the readers' mind-set and tell you what they're concerned about.

—Leila Zogby, president of Leila Zogby Business Writer, Inc. (www.leilazogby.com)

For most professional writers, once the lead is determined, the rest of a message tends to flow organically, with some tweaking. The content of the Entrepreneur Group memo was basically determined by our simple brainstorming list. But leading with strength meant starting with the "contact with important people" carrot, so the rest of the list needed juggling.

Journalists were traditionally trained to write in "inverted pyramid style"—that is, to start with the most important story element and then successively work down to the least important facts or ideas. The reason: Editors prefer to trim articles to fit by cutting as much as necessary from the end, rather than reading every story through to find the most expendable bits.

News articles are still generally written this way, and the method applies nicely to most business writing purposes.

Takeaway: Craft your lead thoughtfully, then use your ideas, arguments and facts in the simplest, most straightforward way that works.

In the case of an e-mail, letter, or online communication, this means sequencing your brainstormed list. In the case of a lengthy document, it means staying clear on the major subtopics or sections and putting them in a logical order.

It's useful to think about everything you write as three parts:

1. The lead

2. The end

3. The middle: everything that goes between the first two elements

When I'm interviewing people, I like to give them a writing test . . . I find that you can tell a lot more about a person's personality from a few paragraphs of their writing than from a lengthy verbal interview. Many people can pretend to be something they're not in person, but very few people can do so in writing.

—Phil Libin, CEO of Evernote, in *Inc.*

The "middle" may consist of a paragraph, or 50 pages; either way, it typically contains the informational content. For example, a memo explaining how to fill out a form would lead with a statement about why an employee is getting these instructions ("On March 3, you must begin using a new system for purchase orders"), and end with a statement about what is expected ("I count on your office switching to the new system on March 3. Of course, let me know any questions about it ASAP").

In between would come the details about how to implement the system.

CHOOSING YOUR BEST OPTIONS FOR ORGANIZATION

Even if you've always felt that organizing a piece of writing was hard, you may find that thinking through the content before you write eliminates the problem. If more structure is helpful, here are some options.

Use a Formal Outline

If the classic outline many of us practiced in school works for you, with major categories identified by numbers and subsections identified by letters, by all means use it. For an alternative that's specifically geared for business writing, try the approach described in "View From the Field: An Easy Organization Technique." Many people find this strategy helpful and it adapts to a wide range of purposes.

VIEW FROM THE FIELD: AN EASY ORGANIZATION TECHNIQUE

Most people plunge into writing without planning—which is fine for a two-sentence e-mail, but not for writing that is longer than a paragraph or two. They write one sentence at a time without being sure where they're going, and probably will cut and paste throughout their writing. This "plunging-in approach" will get the work done, but it's a long and painful experience.

It's better to do an outline. Come up with your main point, one that describes what your piece of writing is about. It should contain a key word that is generally a plural noun that relates to how the piece will be broken up. For example, if you're writing to communicate the reasons for something, the key word is "reasons." Or, depending on your main point, the key word might be "benefits" or "steps" or "procedures" or "advantages." Determining your main point and the key word within it helps you construct an outline, and the writing becomes easier.

Generally, your main point should appear as the last sentence of the first paragraph. Preceding your main point is a first sentence or two that explains why you're writing this e-mail or letter. Often it is in response to a person writing to you. At other times, you may be asked to do a piece of writing, or you may see a need to put something in writing.

Based on the above suggestions, here is an example of an introductory paragraph:

Two years ago, our firm instituted a certain procedure for cashing checks. Unfortunately, serious problems have arisen with that procedure, and we have been forced to change the process. Below are the three steps that you should now follow to cash checks.

Now you know what the next three sections, usually paragraphs, need to be. That is, each paragraph will deal with a new "step," which is the key word.

The key word approach can help you create a good flow if you make sure to use transition words between sentences and paragraphs so people see how one statement relates to the next. Numbers can help: You can begin the second paragraph with *The primary advantage is . . .* The third paragraph can begin with *Secondly . . .* And so on.

—Dr. Mel Haber, president of Writing Development Associates

Organize by Telling Your Message to Someone

This technique helps the brain bypass the part of the brain we use for writing and go straight to the part we use when talking. Oral communication probably preceded writing by a few hundred thousand years, so we're better at it. Most people create first drafts that are complicated, wordy and confusing. But if we tell our story to someone else, we can typically be clear and to the point.

So talk it through with someone. If the person is not steeped in your subject, all the better. Start specifically, with something like "I want a new office and to convince my boss I need to tell him . . . " or "My suggestion for solving the problem is," according to the situation. You're likely to find that you can relay the reasoning or idea fine and that the process shows you your main point and how things fit together. You also discover anything extraneous and any gaps.

This is not, by the way, an unsophisticated technique. Feature writers use it all the time to figure out what's most interesting about a story they're developing or to understand where the story's heart lies. Then they know how to develop a piece they are happiest to write and that has the best chance of satisfying the audience.

Organize Through Graphic Techniques

Whether your document is short (like an e-mail or letter) or lengthy (like a report or proposal), you'll find it helpful to stay organized by building in graphic options. This has a big payoff; it makes everything, regardless of length, more easily understood by readers. In fact, if you don't build in graphics while you're writing, you may have to add them later anyway.

Graphic tools are even more important to online writing because people tend to scan and their attention must be captured and managed. Website designers use graphics quite systematically to attract a reader's eye and move it from point to point, taking account of typical viewing habits, which are researched. Online articles, blogs, profiles and other materials all benefit from the use of graphics.

To structure a document—or whatever the medium—many writers create a series of subheads before writing anything. This lets them build a logical sequence of facts or ideas and—presto!—they have a ready-made outline to follow. This is a popular technique for writing blogs.

GRAPHIC OPTIONS FOR ALL BUSINESS WRITING

Your visual repertoire can be used to make your messages look and feel organized—and, in fact, they'll usually be more organized. Here are some options.

Use subheads to introduce a new thought or section. Choose the format you prefer:

A larger font

A different font

Boldface

Italic

or

Write them in sentence case, with just an initial cap.

or

Write Your Subheads in Uppercase and Lowercase

You can combine some effects—bold with a different font, for example—but you must be consistent.

Use bold lead-ins for the beginning of a paragraph or section. Boldface, with or without italic, can also be used to **highlight a fact**, figure, idea, or conclusion in the body of your copy. There are also times when underlining is a good way to highlight, but this can look outdated or falsely suggest that the phrase is a hyperlink. And of course color works, if the medium accommodates it.

Use bullet points, but remember that they have their pros and cons. They are good for

- Listing ideas or facts telegraphically
- Summarizing
- Saving space
- Presenting at-a-glance facts or ideas

But do not depend on bullet points too much. While bulleting is a good way to present information for an audience with a short attention span—which, admittedly, is most of them—bullets need narrative context to have meaning. Further, readers can't really absorb more than perhaps four to seven at a time, depending on the material. Check out how you respond to bulleted lists yourself. Recall tends to be poor, because as stand-alone items without context or detail, bullet points give the mind little to hold on to.

This applies to all media, including résumés. Listing responsibilities or accomplishments in bullet form doesn't work without narrative-style paragraphs to interpret the big picture. Remember, never expect readers to draw conclusions for you. They may draw the wrong ones.

(Continued)

(Continued)

You may want to number your points. This can work well to pull a reader through your information or argument. Some reasons for this:

1. People like to know how much is ahead of them.

2. It's satisfying to feel a beginning and an end to a message.

3. A clear sequence can be easy to absorb and remember.

So, in print or speech, statements like "We can expect three basic results from this action" or "Here are the seven steps to filing the new form" are quite effective, followed, of course, by steps one, two, three and so on in logical order.

Graphic techniques also include the use of boxes, sidebars and pullout quotes—all demonstrated throughout the book you're reading right now. These give you good ways to incorporate relevant information without breaking the flow of a narrative.

Always, extensive and strategic use of white space is critical to accessibility and eye appeal of EVERY message. This is particularly true of long documents but should be taken into account even with brief ones. Short paragraphs contribute to this cause. And, of course, whenever you have options for making your point visually, through a chart, graph, or image, consider that. But keep the document consistent and keep visuals relevant.

A word on font, or typeface: Be sure you're using a very readable font and refrain from using capitals, italics, or boldface for entire e-mails or large portions of text. Don't mix more than two fonts as a general rule. (For advice on fonts and other graphic basics, see "View From the Field: A Graphic Designer's Advice on Good Presentation" in Chapter 9.)

Takeaway: Use formatting techniques in all media to clarify your message and make it more accessible.

SUCCESS TIP

WE'RE ALL SCREENWRITERS

Writers today must take account of how on-screen reading has transformed reader expectations for print as well as electronic media. Especially because we read so much material on miniature screens, we have become scanners. We check for what's relevant or interesting to us individually. We "dive" for information rather than systematically reading almost anything. We demand choices. We bring this new attitude to all media and messaging.

Notice that few magazines or newspapers present us with dense, unbroken copy anymore. They use photographs, illustrations, pre-article summaries, charts, graphs, captions—deploying all the access points they can devise to pull impatient people in and feed them at least a piece of the story.

A growing number of books (like this one) do the same. And note how sales letters and charitable solicitations are brimful of headlines, subheads, underlining, pullouts, "handwritten" notes and other devices.

Creating websites has been described as "packaging information," and this is a helpful way to think about most of what you write. Don't focus only on the words. Consider the graphic presentation, your audience preferences, and every technique you can draw on to deliver your message in a clear, attractive and compelling manner.

Finally, End Well

Note that in our Entrepreneur Group memo, the final sentences circle back to the lead and tell readers how to follow up.

Takeaway: End every document to reflect and reinforce your goal.

Some examples: "Please let me know if you are available to meet on March 2" or "Contact Jane if this new process isn't clear" or "I look forward to receiving the application." When possible, end with a "call to action"—a clear statement of what you want the reader to do. But be sure this suits the task: Telling a prospective employer to "call as soon as you receive this résumé" isn't a good idea.

ADOPTING THE RIGHT TONE

As we've seen with some of the examples, a document can look well planned and written but still fail if the tone, or "voice," hits the wrong note for readers. Just as with live interaction, the general feeling you project in a written message strongly affects how your words are received.

In a person-to-person situation, tone clearly results from, well, tone of voice. The same words can mean many different things according to our voice's pitch, rhythm, speed and so on—factors that reflect our state of mind and attitude. Moreover, in communicating face-to-face, we read facial expression, body language, conversational pauses and a whole host of cues that convey interest, astonishment, disagreement or dozens of other feelings.

With writing, none of these elements exist. A message's effect may be subliminal; it can be hard to pin down exactly what creates a message's emotional content. But controlling tone is critical. When you're asking for something, obviously it's counterproductive to show disrespect for the other person—or anything that he or she might interpret as disrespect.

If your messages are influenced by texting and casual social media exchanges, you may write letters and e-mails in a style that strikes people over 30 as abrupt, discourteous and rude. (In business settings, it usually doesn't serve you well with younger people, either.) If you're part of a generation that doesn't grant automatic respect to authority you may make this mistake—and never realize why you're not getting where you want to go.

Takeaway: Choose your tone carefully, and keep it in line with your goal and audience. Everything you write should reinforce and build positive relationships. How can you sharpen your writing ear to achieve the tone you want?

1. **First, recognize that just as with face-to-face interaction, your tone usually conveys your actual feelings.** So if you're writing to a boss or client you don't much like or respect, take particular care with what you say and how you say it.

2. **Anticipate that people older than you and higher on the totem pole expect "good manners" in person and in writing.** Use the full trappings of courtesy and respect to stand out when you write to people over 30.

3. **Remember that tone is contagious.** Projecting a negative attitude will provoke the same from your reader. That never helps, so try to communicate with a positive spirit. If you want an enthusiastic response, show your own enthusiasm. Friendly and respectful are generally good hallmarks to strive for.

4. **Be appropriate to the subject and relationship.** If the topic is serious, it's better not to be breezy. If you don't know the person, err on the side of formality, and think twice about using her first name.

Unless the situation and reader truly merit an informal message,

- Write *Dear* in the salutation, or *Hi,* or something similar.
- Use full sentences, not telegraphic texting-style statements.
- Edit and proof scrupulously (even if the VIP sends careless e-mails full of errors).

End with a conservative sign-off—for example, *Sincerely, Best regards, Thanks*—though it's worth noting that e-mail lacks a repertoire of good sign-offs. Here are some don'ts:

- Don't make assumptions not appropriate to the relationship (like setting the time for a meeting with your supervisor).
- Don't issue peremptory orders or express impatience (even with a subordinate).

VIEW FROM THE FIELD: TONE IS CRITICAL WITH CLIENTS

Many people I supervise use the wrong tone when they write to clients. If a client owes you a response, that's never an excuse for an e-mail that sounds like you are barking orders. Start off requests with the magic word, please; end any request with thank you; and always indicate that you are prepared to help facilitate whatever response you need. If an e-mail to a client on any topic sounds like something a parent would say to a child, a drill sergeant would say to a new recruit, or your boss would say to you—it needs to be rewritten.

—Arik Ben-Zvi, managing director of The Glover Park Group

---

5. **Don't antagonize your readers, whatever your relationship to them.** This is as true for peers and people who report to you as it is for people who you report to. So avoid being judgmental, critical, sharp, or unnecessarily abrupt.

6. **Practice feeling genuine consideration for the person or group you're writing to.** Take a moment to say something that feels like you have a personal relationship with the person, even if it's banal:

I hope this finds you well.

Did you have a good holiday season?

Hope your weather is good. It's terrible here!

Better yet, when possible, make a personal connection or relate directly to the reason you're writing:

It was great seeing you at the regional meeting last week. I'd like to follow up on . . .

Thanks for the note. I'm happy to answer your question about upcoming deadlines.

Remember that everyday written messages are often the only way we connect with other people. A relationship, and the trust that goes with it, builds gradually over time. If you take the initiative to humanize your messages—carefully, and when appropriate—you contribute toward creating that relationship. But never take liberties or become personal in a way that might offend.

7. **Adapt to the corporate culture.** E-mail sent by Citibank staff may differ in tone quite a lot from messages written by employees at Facebook or a nonprofit, or it might not. An organization can be formal or informal

based more on its own history and the nature of its leadership, rather than the industry it's part of. In a new work environment, it's a good idea to spend some time analyzing the degree of formality, general style and appropriate subject matter of the written communication you see. Then adjust your writing.

8. **Adapt to the medium.** Generally, a letter needs to be more formal than an e-mail. A report or proposal is typically more formal yet. Online writing, such as for websites or blogs, generally works best when it feels more casual, friendly and individual. A good website looks very accessible and spontaneous—though in fact, these qualities are always achieved through the most arduous planning and rewriting.

TESTING THE IDEAS

A Workplace Recruitment Challenge

Let's check out how the principles translate to a workplace memo. Ellen's consulting firm has asked her to head up an internal research project to revamp the summer associate program. This involves some tedious research and writing, so she needs to recruit a team.

The challenge: Ellen's colleagues are already pretty overwhelmed with client work, which makes the money. What can she give this audience in order to achieve her goal, recruiting help so she can turn out a good report?

She brainstorms a list of factors:

1. A consultant's evaluation and prospects are partly based on participating in internal "volunteer" projects.

2. This project is relatively high profile.

3. The work could shape and improve a program that many staff members experienced themselves.

To lead with strength, Ellen opens her e-mail with the most emotionally appealing element.

Subject line: Project opportunity: Revamp summer associate program

Dear Colleagues: I'm looking for three people to work on a new internal project that might recast the entire summer associate program.

Middle: The team, which I'll head, is charged with reviewing hiring strategies, salaries, the learning experience the program provides and the impression made on associates. Top management will review our report and I expect our recommendations to be seriously considered.

If you had reservations about your own experience as a summer associate, or observed shortcomings in how the program is run, this is a chance to make a real contribution. We can come up with a plan the firm will use as a blueprint— a great addition to your portfolio.

Close: Please call with any questions. Let me know by February 7 if you're interested.

Convincing? Ellen isn't so sure. So she considers what could make her project more attractive than competing opportunities. Reconsidering the #1 problem for her audience—time pressure—she opts for a larger committee and to hit the time problem head-on. She adds this in the middle:

I've planned the work to give team members a lot of flexibility in allocating their time. Only two face-to-face meetings will be scheduled—to launch the project and review results at the end. You can do your share independently on your own schedule, and that should take about four hours per week for two months. We'll teleconference weekly to be sure we're all on track.

Because many company projects require an open-ended commitment, this tack gives Ellen an important competitive advantage.

Draw Important People to Campus

Let's try another example and see how the principles can be used to write speaker invitations.

The Entrepreneur Group is ready to write to the selected business leaders. What could entice these people to accept a speaking invitation?

Start with brainstorming what they have in common. Most probably, they all

- Have extremely demanding schedules
- Like to be recognized as leaders
- See community connection as important
- Share an interest in supporting the region and the schools that foster growth and make it a good place to live
- May be interested in hiring future graduates, connecting with faculty, and/or interacting with young people

Here's one way to write a "generic" version of the letter.

Dear _____:

The Green University Martin School of Business is inviting the region's most prominent business leaders to address our students and faculty this coming year. Recognizing how important Premiere Industries is both to our area's economy and the community we share, and your own contributions as a leader, we hope you will accept our invitation to be part of the Executive Speaker Program.

We ask for just an evening of your time. In addition to an address of approximately one hour, we'd like you to be our guest for dinner and meet leading members of our business school community. We would be delighted to schedule your appearance for March and can offer you a choice of dates during the month.

The Executive Speaker Program will give our aspiring business managers the chance to become acquainted with the Quadruple Cities' most inspiring leaders. The Martin School of Business has worked hard to earn an impressive ranking internationally, and I believe you'll also find the evening stimulating.

With your permission, we plan to publicize your appearance with the local media and videotape your presentation for our heavily used archive. If helpful, committee members will be happy to work closely with you to support you in what you choose to present.

I'll plan to call you next week to ask if you are able to accept our invitation and answer any questions. Or if more convenient, please call me at any time before then.

The letter takes account of the recipients' busy schedules and makes their commitment as convenient and pain free as possible; reminds them of the community and giveback context of a university; flatters their importance; and suggests some tangible benefit in the way of positive press and contact with faculty and select students.

It could work. But is it good enough?

Takeaway: Writing is more powerful when you personalize your message to the individual. When the stakes are high, take the trouble to know what the person values.

How can you do this if it's someone you've never met? Start with questions you can answer with a little effort. In the case of our theoretical guest speakers, for example, you could ask:

Is he or she

- A graduate of the school or parent of kids who have been or might be?
- A former business major? MBA?
- A donor to the university or school?
- Connected with any particular community cause?
- Proud of something in particular? Known for something in business circles?
- Passionate about his or her work?

Does the company

- Hire your university's graduates, or those from your school?
- Send employees to any university program for training?
- Sponsor any campus programs?

Research the answers—online and by finding people to talk to who know the person or the company. Identify a professor, board member or school supporter who knows the individual personally or can connect you with someone who does.

This thinking applies to every occasion when you're requesting something important. Look for ways to successfully relate to your audience. Obviously, it helps if your potential speaker has direct ties to your school, a relationship with a professor or a strong community spirit. In each case, you'll use this information prominently, probably in the lead. One example:

I'm writing to you as a Green U. alumnus because we'd very much like to include you as a Martin School of Business guest speaker.

A basic letter can be adapted to each recipient's characteristics. Read the "Three Ways to Personalize Messages" box, and add the ideas to your tool kit. They work well for many documents, including job-hunting letters.

THREE WAYS TO PERSONALIZE MESSAGES

1. **Name-drop in any available way.** In business, people respect connections and references because it's far more comfortable and trust inducing than dealing with total strangers. If you have (or can find) a mutual connection, use it and use it early. For example:

At John Black's suggestion, I am writing to ask . . .

Professor Blue, whose class on corporate culture I am currently enjoying and with whom you also studied at White, believes I would be an excellent candidate for the internship your company is offering.

(Continued)

(Continued)

2. **Do your homework, and be sure it shows.** People like to know they're recognized or that you took the time to find out about them or their organization—especially when you can identify something they're proud of. Two examples:

Our selection committee was particularly impressed with how you've established Brown Industries as one of the top in its field nationally in only 10 years.

In addition to your business leadership, your support of the community through the scholarship program and hospital building fund makes you an exceptional model for future corporate leaders, so we will especially value your participation.

3. **Use compliments; they may work magic.** Even VIPs like to feel good about themselves and know that other people recognize how special they are. This is not to suggest twisting the truth but rather, that you find something nice you can say with sincerity. (Try this technique sometime with a hostile boss or colleague and you'll be amazed at the turnaround.) Examples:

Several classmates have told me that you are an exceptionally interesting and inspiring speaker, so I'm very pleased to extend this invitation.

I'd like to share that when we canvassed the committee members for their top speaker picks, your name came up repeatedly.

A Bad News Message

Let's test these various principles out in a different context, communicating news that's unwelcome or outright bad.

Let's say it's your unhappy lot to develop a memo announcing that the company will cancel its tuition reimbursement benefit. Your boss gives you the draft she began:

To: All staff

Subject: Cancellation of tuition reimbursement

Please be advised that economic conditions dictate some employee benefit cutbacks. As of June 30, Rose Co. will no longer provide tuition reimbursement. It is regrettable if this causes inconvenience, but as you'll understand, the decision is in the company's best interest.

—Talent Management Dept.

Here's why the message fails both in tone and content. The writer needed to consider two basic audiences—those directly affected and those who are not. A program beneficiary is bound to be upset when an entitlement is taken away arbitrarily. Worse, it sounds like more benefits may be on the chopping block—maybe even jobs. If you're someone not directly affected by this cut, you'd have the same uncertainties.

Further, because the bad news is delivered so impersonally—no one is even taking responsibility for the decision—you're likely to think bad thoughts about your employer. Not to mention that it sounds like the company is on the downslide, and more than one member of the audience might come to the same conclusion: time to update the résumé.

Studies show that the manner in which bad news is delivered, even in worst-case scenarios like layoffs, strongly affects how employees perceive a company and feel about their jobs. This is no small matter because when times are tough, management needs to build an everyone-must-pull-together spirit.

Good managers, therefore, put a lot of thought into anticipating reaction to bad news, figuring out how best to frame it, and determining whether anything can be done to offset the negative impact. And plenty of consultants find their bread and butter in telling executives how to handle these situations.

In the example we're using, then, the goals are:

- Deliver the bad news in the most acceptable manner possible.
- Be honest and realistic (anything else will backfire).
- Express empathy in a businesslike way.
- Reassure employees that there are no current plans for more cuts.
- Assure everyone the company has a good future.

Because you're not speaking for yourself in this case, which is often the situation, you'll need to gather information.

You might want to find out:

- Who made the decision?
- Exactly why was it made?
- Might the benefit be reinstated someday?
- Are other benefit cuts being effected or contemplated?
- Might layoffs follow?
- Is the firm's situation precarious? To what degree?
- What can be said about the company's communication history and treatment of staff?
- What are the options for the message's authorship?

Here's one way to reframe the message.

To: All Rose Company Staff

Subject: Suspension of tuition-reimbursement program

Dear Colleagues:

I'm sorry to tell you that as of June 30, the company will not offer tuition reimbursement.

As the management team has communicated over the past year, the Rose Co. has lost several important clients because of the overall poor economic climate. Additionally, a few clients have had to temporarily reduce their service level.

We're working hard to broaden our client base and diversify services, as you know, and see a promising business uptick. But right now we must effect some economies. We don't want to reduce staff beyond natural attrition. And we don't want to trim benefits like health insurance that are critical to our corporate family's well-being.

Accordingly, we have decided to reduce new equipment spending, cut conference travel, and suspend the tuition program. We realize that losing the program will disappoint many of you and we continue to value our staff's commitment to continued learning. We'll be happy to reinstate this perk when it becomes practical to do so.

Meanwhile, I trust you'll agree with our priorities and our commitment to sharing the news with you openly and honestly. I know that with your help, Rose Co. will weather the current industry downturn and provide a supportive employment climate for all of us.

I'll keep you closely informed of our progress.

Sincerely,

Ed White, CEO

This memo tells readers why the cuts are being made and puts them in context, establishes a team feeling, reassures readers about the company's future and makes them feel valued. It's hard to disagree with the expressed priorities. It sounds like management is handling the economic challenge well and staying with the ship is a good bet. And employees can trust company leaders to communicate straightforwardly.

Note that there are various strategies for communicating bad news, such as "sandwiching" it between positive statements. (For example, "Bob, it's been terrific to have you as a vendor all these years. But the company has grown and we're moving on. Let's remember the good times.")

But this cushioning approach ill suits today's skeptical, impatient, even cynical audience. It's much more successful to impart the bad stuff immediately. Show caring, and give reasons when you can. Try to find something truly useful to offer rather than just empty rhetoric. "I can suggest a contact who may have a job lead for you" or "We're bringing in some job search experts for you to consult with" is a lot better message than, "With all your talents, I'm sure a great future awaits you."

These principles should help you avoid a bad news messenger's worst fate in most situations where you have that role. As you move up the ladder, remember that up-front honesty and compassion for others should guide your response to crisis. Introduce mitigating factors when possible. Where an apology is in order, make it. Unfortunately, this lesson seems never to get learned in the corporate and political arenas.

The experimental memo from "Ed White" claimed a good communication history for the company only because I chose to assume that was true. Just as in personal life, good relationships must be built over time. This is true for external communication as well as internal. An institution needs to foster employee, public and media trust over the long run through good communication to successfully weather a crisis.

VIEW FROM THE FIELD: NEED TO APOLOGIZE? HERE'S HOW

Visiting hundreds of companies and writing about their crisis du jour, I noticed that organizations that apologize have better outcomes. And individuals who do it well rise higher and have better relationships. Clearly accountability—taking responsibility and rejecting defensiveness—is an important skill. So I started to put it together into a systematic approach, the 5Rs model:

- Recognition—acknowledge the specific offense
- Responsibility—accept personal responsibility, no excuses
- Remorse—there's no substitute for "I apologize" or "I am sorry"
- Restitution—here's what I'll do about it, concretely
- Repeating—I promise it won't happen again

(Continued)

(Continued)

You never know when the need to apologize will come upon us, but if you're not prepared, instinct kicks in—we want to defend ourselves, hide, deny responsibility. But the cover-up is always worse than the crime. Train yourself in small things and it will be easier to apply to big things.

Written apologies are more formal than spoken but work about the same.

These days, apologizing is a leadership skill. We see our decision makers dodging and weaving instead of accepting responsibility, and that disappoints us. We don't expect them to be perfect, just willing to learn. In the long run apology leads to better outcomes and more durable relationships.

—John Kador, author of *Effective Apology* (see his blog,
www.effectiveapology.com, for interesting comments on the public apology)

Final Takeaway: Be as honest, straightforward, and authentic as you can in every message you send and every document you create. Using this book's techniques to produce a communication that will succeed with your reader is not manipulative. Identifying the WIIFM—what's in it for the other person—and writing your message within this frame is respectful. It recognizes that people are different and that their viewpoint is valuable. If you doubt this, review some messages that you've responded to favorably to identify the reasons. And do the same with messages you didn't like.

In the next chapter, we'll start to look at concrete ways to improve the mechanics of what you write—the engineering. Good planning and substance are essential, but you also need to craft good sentences, choose the right words and produce cohesive documents.

PRACTICE OPPORTUNITIES

I. Write a Better Note for Amy to Send to Her Subordinate

It should ask Susan to deliver a report by a specific time in a way that will make her feel appreciated, part of a team and happy to work hard on Amy's behalf.

II. Group Work: Plan and Pitch an On-Site Visit

As a group, brainstorm to identify an interesting local company to visit. Come up with as many reasons as you can to justify the time required to plan, organize and make the visit.

1. Collaborate on a letter making your case to the professor.

2. Write a letter to the appropriate person at the company asking that the firm host the class.

III. Write a "Stop Order"

Write a convincing e-mail to the class telling everyone to stop texting, tweeting, Facebook viewing and so on during class time or business meetings.

IV. Draft a "Please Rescind"

Write an e-mail to a supervisor asking that the rule against texting, tweeting, and Facebook monitoring during work hours be rescinded, explaining why.

V. Create a "How To"

Write a detailed document telling someone exactly how to do something practical, step-by-step. Make it as clear as you possibly can by the way you write it and the use of graphic techniques. Possible subjects include explaining how to use the newest smartphone; fix a computer, car, or plumbing problem; make oatmeal cookies or a paper airplane; choose a new computer; build an aquarium; train a dog to fetch; or pick any subject related to your interests or knowledge. Choose something you already know about or would like to research.

VI. Sum Up This Chapter's Content

Draft a 300- to 500-word summary describing the most important takeaways from this chapter. Create a complete message using the strategies explained in the chapters and at least five of the graphic techniques. Exchange your draft with another student and talk about the similarities and differences in content and how each of you handled this task.

VII. Find What's Wrong and Fix It!

Here are some real e-mails with inappropriate tone that I recently received myself or observed. For each, identify the problem and fix it.

1. To a supervisor:

   Dana—I have a great idea for solving the problem we talked about last week. Let's meet on Thursday at 3:00 p.m. We can talk all about it.—Robin

2. To a professor:

   Dear Prof—I looked online again for the syllabus you were supposed to post and couldn't find it. I need it by tomorrow—so last chance.—Mike White

3. To the employer's client:

   Dear Mr. Black—I sent you the Kittredge draft last week but have heard nothing. Did I miss something? The deadline is close. Please advise.—Mark

4. From a travel agent to a client prospect:

   Hello (no first name) Kennedy—Previously I had e-mailed you regarding your request for a quote for Waterworld Cruises Russia trip. There were a couple of questions that I needed answered in order to provide you with a more accurate quote. When is a good time to discuss your vacation plans?

   I certainly can understand your being busy, or perhaps you did not get the e-mail. So if you can get in touch with me at your convenience, I would like to provide you with all the pricing, discounts, and details. —Jenny Jay

5. Dear Ms. C:

   Long time no see! You'll remember me as VP of marketing for Digital Extreme—you wrote a script for the company video under my direction about 10 years ago.

   Now, alas, I've been downsized and am looking for new opportunities. Do you know of any job openings for people with senior experience like mine? Or can you give me some industry contacts to call?

   Thanks—much appreciated!

   Mary Nova

PART II

PRACTICAL TECHNIQUES TO SHARPEN AND IMPROVE YOUR WRITING

Chapter 4

GOOD SENTENCES, THE RIGHT WORDS

The Heart of Good Writing

LEARN HOW TO . . .

- Assemble strong sentences
- Adopt practical guidelines for readability
- Choose the right words
- Use vigorous verbs
- Correct common shortcomings

If you can't explain something simply, you don't understand it well enough.

—Albert Einstein

The sentence is the building block of written communication. I won't define the sentence, which is a lot more slippery a job than your early grammar lessons probably led you to believe. But when you write better sentences, combine them effectively, and use the structured thinking principles covered in the last two chapters, you're en route to becoming a powerful, flexible writer.

This book does not focus on grammar; if you think you'll benefit from mastering rules and a more formal foundation, check out the resources listed at the end of Chapter 5. All are excellent, and you can find an approach that suits you to supplement the practical strategies we'll pursue here.

Let's look first at your choices for how to build a sentence.

ASSEMBLING GOOD SENTENCES

> *If a sentence, no matter how excellent, does not illuminate your subject in some new and useful way, scratch it out.*
>
> —Kurt Vonnegut

In the beginning, there is the simple declarative sentence: Someone is doing something, or something is happening.

Here are examples:

Jack wrote the report.

Ellen is Mark's supervisor.

Ellen read the report.

The auditors found a mistake.

Jerry denied responsibility for the mistake.

Jerry was caught.

Jerry apologized.

Then there are sentences with more than one phrase, or clause (which is a phrase that includes a verb), often separated by commas. Here are some two-part sentences:

Jack wrote the report and submitted it to his supervisor. The auditors found a mistake, but Jerry denied he was responsible.

A more complex, longer sentence can have three or more parts or sections:

Jack wrote the report and gave it to his supervisor, Ellen, the next day.

After the auditors found a mistake, Jerry denied responsibility but eventually had to confess his error and apologize.

Or

Jerry apologized for the accounting error, although earlier, when it was discovered, he had tried to evade responsibility.

Which sentences are correct? All, of course. It depends on the information you're delivering, the tone of what you're writing, and so on. But note that the longer sentences enable the writer to make connections between events more clearly without repeating words and ideas. And if you read the sentences aloud, their rhythms are quite different.

When simple declarative sentences dominate your writing, it sounds childish— much like a first-grade reader or many sixth-grade social studies textbooks. On the other hand, when writing consists entirely of long, complicated sentences, it becomes hard to follow and, pretty soon, boring. It picks up a rhythm that, well, puts the reader to sleep.

For example,

Wanting to express subtle thoughts and ideas, Alice often used lengthy, complicated sentences in her business correspondence. When this problem was brought to her attention, she responded that she preferred not to insult her readers' intelligence. She was told that people found her messages confusing and might not read them to the end. After thinking about the issue further, she decided to rethink her premise.

In fact, more of us share Alice's writing problem than the "first-grade" approach: We tend to begin writing a message or document in a complicated, even convoluted way, disregarding how it "sounds," and need to work our way to simplicity and good rhythm. That's one of the main reasons you need to see every message as a first draft and plan to edit it.

How could the paragraph about Alice read better? Here's one way.

Alice often used long, complicated sentences in her business writing. Told that this was a problem, she explained that she wanted to express subtle ideas and not insult her readers' intelligence. But her messages confused people. Often they didn't read them to the end. Confronting these facts, Alice decided to change her writing style and use sentences of varying length. She finds this technique much more successful.

Note that the two versions are almost exactly the same length, so the changes in this case don't save space. And the same information is delivered. But do you agree that the second version is more engaging? The reason is simple but important: Version 1 repeats the same sentence structure, sentence after sentence—each is perfectly correct but together make it tough for the reader. Version 2 deliberately breaks the pattern by combining sentences with different structures.

If you don't want to think about structure at all, just consciously try to begin each sentence differently. In the second version, for example, the simple sentences like the first one usually alternate with more complicated ones that require commas.

Absorb this basic idea, and your writing may improve dramatically. It's easier to keep your reader's attention and sound interesting just by alternating the length and structure of your sentences. This pulls people along. *We live in an age of speed readers and scanners. The faster people can read what you write, the more successful your message will usually be.*

Fortunately, you don't need to think about grammar to do this. But you do need to reexamine what you want to get across and see if you can recombine the ideas, wording, and sentences so the sum of the parts makes a better whole. You may also need to cut sentences up to make some short and punchy.

In your own writing and everything you read, make it a point to train your ear. *Read your writing aloud.* Be aware of rhythms: when they work and when they don't. Listen for the oral stumbling blocks that tell you that words and structures can and should be better.

APPLYING READABILITY GUIDELINES

How Long Should Sentences Be?

There is actually a semi-scientific answer to this question. It comes from readability research on what makes writing most understandable. As the sidebar feature on "The Shrinking English Sentence" shows, the average number of words per sentence in written materials has radically fallen over the centuries. Today there is more or less agreement that sentences should *average* between 14 and 18 words to be most comprehensible.

And speech? Linguists have determined that the spoken sentence typically consists of 7 to 10 words.

How about online material? Somewhere between what works for print documents and what's typical for speech.

THE SHRINKING ENGLISH SENTENCE

People began studying readability and its relation to sentence length in the late 19th century. An English literature professor named Lucius Adelno Sherman analyzed sentence length historically and found (in his 1893 book *Analytics of Literature*) the following averages:

Pre-Elizabethan times	50 words per sentence
Elizabethan times	45 words per sentence
Victorian times	29 words per sentence
Late 19th century	23 words per sentence

Sherman observed that over time, sentences had become simpler and more concrete as well as shorter. He noted that this was because spoken language was affecting written language—as it should: "The oral sentence is clearest because it is the product of millions of daily efforts to be clear and strong. It represents the work of the race for thousands of years in perfecting an effective instrument of communication."

Today, journalism experts believe sentences should be as short as 14 words on average for maximum readability. But not all written documents need to be understood by everyone.

Since the research agrees that sentence length is one of the two key ingredients of readability (word length is the other), it's important to consider these guidelines seriously.

Here are a few takeaways for the business writer:

1. Academia remains partly immersed in pre-20th-century writing, especially for English majors. So the writing style encouraged by some professors reflects an earlier time and may be at odds with this book's guidelines, which are grounded in practical writing for today's high-speed digital world.

2. The "rule" doesn't mean that every sentence should be at least 14 words and no more than 18 words long. It means the average length should fall within those limits. For example, the last few paragraphs here—from the "How Long Should Sentences Be?" head through the end of this sentence—average 17.9 words per sentence. But one sentence is 41 words long and some have fewer than 10 words. Using average length in this way promotes the alternating rhythm recommended earlier.

3. It's fine to vary the general rule according to your own writing style and the nature of your audience. Obviously, highly educated readers will understand difficult material more easily than less educated ones. If you're writing to an

audience that ranges, say, from factory workers to managers, or you'd define the readers as average, keep in mind that the "average American" is estimated to read at a seventh-grade level. *And just because people with a lot of education can understand something difficult doesn't mean they want to read it—or will stick with it.*

After all, we're not talking about writing required textbooks. Virtually nothing you'll write is mandated reading. There are no captive audiences in the business world: You have to earn your audience with just about every single document you create by writing it well.

4. To check how you're doing, you don't need to count the words of every sentence. Your Microsoft Word program, and others, gives you a marvelous tool that does this for you. It's the Readability Statistics Index, and you can ask your computer to bring it up every time you use spell check. The box materializes immediately after the spelling and grammar check and tells you the average sentence length of the document or highlighted piece, along with additional useful information.

Using the Readability Statistics—sometimes called the Flesch Index—is a great stress-free way to monitor and improve your own writing.

HOW TO USE THE READABILITY INDEX

The Readability Index gives you an instant way to check how readable your writing is, along with helpful clues about how to fix it.

To access it in Microsoft Word, bring up Preferences, and under Spelling and Grammar, make sure the "Show readability statistics" box has a check mark. Then it will automatically come up after you've checked spelling and grammar. You can also highlight a section of a document and get this information. As you see in the examples shown, the statistics include number of words and number of characters, paragraphs and sentences. More useful is the "averages" section. These figures tell you whether your writing reflects the guidelines recommended here:

14 to 18 words per sentence, averaged

Short words, short paragraphs (more on this in Chapter 5)

Better yet, "readability" tells you percentage of passive sentences (the lower the better; try for under 10%), Flesch Reading Ease (meaning the percentage of people who will understand the piece), and Flesch-Kincaid Grade Level: how much education someone needs to

(Continued)

> (Continued)
>
> understand your document. You may find it hard to write for less than an 11th-grade reading level, depending on your subject. Don't worry about this particular statistic unless you're writing for a relatively uneducated audience. However, the *Wall Street Journal* has claimed to be written at an eighth-grade level.
>
> Following is a demonstration of how the Readability Index can help you. First, there is a not-very-well-written piece of prose along with the index stats. Then there's a rewritten version, with a new set of stats to match. It shows the difference achieved by editing and rewriting.
>
> When you write, try checking the readability stats. If you're not satisfied with the outcome, experiment with fixing your sentences and word length—the major elements the system measures—and check again. If the document is important, you may want to go through another round of stats and look at the index again.
>
> The good news: The guidelines eventually become built into your writing process, and you instinctively write better.

Example

Text Version 1—Original

There have been a diminishing number of young people in the region, according to a variety of studies that have been issued on the subject by organizations ranging from smart growth groups to the offices of the county executives. Universally, it is agreed that a brain drain is untenable. The impact of losing our best and brightest would be that the region could become less vital and would offer fewer opportunities, which can only increase the problem. If this happens, Green Island is going to become a place that is dominated by an aging population, a situation that would have dire economic and social consequences. To solve this challenge, we need to be able to understand the perspectives of a variety of stakeholders and determine what program we can put into place in order to move forward.

Readability Statistics

Counts	
Words	137
Characters	660
Paragraphs	1
Sentences	5

Averages	
Sentences per Paragraph	5.0
Words per Sentence	27.4
Characters per Word	4.8

Readability	
Passive Sentences	60%
Flesch Reading Ease	44.4
Flesch–Kincaid Grade Level	12.0

OK

Text Version 2—Rewrite

Young people are moving away from the region, a number of studies confirm. We all agree that preventing a brain drain is essential. If we lose our best and brightest, Green Island loses its vitality.

As young adults find fewer opportunities, more and more will look elsewhere, leaving us with an aging population. This outlook threatens our economy and social well-being. To address the challenge, we must understand the different stakeholders' perspectives and decide on a program so we can move forward.

Choose the Right Words

The second factor in calculating readability is word length. Research on this tells us that the short words are most understandable to the most people. That's no surprise. But how short? One or two syllables.

In business writing, unlike parts of the academic world, you don't get rewarded for using long, "sophisticated" words. Instead, you lose readers.

Does this mean you need to simplify your thoughts? Absolutely not. It means that while you have a wealth of choices with which to express your precise meaning, you must work to be as clear as possible through words that really communicate this meaning to other people.

The English language was built on short words (see the sidebar on "Why English Has So Many Words and How That Affects Your Writing"), and to this day, we seem to trust those words most and find the "fancy" words suspicious or even pretentious. *To succeed, use the one- and two-syllable words as much as you can and consciously use the longer words when you need them because a shorter word won't work or you want the effect.* Just as sentence variety adds interest to what you write, a peppering of longer words can spark things up.

Readability Statistics

Counts

Words	80
Characters	409
Paragraphs	2
Sentences	6

Averages

Sentences per Paragraph	3.0
Words per Sentence	13.3
Characters per Word	5.0

Readability

Passive Sentences	0%
Flesch Reading Ease	54.7
Flesch-Kincaid Grade Level	8.9

OK

I am a bear of very little brain, and long words bother me.

—Winnie the Pooh
(by A. A. Milne)

WHY ENGLISH HAS SO MANY WORDS AND HOW THAT AFFECTS YOUR WRITING

The English vocabulary is unusually rich, and there are often abundant word choices for expressing the same thought. For comparison, English has about 200,000 words while French has half as many.

(Continued)

(Continued)

The short words mostly come from our Anglo-Saxon legacy, the original base of English. These include words like *man, bad, good, work, dog, big, eat, love, in, out.* Some Scandinavian additions arrived with the Viking invasions (*leg, crawl, trust, take*).

But many of the language's longer words derive from Latin, or French—via the Norman invasions—and because the Normans occupied England as ruling aristocrats, they introduced words relating to government, the military, abstract ideas and sophisticated living. For example, *justice, fraternity, sovereign, materialism, casserole, elegant.*

It's estimated that while the Anglo-Saxon words compose only 1% of today's English, they remain the fundamental words and half of what we typically write consists of those words. As Bill Bryson says in his interesting book, *The Mother Tongue: English and How It Got That Way,* "To this day we have an almost instinctive preference for the older Anglo-Saxon phrases."

Old words are best. And old words, when they are short, are best of all.

—Winston Churchill

Find the Words You Need

A big part of editing your own work—as well as other people's writing—is to review the document and substitute short plain words for the long complicated ones. This is a basic way to achieve the rhythm you want: the word movement that sounds smooth when read aloud and pulls people through your message at warp speed.

Here are some frequently used words and better alternatives.

Instead of . . .	Use . . .
Approximately	About
Demonstrate	Show
Utilize	Use
Subsequently	Next
Construct	Build
Assistance	Help
Competencies	Skills
Initiate	Begin

See the activity at the end of this chapter for more ten-dollar words to watch for. Note that you don't necessarily need to always use the shorter versions. I've chosen to use the long way round a number of times in this chapter, and throughout the book. But your choices should be deliberate.

How can you find the right words? Build a repertoire of useful, short words that are often needed in everyday business writing, and make a habit of using them. For example, *hard* generally works better than *difficult.* It's better to *"fix"* a problem than *"remediate"* it. Instead of *investigate,* you may want to say *study* or *track* or *look into* or *follow up.*

Notice, too—as is the case with *investigate*—a simpler way of saying something may mean using a phrase instead of a single word.

And use a thesaurus—nothing could be easier to do online. Just Google the word plus "synonym," and a choice of free resources pops up with enough choices to overwhelm.

As you write or after you've finished a draft, check the Readability Statistics box. If it shows that your piece is 12th-grade level and will only be understood by 20% of readers, note the stat for word length—how many average characters per word your sample contains. To improve your readability, substitute shorter words and shorten your sentences.

Employ Colorful Words

Let's agree at the outset that colorful language is not needed for most business writing. You want to use concrete, familiar words and not come across as pretentious. This helps ensure that a range of people will understand your messages, including those whose native language is not English.

However, graphic wording is important when you want to stimulate readers' imagination or influence them. This is often desirable in marketing copy, presentations, and any writing where it's important to be vivid and memorable. It helps to notice some techniques that creative writers use, even though you may not routinely draw on them. Also, build an awareness of how writers in various media use language to influence you. Here are some techniques to enliven your writing.

Choose specific, concrete words with more "atmosphere" to liven up material. Since English offers so many options, check for similes as you write or once you have the first draft down.

Use interesting modifiers—descriptive words. In general, business writers are told to minimize use of these adjectives and adverbs. This is valid: They slow reading down and often create a sense of overkill.

Mark Twain's statement—"If you find an adjective, kill it"—is often quoted by writing instructors. But he didn't mean that all adjectives and adverbs should be cut, just the unproductive ones. In business writing, modifiers used well help bring copy alive. A good way to go about this is to choose words that engage the senses and lead the reader to taste, see, hear, feel, and even smell what you're writing about. This is a staple technique for fiction writers.

For example, you don't need a context to form mental images for words such as:

- glittering
- squeamish
- sluggish
- tangy
- salty
- heroic
- gaunt

- grungy
- sneakily
- slimy
- razor-thin
- twitchy
- squishy
- cranky

Your thesaurus is your friend here. Look up *big,* for example, and you'll have a choice of *enormous, huge, colossal, astronomical, titanic, mountainous,* or *ample, broad, stout* and much more.

Notice that some of these words are "prejudicial": They incline readers to see what you're describing in negative or positive ways. To say that a report's documentation is "razor-thin," that the market is "twitchy," or that a new company venture is "heroic" carries more meaning than if the documentation is simply "light," the market "uneven," or the venture is merely worthwhile. Avoid such words if you don't want the connotations.

Actively create extended graphic images. Think of a helpful comparison. A newspaper article about a fossil discovery, for example, does this simply: " . . . the dinosaur, the size of a gigantic turkey, was a meat-eating creature that lived more than 65 million years ago." Giving people graphic images can make concepts easier to grasp and more memorable.

Here's a sentence I wrote recently:

Long Island established the American suburban pattern, characterized by numerous small communities, each absorbed in its own local affairs.

The revision:

Long Island set the pattern for America's suburbs: an enormous patchwork of small communities, looking inward.

For some people, using graphic language, whether in print or speech, is a natural talent. The best storytellers flaunt this skill and we love them for it. But don't kid yourself—it's also very hard work. It demands moving a step or two beyond the clear and simple. It takes extra time to plumb the depth of your meaning, connect disparate ideas imaginatively, and, probably, research the wording options.

And yes, when you aim for more specific words, you often end up using the long French or Latinate words that I cautioned against. But there is a loophole—*sprinkle your writing with the more complex, specific words when that serves your goal and suits your audience.*

And keep in mind that the true masters of writing can stick to the simplest language and yet paint unforgettable mental images. Consider these lines by the 19th-century American poet Emily Dickinson:

> *Hope is the thing with feathers that perches in the soul/and sings the tunes without the words/and never stops at all.*

Build With Vigorous Verbs

Using strong, active verbs is another way to inject life into all your writing and by far the best way to spark it up. Unless it creates an effect that doesn't support your goal, when you can deploy a strong verb, just do it.

Using Action Verbs

Consider *grumble, squash, enflame, twitch, droop, tantalize,* and *mope*—they create mental images and a feeling of action or "being there." But you may not find many occasions to employ such verbs. How does the active verb idea apply to your everyday business writing? You have a mountain of choices. For example:

Instead of *move,* you could say *galvanize, rush, accelerate, lunge, streak,* or *scramble.*

Instead of *tell,* consider *expose, instruct, enlighten, narrate, recount,* or *lecture.*

Instead of *introduce,* consider *unmask, reveal, uncover, divulge,* or *bring into play.*

Instead of *make,* consider *originate, invent, compose, build,* or *fabricate.*

Instead of *stop,* consider *halt, pause, conclude, block, stonewall, drop,* or *shut off.*

Instead of *hesitate,* consider *dither, hedge, vacillate, teeter, waver, wobble,* or *pussyfoot.*

Instead of *decide,* consider *map, settle on, mull, figure, ponder,* or *weigh.*

Improving the way you use verbs is the single best tool for improving everything you write. Here are some techniques to know about.

Use Verbs to Carry the Weight of Every Sentence, and Use the Simplest, Most Active Form of the Verb

When you center on the action and simplify the verb, it's easy to cut unnecessary wordiness and build a forward-moving rhythm that keeps readers with you. Notice how much more direct and compact the second sentence is in each case.

We are taking forward leaps.

vs.

We're leaping forward.

Many people are resistant to reading on screen.

vs.

Many people resist on-screen reading.

Often if you take a moment, you can think of more graphic verbs that don't need modifiers to make the idea clear:

The company's sales figures usually rise substantially in the first quarter.

vs.

Company sales usually zoom in the first quarter.

Here's a more complicated example that is common to a lot of business writing:

This mistake has put us in the position of having to explain why business in the last quarter went down radically.

Notice the clues that tell you this sentence needs help. Read aloud, it dictates the singsong cadence of poor writing. When you review it visually, you see that some parts are awkward and wordy.

Spend a few seconds thinking about what the sentence means and you'll see other alternatives, such as,

This mistake *forces us to explain* why business in the last quarter *plummeted.*

Simply substituting these stronger verbs for the roundabout versions cuts the word count from 21 to 13, produces a fast read with a natural rhythm, and gets the idea across more vividly.

Notice that many sentences with weak verbs and unnecessary wordiness can be fixed by using the present tense. Resist works better than "are resistant to"; "forces us to explain" is much better than "has put us in the position of having to explain." Look at how these sentence pairs differ:

This rule can be applied to the problem we are confronting.

vs.

This rules applies to the problem we face.

This ability is the result of having the foresight to come to the table well prepared.

vs.

This ability results from coming to the table well prepared.

A subject line should really be focused on letting people know what the message is about.

vs.

Focus subject lines on what the message is about.

To write a better e-mail, it's helpful to plan your message first.

vs.

To write a better e-mail, plan your message first.

We also dilute verbs by hedgy, lazy phrasing with words like *make, can,* and *get.* For example,

He made an announcement that Tim won the award.

vs.

He announced that Tim won the award.

She's making a decision about how to proceed.

vs.

She's deciding how to proceed.

You can handle the challenge this way.

vs.

Handle the challenge this way.

I need to get acclimated to the situation.

vs.

I need to acclimate myself to the situation.

How do you get started on this project?

vs.

How do you start this project?

You should add some long words to make copy more colorful.

vs.

Use some long words to invigorate copy.

One more "do not": Resist temptations to use passive-sounding verbs to avoid taking responsibility. This approach is sometimes called "the divine passive." A fact or event is presented as if it were an act of God. It doesn't work in the business world. For example:

The wrong decision was made and an unproductive path was chosen.

Who made the decision? Beyond creating an impersonal tone, this evasion undermines credibility and does the cause no good. Here's an irritating quote reported by the *Wall Street Journal*, said by a News Corp. executive when his editor was convicted of hacking voice messages:

"We said long ago, and repeat today, that wrongdoing occurred and we apologized for it."

See the Clues to Wordy Sentences

> *We are a society strangling on unnecessary words, circular construction, pompous frills ad meaningless jargon.*
>
> —William Zinnser, in his
> classic book, *On Writing Well*

Here are some more clues that you're weakening your sentences with clutter and some instant improvements:

Too many words ending in *-ion.* For example,

The function of the communications department is the production of newsletters.

Better:

The communications department's job is to produce newsletters.

Generally, try to use only one *-ion* word per sentence.

Too many words ending in *-ing* (gerunds), such as,

We're implementing a system for tracking how well we're measuring performance.

Better:

The new system will track how well we measure performance.

Restricting yourself whenever possible to one *-ing* word per sentence can help readability a lot. Check whether you can cut most *-ing* words by using the present tense instead.

Too many words ending in *-ed*:

The lead of a press release should really be aimed at telling readers something they might be interested in knowing.

Better:

Focus subject lines on what interests readers.

You'd also find these wordy and passive-sounding phrases by listening to their cadence when read aloud. The nice thing about improving your sentences in these commonsense ways is that you can identify how to improve them from many angles. Observe which clues work best for you, and practice finding the weaknesses that way. Once you pinpoint the problem, you're 75% toward the solution!

Too many words like *of* and *to* and *in* (prepositions):

Our office is ready to advise staff members on how to use the benefit program to the maximum degree.

Better:

We advise staff members on how to best use the benefit program.

To measure the progress of the project, a system of documentation will be implemented.

Better:

To measure the project's progress, we'll document it.

In case the contract doesn't reach you in time, please look into the reason and keep me in the loop.

Better:

If you don't receive the letter in time, please find out why and let me know.

In cases where you repeat *to, of,* and *in* constructions, you can often cut what isn't needed or substitute words that make reading easier. Eliminate *of* phrases by using an apostrophe + *s.* In the second example, "progress of the project" became "project's progress." "The contract of the CEO" works better as "the CEO's contract."

Too many *and*s that interfere with understanding:

We're ready to communicate to all stakeholders and interested parties and will ensure that good information and current thinking are available to the media and the public.

The solution here is often to break sentences up. Substituting words and phrases such as *also* and *as well as* can help, but don't depend on them too much. And as in all the examples, think about another way to say the same thing more clearly. For example,

We're ready to communicate to stakeholders and interested parties. We'll deliver good information and current thinking to the media, plus update the public.

Too many sentences built on "to be" verbs—*is, were, will be, should be,* and *has been.* And too many built on "to have" verbs.

Without struggling to understand the passive voice, which is slippery, develop an awareness of the traps that inactive constructions drive you into. Usually, when you see more than one "to be" or "to have" verb in a sentence, change it. (Once may even be unnecessary.) Consider

There are strong indications that this is not the best time to ask for a raise.

vs.

Clearly, this is not the best time to ask for a raise.

It's hard to measure how much the community was pained by the decision.

vs.

The decision pained the community immeasurably.

To have edited your work after having written it is always advised. Upon review, you'll find that mistakes have been made.

vs.

Always edit your work after writing it. You'll find that you've made mistakes.

But editing is not a subject many of us were ever taught in our lives.

vs.

But few of us ever learned to edit.

Also develop your inner ear for sounds that repeat. Too many words ending in *-ly* or *-y* make sentences awkward and indicate adjectives or adverbs that should be cut. Repeating the word *by* also sounds bad and suggests a need to rework. Here is an extreme example:

The report by the committee was fortunately generally positive and gave us a blueprint to revamp policy by rethinking the guidelines.

How would you rewrite that?

EDITING: MANY WAYS CAN WORK

Keep in mind that there are nearly always more ways than one to solve a problem, in writing as in life. Editing is nowhere near a science, though you may want to argue whether it's an art. Certainly it rates as a craft.

Here's a sentence that I asked a group of professional writers to rewrite:

A performance system will allow the development of innovative training techniques and methodologies and allow companies flexibility in tailoring their training to the specific job duties of their employees.

Here are three different results. All are workable.

1. A performance system will allow companies to develop innovative and job-specific training techniques for employees.

2. A performance system gives companies access to new and innovative training techniques and enables them to tailor learning to specific responsibilities.

3. A performance system allows companies to develop new training techniques. Companies also have more room to create customized training for each job.

Notice that each interprets the original sentence somewhat differently. Editing other people's work is often a challenge. If it's poorly written, the meaning can be hard to pin down, and a rewrite might slant it wrong. When you revise your own work, it's a relative snap—you usually know what you meant.

In the next chapter, we'll move on to the bigger picture and turn sentences into paragraphs and paragraphs into whole documents.

PRACTICE OPPORTUNITIES

I. Sentence Rhythm Practice

A. Choppy Cadence

Rewrite this paragraph. First read it aloud to identify the problems. When you've written a new version, read that aloud as well and see if you're satisfied.

Carol is working on an MBA. She finds the pressures very demanding. She has almost no time to spend with friends. She doesn't even have time for phone calls. She doesn't have much time for e-mail or keeping up with Facebook either. The only time she sees other people is in class or team projects or study groups. She recently decided to change this pattern. She'll begin by brainstorming ideas for how to set aside some personal time each week. She also needs to think about whom she can spend that time with. Everyone she knows is constantly working.

B. Monotonous Cadence

Rewrite this letter asking for a recommendation. Again, read the before and after versions aloud.

Dear X,

Not only are you an exceptional business adviser whose unique vision adds significant value to the company but your constructive management style helps the entire team to develop new skills each day. Because you are a leader in your field, I was wondering if you'd write a letter of recommendation supporting my application to the Green University International MBA program.

While this job affords me constant learning and I continue to enjoy my experience here, I hope that gaining an MBA will enhance my management skills at the international level. It should also prepare me for a future in management, since I hope to become a great manager, like you, one day.

I realize that my acceptance would mean my departure from the firm, but there should be ample time to train a replacement. If permitted, I would love to help secure a replacement and provide thorough training as well as feedback to ensure that the new role maximizes efficiencies and focuses on future growth. And after I've completed my schooling, I hope I have the opportunity to work with you in the future.

If you do decide to grant me this request, I have prepared a folder that includes a letter outlining specifics and a prepaid envelope for mailing. If for any reason you don't feel comfortable writing a letter on my behalf, I completely understand.

II. Play With the Readability Index

A. Use your Microsoft Word program's Readability Index to determine what grade level your favorite magazine is written for. Then check out the *Wall Street Journal,* your city's daily newspaper, and online publications and blogs that you like.

B. Discuss results in class: What surprises you? Were the publications consistent in their grade-level appeal, or did different parts of them vary? Did the online media produce indicators different than print?

III. Compare Readability Tools

Check out the Gunning-Fog and SMOG indexes, and compare them to each other and the Flesch. Are the formulas different? Which is most useful and why? Are there any others you prefer? Write a report suitable for a blog.

IV. Substitute Short Words for Long Ones

Think of short-word alternatives for the words in the list that follows. Expand the list with more frequently used long words and their substitutes based on your own writing and your everyday reading. A volunteer, or a small committee, can take charge of integrating the lists to produce a helpful resource for everyone.

Substantial	Prevalent
Subsequent	Verbose
Indication	Fundamental
Aggregate	Additionally
Culmination	Fraudulent
Disseminate	Initiate
Subsequent	Optimum
Eliminate	Curriculum
Construct	Assistance
Convoluted	Substantiate
Imminently	Component

V. Rewrite Exercise

Select one page from a recent piece of your own writing; classwork is fine. Improve it according to your best judgment based on the principles covered in this book so far. Aim for better sentences, word choice, and use of verbs.

Then use the Readability Index to check out the stats on your original piece and the newer version. Is there a difference in the word length, words per sentence, total number of words, percentage of passive verbs, and the readability indicators?

If you do not yet have an average of 18 or fewer words per sentence, and/or the percentage of passive verbs is more than 10%, rewrite the selection again and see if you can hit these targets.

VI. Practice Editing

I wrote this paragraph for the preceding chapter and upon review, found it awkward. Circle the problems and edit the sentences. To see how I rewrote it, find the paragraph in this chapter.

However, graphic wording can be useful in marketing copy and other writing where you want to stimulate readers' imagination. It's helpful to be aware of some techniques that creative writers use, even though you may not often draw on them. Also, developing your awareness of how language is used to influence you is worthwhile.

VII. Write a Memo to Yourself

We all have our own individual writing problems. Self-editing is much easier once we recognize those problems and notice how we repeat the same mistakes. So review this chapter against your own writing patterns, and think about which specific ideas can help you improve. Then write a memo to yourself describing how you plan to make your writing work better in terms of sentence structure, rhythm, word choice, use of verbs, unnecessary use of gerunds, and so on.

VIII. Sentence Fixer-Uppers

Try your hand at improving these sentences. Focus on improving the verbs, but also cut unnecessary words, use shorter words where possible, and simplify each sentence.

Watch for the clues, including intrusive use of *-ing, -ed, -ion* and the constructions involving *has, is,* and other inactive verb forms.

1. There isn't an exact number yet of how many people we will need to hire, but we are going to try to keep the number as minimal as possible.

2. It has become a rather difficult time for our industry.

3. We're very appreciative of your interest in the products our company produces.

4 Want to put your expertise in the spotlight?

5. Please note that the central speech you will present should focus on the new style of leadership.

6. We gave them warning that it would be necessary to develop additional funding sources to establish the new service.

7. You might have hobbies that lead you to an in-depth understanding of a subject.

8. When writing to a prospective employer, ask yourself, do they have a need that they may not have perceived yet that I could fill?

9. In addition to their financial contributions to the candidate, the support group had the intention of increasing her public profile.

10. His presentation on the skills of negotiation has been scheduled to be delivered in March.

11. We need to be able to understand the perspective of a variety of stakeholders and what needs to happen in order to move forward.

12. New development is making our suburban sprawl become even worse.

13. Few things affect the quality of our life as much as the removal of intrusive sound in our environment.

14. People who do not have the support of a partner accord more value to their friends.

15. The work of the lab is to develop nano-engineered particles that can be much more powerful in catalyzing combustion.

16. Our greatest awareness of the complexity of movement is a by-product of watching babies' development.

17. Jones needed to do something to revitalize the association.

18. We review your publications and websites and advise you on how to improve them.

19. The supervisor did an investigation of the accident and came to the conclusion that the agency had been in violation of safety regulations.

20. A decision was made by the nominating committee that due to the fact that applications were tardy, an extension of the application period would be made.

Chapter 5

THE WHOLE PICTURE

Pulling Your Best Message Together

Simplicity is the ultimate sophistication.

—Leonardo da Vinci

WRITING THE SHORT PARAGRAPH

Now that you know how to build sensible sentences, it's time to move on to the larger unit.

You may have been told to develop a "topic" or "thesis" sentence for each paragraph, build a single idea on it and end with a conclusion. If that approach helps, use it. Alternatively, start with the readability premise. Research tells us that the best length for a paragraph is three to five sentences. In many cases, even fewer sentences are best for the first paragraph—the lead—and for online copy like websites and blogs.

Luckily, when you keep your paragraphs short, it's easier to stay on track and recognize when you stray off your intended path. It's also easier to know when to break your paragraphs, or "grafs." Basically, start a new graf when it feels logical to do so. Typically, this is when you're beginning a new thought or subthought, or moving to a detail or clarification.

If you're the kind of writer who tends to spill it all out in a few long, breathless gasps, no problem: Consistently review your draft with an eye toward the white space. Have you produced a dense document with long paragraphs that break only a few times per page? Then splinter the material into shorter paragraphs of three to five sentences. Next, look at each paragraph to see if it makes sense or needs to be clarified.

Every document gains from short paragraphs in a number of ways:

1. They more readily engage the eye and therefore readers' interest. A packed message skimpy on white space challenges and may even prevent them from reading the message at all.

2. They increase the likelihood of keeping your reader with you, because the message seems to move so much faster.

3. They produce a "spacey" document that's far easier to grasp than an unbroken dense one and is therefore more likely to succeed, whatever the goal.

In addition to checking that each graf works, check whether each leads logically to the next one and all relate neatly. Brief paragraphs are easy to move around so you can experiment with making your message flow more logically. You'll often find that the last sentence of one paragraph works better when you move it to begin the paragraph that follows.

And there's a magic tool for melding all those paragraphs into a fluent, convincing, logical message that makes what you write seem persuasive and even inevitable: the transition.

USING TRANSITIONS: WORDS, PHRASES AND DEVICES

Transitions are an important part of the infrastructure that connects your ideas, examples and overall argument. Take care with them, because successful writing requires that all connections are clear to your audience. You never want your readers to wonder, "Why is she telling me that?" or substituting their own reasoning for yours, even unconsciously. Ambiguous connections create misunderstanding, or indifference.

Good transitions, on the other hand, instantly improve all your writing because they smooth it out and eliminate the choppy, disconnected effect that signals poor writing (and thinking).

Transitions are critical at the sentence, paragraph, and full-document levels. For example, you could write,

John doesn't like classical music. He went to the concert his friends chose.

The two thoughts don't connect. Instead they could read,

John went to the concert his friends chose, *even though* he doesn't like classical music.

or

John doesn't like classical music. *Nevertheless,* he went to the concert his friends chose.

On the sentence level, we typically use transition words instinctively. Simple words like *and, but, or* and *because* are handy—and may be used to begin sentences in all but the most formal documents. But connecting paragraphs well can take more deliberate thought.

It may be appropriate to end a paragraph with a transition, as an introduction to what comes next. Note the transitions between sentences as well as at the end of the paragraph:

The White Contract is scheduled for signing on the 30th. *However,* some problems have come up that we should discuss at Friday's meeting. *In the meantime,* we can prepare for that conversation *with the following procedure.*

In many cases, transitions should be used to begin a paragraph so it links to what preceded it. Among the useful words and phrases to draw on for both opening and closing a graf are,

To sum up . . . in review . . . finally . . . in general . . . in other words . . . equally important

To the contrary . . . on the other hand . . . conversely . . . nevertheless . . . in spite of . . . otherwise . . . unfortunately . . . regrettably

Also . . . additionally . . . further . . . specifically . . . for example . . . accordingly . . . moreover . . . besides

Later . . . the next step is . . . recently . . . in the future . . . afterward . . . at that point . . . so far

To illustrate . . . for example . . . similarly . . . conversely . . . accordingly . . . in conclusion . . . finally

Some transitional words and phrases carry connotations that can help convey the tone you want:

Best of all . . . in fact . . . truthfully . . . of course . . . naturally . . . chiefly . . . inevitably . . . and yet . . . happily . . . it goes without saying . . . surprisingly. . . fortunately

In any message that matters (and as you know, I think they all do), check how each paragraph connects to the one that precedes and the one that follows. If you can't make these relationships clear, you may need to rethink your content and your own understanding of the subject.

In long documents like reports and proposals, use transitions to ensure that the sections connect logically. Go out of your way to clarify the links with phrases that act as transitional devices:

Here's why . . . the result . . . our conclusions . . . there's more . . . What did we learn? . . . How will this help you? . . . the solution

You can also use whole sentences to introduce a section and tie it into the document's logical pattern. Apply some creativity to these transitions, and they'll really advance your cause:

Our conclusions are based on the following trials.

We've focused on similar projects for five years and learned a number of lessons.

The sales projections are especially interesting.

Here are the questions most frequently asked—and the answers.

Here is a brief review of the problem's background.

It sounds great. But . . .

That's what we used to think, too.

Setting up a sequence via a numbered list is another good tool for promoting clarity and holding a document, or section, together:

Four factors weigh most heavily in making the decision.

The process can be completed in seven stages.

Here's the plan for the next eight months.

One more great benefit to transitions: Consciously used to better communicate a message, they can help you organize your material more easily. And for your reader, a message that feels clear, logical, and cohesive is much more convincing than one that holds together less tightly.

AVOIDING WORD TRAPS: BUZZWORDS, JARGON, IDIOMS

Buzzwords and Jargon

As you write, keep some important principles of word choice in mind.

Avoid clichés, buzzwords, jargon, and just plain overworked phrases whenever possible.

Why? They bore, confuse and conceal meaning. Whatever industry we belong to, we typically absorb a specialized repertoire of words and terminology. This is necessary and positive. It enables us to exchange specific information built on common understanding. A lawyer's "inside" language naturally differs from a biologist's, a financial manager's, a graphic designer's, and so on.

But industry shorthand can create problems.

Problem 1: Using a private industry code to communicate with a client, a funding agency, a journalist, investor, other stakeholder or the public.

Here's an example from education, a passage (admittedly out of context) from an alumni magazine issued by a major university's Department of English. The article is about how writing instruction must adapt to changing technology.

Apply this domestic generational paradigm to the English Department and we begin to see how the ethos of space might affect students and teachers, perhaps even an entire discipline.

It's easy to laugh at how people in other industries use jargon but harder to notice when we do it ourselves. Here is a business example:

This change will allow us to better leverage our talent base in an area where developmental roles are under way and strategically focuses us toward the upcoming Business System transition where Systems literacy and accuracy will be essential to maintain and to further improve service levels to our customer base going forward.

SUCCESS TIP

BE PART OF THE SOLUTION, NOT THE PROBLEM

During the past decade, numerous corporate catastrophes, from oil spills to CEO personal scandals to fraud revelations, have led the public and government to distrust business. Government leaders and agencies have enjoyed their fair share of major embarrassments as well. To establish or reestablish credibility demands that organizations be honest, transparent, and clear. Writing jargon-laden drivel makes you part of the problem. Writing well makes you part of the solution—whatever work you do.

Problem 2: Using code words with ambiguous meanings that can be interpreted in different ways undermines clarity. *Protocol,* for example, has different meanings to a diplomat, medical researcher and computer specialist.

Consider the word *overload.* To physical trainers, it means building fitness through progressive weight bearing. To computer scientists, it's the use of a single definition for different classes of objects. To some college professors, *overload* means teaching more courses than the base number required—not to mention that *overload* is also a specific chess tactic, and a Pakistani band.

Of course, context usually tells us which meaning is intended, but if we're talking to someone from a different field of expertise, or the public, this can be a costly assumption.

Problem 3: Using jargon and buzzwords to veil our meaning or avoid having one—such as when we say nothing at all in a supposedly impressive way. Take a phrase like "cost-effective, end-to-end, value-added services." Hundreds of thousands of companies describe themselves this way in print and online: What have they said? Nothing, or worse, because using the same jargon for every service makes them sound identical.

Here's an example from another annual report:

The company is maniacally focused on ensuring that all of this software meets stringent benchmarks and product criteria for best-in-class ease of use, simple installation and overall ease of ownership to ensure that mission-critical networks are safeguarded and protected not only by redundancy, but also by the most innovative technology available today.

Train Yourself to Recognize Buzzwords

I don't know the rules of grammar . . . If you're trying to persuade people to do something, or buy something, it seems to me you should use their language, the language they use every day, the language in which they think. We try to write in the vernacular. Our business is infested with idiots who try to impress by using pretentious jargon.

—Advertising pioneer David Ogilvy, quoted
by Kenneth Roman in *The King of Madison Avenue:
David Ogilvy and the Making of Modern Advertising*

A first step toward resisting buzzwords is to recognize them in your own environment. Here are a few business expressions to sidestep when possible, along with better alternatives. For more examples, see the Practice Opportunities section at the end of the chapter. Don't be surprised at how hard it is to find less clichéd substitutes. In many cases, it will require more words to express the idea.

Instead of *core competency,* try *skill.*

Instead of *thought leader,* try *expert* or *authority.*

Instead of *proactive,* try *take the lead.*

Instead of *doubling down,* try *work harder.*

Instead of *curriculum,* try *content.*

Instead of *optimum,* try *ideal* or *best.*

Avoid Empty Rhetoric

When you make meaningless claims without substance or backup, you typically end up with a pile of jargon and buzzwords that communicate nothing: statements like "synergistic out-of-the-box best practice." You can have some fun and play with online "buzzword generators." But many businesspeople generate the meaningless combinations with no humorous intent whatsoever.

How Do You Avoid the Jargon Trap?

It can be challenging. One signal that you need to rethink your language is when your statement could apply equally to any number of businesses and industries. Here are some tactics:

1. Know what you really mean and figure out how to say it most clearly. When you're drafting generalizations that have no true substance, face it and think, How exactly would I explain this to a friend, using simple language that requires no translation?

2. Be as concrete as you can. What is truly original or different about your product? What does it do? What do *you* do? What can you really offer?

3. Find the facts and use them. "97% of our customers told us they'd buy our product again" is a lot better than "We've got a phenomenal satisfaction rate" (provided you can actually cite such a study).

4. Go for evidence of some kind. "We've been recognized for innovative products three times in the past five years by the Consumer Advice Board" is more convincing than "We are the most innovative." "We have partners in 23 countries on five continents" works better than "We're really international."

It takes thinking to figure out what you want to say and the best way to say it. Spouting vague generalities is the easy way out. Determine not to take that path.

Recognize Idioms

Idioms—phrases that we use all the time that mean more than the sum of their words—are so built into the English language that we hardly notice them. Many of them are more graphic than "straight" wording, and even though they're overworked, they tend to add color to our interactions and speed them up. However, because they are generally untranslatable, many nonnative English speakers have no idea what they mean and may totally misinterpret them.

Since so much of what we write will be read by an international audience, it's important to take care with idioms and jargon. Moreover, today most organizations' internal audiences include many nonnative speakers. So you must often find alternative ways of expressing an idea rather than taking the first one that comes to mind.

Here are a few idioms that can confuse readers whose first language is not English.

Against the clock	Set the record straight
Draw the line	On the shelf
By word of mouth	In a nutshell
Face value	Get to the bottom of
Lose track of	Let something ride
Make a stand	Across the board
Zero in on	Change of heart

Be especially wary of analogies that derive from sports that may not be popular outside your own country. American English is rife with expressions that are opaque elsewhere: "end run," "hit it out of the park," "thrown for a loss," "step up to the plate," "out of left field," and "Monday morning quarterback." British idioms drawn from cricket—such as "gola," "sticky wicket," and "hit someone for six"—are foreign to Americans as well as people in other countries where cricket isn't played.

Even this smattering suggests how entrenched many idiomatic expressions are in our language. Eliminating all of them, even from a short document, is a challenge. But when your audience is diverse or the document will be translated, try to use them sparingly.

Once again, the antidote is to delve behind the meaning of what you want to say and find the clearest, least ambiguous way to put it. Look with a critical eye at multiword expressions, and write more basically.

Will the writing lose color and interest without idioms? For native English speakers who read well, yes. For all others, the loss of color matters much less than clarity. This is one more reason to shape your writing to your audience.

SIDESTEPPING TONE TRAPS: HUMOR, EMOTION, PRETENTIOUSNESS, THE IMPERSONAL

The Meant-to-Be-Funny

Humor is a tremendous asset for a speech, a presentation, or a conversation. Unfortunately, unless you're a talented and confident humor writer, it's risky to use it in writing.

A piece of writing lacks the advantages of personal interaction. There is no facial expression to underscore or counter the words; no subtle body language to suggest your true meaning; and, above all, no tone of voice to communicate the real message.

This is a particular drawback with using irony and sarcasm. There's no way to indicate that you're "just joking" and no way to soften the message. What would be funny in person can easily come across as insulting or cruel. Especially because e-mail (like social media) is infinitely forwardable and accessible, a moment's entertainment can have unwelcome consequences.

So here is the rule: In business writing, avoid the temptation to make fun of someone or something others might care about. Don't joke at someone else's expense. Be wary of injecting any humor, because your readers may misinterpret it or find it very inappropriate.

Prejudicial Wording

Don't undercut your message by building in a negative slant, consciously or not. Suppose, for example, you receive an e-mail that begins:

As I already told you . . .

This is to reinforce our conversation . . .

You did not provide . . .

You are apparently unaware that . . .

I am at a loss to understand . . .

Don't fail to let me know . . .

As you should have foreseen . . .

Obviously, you're on full defensive even before reading the rest of the message. The takeaway: Avoid this tone and wording. It's not a productive way to address people, no matter what their relationship to you. Amazingly, however, companies will often write to customers in a similar off-putting manner:

This is to inform you that we are unable to ship your product at this time . . .

Our policy clearly states that purchases are only refundable if . . .

For your information, we no longer provide support services for . . .

Please understand that we cannot make exceptions . . .

The substance of a message may in fact be negative, as in the foregoing examples. If this is the case, then take special care to present the information in as positive a way as possible.

SUCCESS TIP

KEEP A LID ON YOUR EMOTIONS

In business, the line between expressing passion and emotion can be a fine one. Your colleagues, superiors, and subordinates certainly want to feel your conviction, enthusiasm and confidence. But these qualities must appear to be based on an objective reality—not personal investment and feelings.

Obviously, it's bad to lose your temper at a meeting, act defensively, sulk or cast blame. In the business world, like the political, such behavior marks you as the loser. Results can be even worse if you send a hostile message. It can circulate or rankle forever.

Never let what you write show anger. Never criticize anyone in writing (unless it's part of a structured evaluation process). Work hard to maintain a balanced, reasonable tone.

Avoid words that can be negatively interpreted. Don't sound judgmental.

Monitor your messages so they don't betray any attitude, emotion or feeling that will undermine you.

Always pause before sending a harsh message and ask if it might damage a relationship.

However: It can be very helpful to *write* a message that tells someone how you feel, just don't *send* it.

Compose and polish a complete e-mail, letter or post and then burn it: that is, file or discard it. Mentally processing an emotional situation this way enables you to put it in perspective and move on, almost magically.

The first statement, for example, might (if the facts justify it) be phrased this way:

We're delighted that you've ordered our Product #65 but sorry that because it's proved so popular, we are unable to fill orders as quickly as we'd like. Each #65 is individually crafted . . .

Here's how one smart retailer responded, in part, to a return:

We'd love another opportunity to please you. Please accept this offer of free shipping on your next purchase in our catalog or online at . . .

Note that if any company produces a flow of impersonal these-are-the-rules-and-we-don't-care-if-you-like-them-or-not messages to its customers, then policies merit review. The marketplace is too competitive for this approach to customer relations.

The Pompous and Pretentious

For me the words should be like a pane of glass that you look through, not at.

—Ken Follett, novelist

We often see overblown, pretentious language that combines long words with awkward construction. This undercuts a message. It also fails to communicate when used in place of real substance. Here are two ways to be pretentious, both of which you should avoid: a flowery sentence full of mixed metaphors and one built on abstractions and adjectives:

Yet the nightmare cast its shroud in the guise of a contagion of a deer-in-the-headlights paralysis.

The nostrum of "regulation" drags with it a raft of unexamined impediments concerning the nature of markets and governmentality, and a muddle over intentionality, voluntarism, and spontaneity that promulgates the neoliberal creed at the subconscious level.

(Both examples are drawn from a financial book quoted in an *Economist* blog titled *The World's Worst Sentence?*)

How to write more clearly? To recap, use simple, short words; simple, straightforward, short sentences; and simple, clear constructions. And remember the clues that tell you to look for a fix: Read it aloud, and notice the long words, bad cadence, and repetitions (in this second example, three words ending in *-ity*). Check the Readability Index as covered in Chapter 4 (which will tell you the sentence has 36 words, requires at least a 12th-grade reading level and 0% of readers will understand it).

Many different signals can tell you that it's time to rewrite.

The Cold and Impersonal

People today value messages that feel authentic and personal. Whether you're writing a memo explaining a company benefit, a promotional piece selling a product, or a letter responding to a complaint, make it personal. Often this means taking the "you" viewpoint:

For example, rather than:

The new policy on filing for overtime claims is . . .

try,

To file an overtime claim, you need to know . . .

For pitching a product, rather than:

The newly designed Inca 247 offers a number of features to help the graphic designer.

try,

Inca 247 saves you 20% of your graphic design project time and . . .

This tactic ties right in with your need to instantly engage readers and pull them through your document. Remember, when people decide whether a message is worth reading, self-interest rules. Figure out how to phrase the sentence, and the whole message, building on the word *you*.

EDITING YOUR OWN WORK

Fix it...NOW! Periods and commas are everything! Attention to detail, grammar and ease of use are the most critical things on the site.

—Noah Kagan, describing Mark Zuckerberg's unbreakable set of "laws" in his article "How I Lost $170 Million: My Time as #30 at Facebook"

Many people are wary of editing, as if it requires some rare mystical skill. But just as with writing, a strategic approach guides you through.

Knowing you will improve your document and fix problems later is liberating. It frees you to be more spontaneous and even experimental when developing a first draft. This is true whether you're a get-it-all-down-at-once type of writer or one who crafts each sentence thoughtfully.

Here is how to think about the editing process.

1. **Plan your time to allow for editing.**

On a typical project, many professionals allocate a third of the available time for planning, a third for drafting, and at least a third for editing and rewrite. If you're developing a big project, build in a good amount of time for editing at the end.

2. **Give it some space.**

When a document is important try to put it aside for a week or a few days, or an hour. Distance helps you be objective. When you read the draft after a lapse, errors of tone and substance will pop out, as well as technical mistakes. Even a significant e-mail should be stashed for a few hours so your eyes are fresh and your emotional antennae are up.

3. **Switch roles.**

To be your own editor, approach the piece as if you've never seen it before. Don't be influenced by how hard a particular section was to produce. In fact, many fiction writers follow the advice "Kill your little darlings," meaning that passages to which they are especially attached are suspect—probably distracting from the piece's overall intent—and should be cut.

4. **Print it out.**

It's tempting to edit onscreen, but material reads differently in print form and mistakes become easier to spot.

I like to cite chapter and verse with all the proper punctuation laid in. If nothing else, it's a demonstration of both your IQ and your writing skills. How can you trust someone who doesn't bother to spell correctly or can't manage to lay out a simple declarative sentence?

—Kinsey Milhone
(fictional private detective in *N Is for Noon* by Sue Grafton)

Of course, you need not do this with routine e-mails. But consider it with letters, reports, blog posts, website copy and more.

5. **Plan to edit important material in successive stages.**

When you make changes, new mistakes are often introduced so you must review your new version. As you do this, you'll always find more opportunities to improve the language and make the content more persuasive.

6. **Find a reader.**

Backup is invaluable—scout your environment for a colleague or friend to read your important documents and provide honest feedback. Find out how they are perceived and how well they are understood. And extra proofing is always an excellent thing. Offer to perform this service in return.

Now let's look at a practical editing strategy to use, complete with some professional tricks of the trade. Note that a garden-variety e-mail might need just a quick run-through, while a major document such as a proposal, or a résumé, or how-to information demands careful step-by-step attention. But do commit yourself to at least rereading everything you write with an eye toward improving content and fixing mistakes.

Practical Editing Stage 1: Review Your Substance

Start by focusing first on the big picture—content and tone. Conveniently enough, you can recap the same checklist that led you through the planning and writing processes:

> **Review *Goal*:** What comes across to the reader? Does the gist of the message embody your goal, the reason you're writing?
>
> Will what's included accomplish your purpose?
>
> Are the points relevant? Anything missing?
>
> Is there too much information? Does anything distract from the goal?
>
> Is the sequence logical? Convincing?

And really important to notice is the overall impact on your company, and you, of broadcasting this information. As companies post more and more content on their websites in the interest of transparency, misjudgment is common.

It's a problem on social media sites, too, for individuals. People post information (and pictures) for an audience of peers but may lose job or promotion opportunities when employers check them out.

Review *Audience*: Is the content right for that audience? Did you assume the right level of detail and knowledge base? Did you consider audience sensitivities?

Review *Tone*: Appropriate to your goal and audience? Right for the relationship and relationship building? Can anything be misinterpreted? Is it courteous and positive in spirit?

Review *Message Structure*: Well organized? Clear, engaging lead? Strong close, with a call to action if needed? Is the response you're asking for perfectly clear?

By now, you should have a good idea of what cuts to make in your document and any additions you need to develop. Move on to sharpening your language.

Practical Editing Stage 2: Improve Words and Structure

Take out your red pencil; you'll need one if you're editing a printout. Or make changes on screen (using the Track Changes tool in Microsoft Word if your document is important or you're collaborating).

Do the content cuts. If you haven't already removed any extraneous ideas, cross out or delete them now.

Add any new and necessary information or ideas.

Scan the result to see how the sentences and paragraphs hang together. Check your transitions, and add new ones as needed so everything connects and flows. Look at paragraph length—find break points for those that run more than five sentences long and intersperse short ones.

Identify where the document needs improvement in any or all of the following ways:

- Read it aloud. Listen to the rhythm—is your voice forced into an up-down-up-down singsongy cadence? Do you hear stumbles and awkward pauses? Does it sound active?
- Check the Readability Index—too much passive? Words and sentences too long? Hard to understand?

- Look for repetition of every kind: words, sounds, sentences that create a monotonous rhythm; the clues outlined in these chapters: *-ing* words, *-ion* words, too many prepositions, and so on.

Make the changes, then proofread. Use your computer software's grammar and spell check to pinpoint mistakes, but don't rely on this help entirely. Your computer won't know that you meant "sole" rather than "soul," for example, or that you've used a specific structure to highlight a fact.

SUCCESS TIP

USE MICROSOFT WORD FIND AND REPLACE

If you repeatedly misspell certain words, click Find under the Edit menu, enter the word, select Replace, and type in the right spelling. Click All if you want to review and correct the whole document. You can also replace phrases this way. A time-saving option is to write in a placeholder when you draft your message and replace it with the correct term later. For example, if you need to put in a long title more than once or don't know it, just type "March book" and later replace it with the correct full name. This helps you maintain your writing momentum.

Especially don't rely on any device's autocorrect feature, which can create notable bloopers. Whole websites are given to such mistakes and while they're funny, they can be damaging, too.

A proofing trick that professionals sometimes use, if they've read material so many times they can hardly see it, is to read it backward, beginning from the end. You can pick up typos and repeats that you wouldn't otherwise notice. This works well for proofing numbers.

One more tip: If you customarily edit on printouts rather than on screen, try using proofreaders' symbols, a shorthand that writers and editors employ to communicate with printers and each other. Just Google "proofreading marks" and you'll find a number of demonstrations. The marks are easy to learn and make the proofing process more efficient—and a touch more fun.

Sentence Sharpening Techniques

When I see a paragraph shrinking under my eyes like a strip of bacon in a skillet, I know I'm on the right track.

—Peter DeVries, comic novelist

Here are examples of what to look for when editing your own material or someone else's and how the problems can be fixed. You already know many of these strategies from Chapter 4, where I talked about writing the draft. Here's how to apply the ideas in the editing stage and turn your document into a winner that reads quickly, clearly, and powerfully.

For each example, try to improve the sentence yourself before reading the revised version. If you come up with a different rewrite, compare it to the one presented. Remember, there's always more than one way to rewrite.

Substitute short words for long ones—unless you're making a particular point, can't find a short one, or a short one doesn't work as well.

The new managers are embarking on a fundamental shift in accounting methodology, in the hope of circumventing financial embarrassment.

vs.

The new managers will introduce a new accounting method to avoid financial embarrassment.

Strip everything that doesn't add to your meaning—ideas, phrases, words—so your sentences are brief and punchy.

All these ideas are excellent, and you can find an approach that works for you to supplement the practical strategy we'll pursue here.

vs.

These ideas are all excellent. Use them to supplement the strategy we've described.

Cut as many of the redundant words and phrases as you can.

This is truly a very good time to think about the newest ideas for innovating a new product line for spring.

vs.

This is a good time to plan a new spring product line.

We can predict the outcome with a high degree of confidence.

vs.

We can confidently predict the outcome.

Replace lifeless, dull verbs such as *have, get,* and *made* with lively, active ones, dumping those extra phrases that clutter our writing.

I suggest we make a decision to have a meeting to discuss the issues that may make our company's image a problem.

vs.

Let's meet to talk about the risks to company image.

Or just take a few seconds to think of a better, more to-the-point alternative.

We need to get ready for the bad publicity.

vs.

We must brace for the bad publicity.

Replace the *of* and *to* and *for* constructions where possible.

The plan for the department is to restructure in order to apply the best principles of management.

vs.

The partners plan to restructure so we can apply the best management principles.

Mark is of the opinion that the council will reconsider the facts of the matter.

vs.

Mark believes the council will review the facts.

Cut down on the phrases that contain too many words ending in *-ed* and *-ing* and *-ion.*

Giving the audience the responsibility of interpreting your writing is a bad idea.

vs.

Don't make the audience responsible for interpreting what you write.

Jane provided us with the information that Jerry has submitted his resignation.

vs.

Jane told us that Jerry resigned.

The intention of providing the information is to provoke a reconsideration of the guidelines.

vs.

We're providing the information because we want the guidelines reconsidered.

Avoid too many *is* and *are* sentences. Particularly beware of sentences that begin "There is" or "There are."

There is a section describing the new technology inside the report.

vs.

The report includes a section describing the new technology.

Different parts of the brain are involved in writing as opposed to speaking.

vs.

We use different parts of the brain to write and to speak.

Look for stock phrases that are wordier than they need to be and simplify them. For example, why say,

We came to the conclusion	Better: We concluded . . .
At the present time	Better: Now . . .
We're in a position to	Better: We can . . .
The question as to whether	Better: Whether . . .
We wish to bring to your attention	Better: Please note . . .
Owing to the fact that	Better: Because . . .
For the purpose of	Better: To . . .

And cut all empty filler—the jargon, clichés, buzzwords, and pretentious expressions so common to business writing. An example:

With risk weighted profitability metrics implemented in a consistent manner across the organization, both financial and staff resources can now be optimally allocated based on maximized overall business performance.

I'm not even going to try to translate that.

Easy reading is damn hard writing.

—Attributed to Nathaniel Hawthorne or Thomas Hood, both 19th-century writers

IDENTIFYING AND FIXING SOME GRAMMAR GLITCHES

This isn't a grammar book—there are plenty of excellent ones listed at the end of this chapter to choose from—but I've observed that even many good writers share some common problems that undermine their professional image. Naturally, if you must take a writing test to qualify for a job, these are the mistakes the tests focus on. So here is some practical advice. If you know your weaknesses, reinforce these quick fixes with other resources.

Commas: The read-it-aloud method will reliably show you where to put commas. Say your sentences s-l-o-w-l-y with attention to what they mean, talking in a natural way. The commas usually go where you want the pauses to be. No pause, no comma.

Read the following sentences aloud to develop your sensibility:

Commas tell readers where to pause, making it easier to understand a sentence immediately.

So it makes sense to use commas carefully, because when they're in the wrong place, you create confusion.

Jack, who studied grammar books for years, failed the writing test because he became so confused he couldn't decide where to put the commas.

A disclaimer: Note that throughout this book I use the "pause" method of placing commas, and a grammarian will find many inconsistencies. My imperatives are clarity and fast reading. In practical writing, both are best served by using commas to signal cadence, and therefore meaning. However, some manuals of styles dictate other practices—such as always using a comma before the next-to-last item on a list (this issue is called "serial commas"). If your company follows a specific style guide, find out, and look to the grammar resources at the end of this chapter for clarification on commas and also any problems you diagnose in your own writing.

Agreement: Pay close attention to nouns and people's names. Then make sure words such as *it, they, he,* and *their* used later in the sentence matches the singular or plural situation. A student kindly included this example of multiple non-agreement:

The blog's main goal is to get their readers to stop lying on social media in order to make their lives appear better than it may be.

Run-on or long sentences: Read them aloud and you'll hear them wander. Or just look at them, especially if your readability index check shows your average sentences are long. Simply break these sentences into two or more.

Danglers and misplaced modifiers: These are sentences that confuse the basic "who did what" structure:

Paddling the canoe up the river, the alligators scared me out of my wits.

The mosquitoes will descend on you while sleeping, so use a bed net.

Walking along the shore, a pig suddenly jumped out of the water.

Obviously, the alligators didn't paddle, the mosquitoes didn't attack in their sleep and the pig didn't fly.

Parallel construction: In all your writing, be consistent in how you use verbs and combine phrases. Here's a favorite example of a terrible sentence from an e-mail I received. It demonstrates a number of awkward constructions:

One of my colleagues is trying to build a Wordpress-based site for a client and a major feature they need integrated is the ability for a client to design a shirt and then the order to be placed—similar to CafePress.

A hint on fixing this: Break it up, and focus each new sentence on "who" is doing "what."

That *vs.* who *vs.* which: When you don't know whether to use *that* or *which,* try *that.* Only use *which* when the sentence sounds really strange with *that.* But please don't use *that* when you're referring to a person—use *who.* The following are incorrect:

ABC members are looking for business professionals that would like to expand their business relationships.

I have a colleague that is also a good friend.

Avoid using more than one negative word in a sentence because it confuses readers. Here is a triple-negative sentence attributed to the comedian Groucho Marx:

I cannot say that I do not disagree with you.

And here is a three-not sentence written by a student, responding to a complaint he received in his work life:

Although the report concluded that there is not enough evidence yet to say whether the dust and smoke cloud produced by the terrorist attack on the World Trade Center caused cancer, it does not mean the Registry or other 9/11 surveillance programs may not find such evidence in the future as a result of our ongoing investigations.

To simplify, sharpen, tighten and energize your writing is always challenging. Fortunately, the payoff is real. People will find you more interesting, credible and professional, and they'll do what you want more often.

Look at editing as a game. You don't need to memorize rules or even systematically attack a piece of writing based on all these guidelines. But follow the clues that tell you when something can be more clearly said, and think about how to say it better.

Every writer has a personal set of repeat problems. Start recognizing your own and consciously make fixes. You'll soon accumulate your own set of solutions.

About Editing Down Long Copy

Sometimes you'll work through a document and find you've occupied more space than allocated for it, or more than your subject is worth. Trimming it back can be hard.

First, apply the guidelines: Cut everything inessential to your goal—ideas and information, words, perhaps whole sentences and paragraphs. If you've shortened your message as much as you can and it's still too long, think about whether you can pull out some material and supply it as an appendix. This works well with a report or proposal, for example. If you're writing an e-mail, the subject might be divided into two or more messages.

One helpful approach is to think about exactly what you need to get across and then, without looking at what you wrote, draft a new version. It will probably be much stronger as well as closer to the length you want.

But resist the temptation to just condense everything you write into a shorter space. This approach often saps all the interest from a piece. Journalists prefer to sacrifice whole sections of a story rather than lose an interesting quote or sidelight that brings their story alive.

Don't try to deliver everything you know about a subject in a document; it's much more effective to deliver less, more powerfully.

In the next chapter, we'll begin to apply the writing guidelines to specific media. First up: e-mail, a channel that is an overlooked make-or-break success factor in most industries. Mastering this short-form message system will give you a head start on the longer "important" documents common to the business world.

PRACTICE OPPORTUNITIES

I. Know Your Transitions

Find an opinion piece such as an op-ed, article or blog that interests you, and scan it for transitional words, phrases and devices. Can you recognize what role each serves? Can you think of alternatives?

II. Diagnose and Rewrite

Individually or in small groups, review the following paragraphs, considering both stages of editing: the Stage 1 big picture (goal, audience, tone and content) and Stage 2, improving clarity and language. Rewrite each example. Then check the Readability Index (see Chapter 4) to compare the old and new versions, and be sure you're satisfied with your version in each case. Finally, proofread: Use your computer software's grammar and spell check to pinpoint mistakes, but remember not to rely on this help entirely.

A. From a Respected Online Newspaper in a Weak Moment

The core values of an effective community leadership program help create among stakeholders and participants a shared sense of destiny in devising strategies for implementing a common set of community goals based on holding the community in trust for future generations.

B. From an Interoffice E-Mail

Dear X Department Staff:

On June 18, at 2:00 p.m., a meeting has been scheduled to follow up on our previous conversation of May 10, and I would ask you to make arrangements to be in attendance. It is anticipated that approximately two hours will be necessary to cover the agenda thoroughly and review the various recommendations that were previously made. Please advise me of your availability.

C. From a Wall Street Journal Op-Ed

At the most basic level, however, capitalism has become the world's economic ideology of choice primarily because it demonstrably unlocks a higher fraction of the human potential with ubiquitous organizational incentives that reward hard work, ingenuity, and innovation.

D. From an Advertorial

With risk-weighted profitability metrics implemented in a consistent manner across the organization, both financial and staff resources can now be optimally allocated based on maximized overall business performance.

E. From a Website

Design happens at the intersection of the user, the interface, and their context. It's essential for interface designers to understand the gamut of contexts that can occur, thereby ensuring they create designs that are usable no matter what's happening around the user.

F. From an E-Mail Promotion of an Event Called The Harsh New Media Reality

Insights on the need for more precise media training that emphasizes a contextual sentence that stimulates a reporters lead and to provide compelling quotes, which together manipulate the reporter's script, giving you the ability to control the edit.

III. Evaluate and Rewrite

Read this message from a company's technical communications department to the rest of the organization, and evaluate—based on the content—where the writer went wrong in terms of goal, audience, tone, and structure. Try rewriting this document. What should the writer have said? What should he have left out? What information seems to be missing? Be alert to spelling and consistency errors as well.

Subject: Videoconferencing

For your information, the Technical Communications Center offers Videoconferencing Service. Next are some guidelines that should be followed when facilitating a videoconference.

1. The enclosed videoconferencing package should contain the following:

    a. Three Registration Forms

    b. Guide to Videoconferencing

    c. Videoconference Listing for the Current Year

2. When you have received this package, it is important to fill out a Videoconference Registration Form. This form must be filled out completely. All information on this sheet is pertinent to the booking.

3. The Videoconference Registration Form should either be mailed, e-mailed, or faxed to our office. Because dates book quickly, it is in your best interest to return the forms to us as soon as you can to insure the booking of your videoconference.

4. Once the Communications Center has received the forms, we will investigate the dates and times you have chosen and the status of your request will be confirmed.

If you have any questions please do not hesitate to contact me at xxxx.

IV. Group Project: Word Review

Here are some buzzwords and clichés often found in business writing. Discuss each one: Can you come up with alternatives? Make a list, and amplify it during the next month. Draw on some of the resources listed at the end of this section to add more buzzwords and better alternatives. (Many will require a phrase rather than a single word.) At the end of the time frame, organize a complete list and distribute to the class as a resource and inspiration.

Value-added	Paradigm shift
Seat at the table	Synergy
Incentivize	Doubling down
Organizational alignment	24-7
360-degree review	Push the envelope
Offline	Ramp up
Innovative	Transparent communication
Solution	Re-engineer
Leveraging	Cascade down
Right-size	Out of the box
Drill down	Outreach
Functionality	Competitive advantage
Matrices	Actionable

After you do the exercise, download this resource from www.plainenglish .co.uk/free-guides.html: The A–Z of Alternative Words. It shows alternatives to many common but overly wordy expressions.

V. Sentence Rewriting (Nobody's Perfect)

Here are some sentences that I wrote for this book—and upon review, rewrote. Figure out how you would express the thoughts better. Work individually, then compare results in small groups and agree on the best solution for each example.

1. Even if writers could restrict themselves to writing only for traditional print form, they'd have to take account of fundamental ways in which on-screen reading (whether computer, etc.) has changed reader expectations.

2. It's a box that appears immediately after spell check.

3. All the approaches are excellent, and you can find one that works for you to supplement the practical strategy we'll pursue here.

4. Have you considered any sensitivities your audience may have?

5. All the graphic tools are even more important because many people are resistant to on-screen reading.

6. Note that the longer sentences give the writer the ability to make connections between actions.

7. Giving the audience the responsibility generates either misinterpretation or indifference. You never want your readers to wonder "why is she telling me that?" or substituting their own reasoning for your own, even nonconsciously. Ambiguous connections generate misinterpretation or indifference.

8. Nevertheless, if you write better sentences, combine them effectively, and use the structured thinking principles covered in the last two chapters, you're on the way to a powerful, flexible writing capability that will serve you well.

9. Improving the way you use verbs gives you one of the best tools for improving all your writing.

10. Try to improve your use of words, create better sentences, and use verbs more effectively.

11. Did you fully articulate your goals?

12. Our assumption was that better writing results from having practiced more.

13. The amount of interaction in contemporary office contexts is continually diminishing, because of technology.

14. This method will demonstrate the need for clarity.

15. The subject line of an e-mail is the biggest factor in determining whether the message gets read or not.

16. Is there anything that can be interpreted as being against the writer's interest?

17. E-mail can be critical in scoring opportunities and in building and maintaining relationships, so examples of messages to support networking are included in some of the preceding chapters.

VI. Create Your Own Writing Improvement Plan

Review the writing and editing techniques covered in this section of the book, and examine some examples of your own work. What consistent shortcomings do you see? Have your professors or supervisors given you input on your writing? Take it all into account and identify opportunities to strengthen your writing. Make a list of your challenges (e.g., sentences too long; too many *-ing* words; too many adjectives). Then for each challenge, write down the solution (e.g., break sentences up so they average up to 18 words per sentence; rewrite sentences that use more than one *-ing*; cut adjectives and make verbs more interesting), etc. Use your plan as a constant guide to sharpen everything you write.

VII. Class Discussion

You arrive at your new job pleased with your ability to write well: clearly, simply, persuasively. But you find that the organization is entrenched in a wordy, complicated, cliché-driven style and that you're expected to write that way too. What's your course of action? Discuss this dilemma in small groups, and then compare the recommendations each comes up with.

RESOURCES FOR PART II

You may want to review the basics, address specific problems in your writing, or just know where the resources are when you need help. Great books are available as well as excellent online advice and reference material. Here are some choices. Check out the ones that sound promising to find those that resonate for you.

Books

Robert Allen, Editor, *Pocket Fowler's Modern English Usage*

A classic, updated with new entries on the language of e-mails and the Internet

Karen Elizabeth Gordon, *The Deluxe Transitive Vampire: The Ultimate Handbook of Grammar for the Innocent, the Eager, and the Doomed*

This book does a better job than you might imagine of making grammar fun.

Patricia T. O'Conner, *Woe Is I: The Grammarphobe's Guide to Plain English in Better English*

An easy-to-read rundown on most problem areas presented with a humorous tone.

Constance Hale, *Sin and Syntax: How to Craft Wickedly Effective Prose*

A guide to English prose drawing on pop culture for a really up-to-date take on language

Lynn Truss, *Eats, Shoots & Leaves: The Zero Tolerance Approach to Punctuation*

An enjoyable review of punctuation in its most correct form.

Joseph Kimble, *Writing for Dollars, Writing to Please: The Case for Plain Language in Business, Government and Law*

Excellent advice on clarifying materials for consumers, a must-read for government agency work.

Richard Lanham, *The Longman Guide to Revising Prose: A Quick and Easy Method for Turning Good Writing Into Great Writing*

A specific system for revision you may or may not like

William Strunk and E. B. White, *The Elements of Style*

The classic case for simple writing revered by all writers

William Zinsser, *On Writing Well*

A fine manifesto on clarity, and you get the message in just the first few chapters.

In Print or Online

The Associated Press Stylebook (www.apstylebook.com)

Merriam-Webster's Collegiate Dictionary (www.merriam-webster.com/dictionary)

Roget's Thesaurus (http://thesaurus.com)

Online Resources

The A–Z of Alternative Words: www.plainenglish.co.uk

See "Free Guides" for this helpful, downloadable pdf showing good substitutes for long words and phrases and other useful writing guides.

Style guide, the *Economist* magazine: www.economist.com/styleguide

Excellent set of brief basics followed by exhaustive alphabetical list of writing problems and advice

Grammarly.com

Grammar errors and check for plagiarism

11 Rules of Writing, Grammar, and Punctuation: www.junketstudies.com/rulesofw

Surprisingly concise problem solver

Hemingway.com

Shows you how to translate your writing to be more like the author famous for his simplicity

Guide to Grammar and Style, Jack Lynch: http://andromeda.rutgers.edu/~jlynch/Writing

An alphabetized list of problem areas

The Guide to Grammar and Writing: Interactive Quizzes: http://grammar.ccc .commnet.edu/grammar/quiz_list.htm

Teaches by quizzing you

The Online Grammar Guide: www.world-english.org/grammar.htm

Another alphabetized list of problem areas

Plain Language "Examples Database": www.plainlanguage.gov/examples/before_after/index.cfm

A payload of terrible but true "before" examples with the illuminating rewrites, a must-see especially if you're looking toward government work. See also www.plainlanguage.gov/examples/humor/index.cfm for examples that make the point by being funny. There are also plain language initiatives in Canada, the United Kingdom, Australia, and New Zealand—check the websites for great "before and after" writing examples and advice.

College and University Writing Help Websites

University of Calgary: The Basic Elements of English

http://www.ucalgary.ca/UofC/eduweb/grammar

Capital Community College: The Guide to Grammar and Writing: The Editing and Rewriting Process

http://grammar.ccc.commnet.edu/grammar/composition/editing.htm

University of Chicago Writing Program

http://writing-program.uchicago.edu/resources/grammar.htm

University of Illinois at Urbana–Champaign: The Center for Writing Studies

http://www.cws.illinois.edu/workshop/writers

Purdue University: Online Writing Lab

http://owl.english.purdue.edu/owl

PART III

THE BASICS OF BUSINESS COMMUNICATION

Chapter 6

E-Mail

Your Everyday Chance to Build a Professional Image

Email remains the most pervasive form of communication in the business world; while other technologies such as social networking, instant messaging (IM), mobile IM, and others are also taking hold, email remains the most ubiquitous form of business communication.

—Email Statistics Report, 2014–2018,
The Radicati Group (www.radicati.com)

START WITH STRATEGIC THINKING

E-mail is serious business in today's workplace. This may surprise you if you haven't yet held a career position in your field and think e-mail is an antique form of communication. You probably didn't need it much in college, and I've yet to hear of a course that covered it. But in fact e-mail is the nerve system that connects the business world. It's how we communicate in all directions, no matter what the nature of the organization.

Despite the inroads of instant messaging and social media tools in some business circles, we depend on internal e-mail to interact with colleagues, supervisors, subordinates, collaborators and services. When we deal with people outside— from clients and prospects to suppliers, partners, media, and industry contacts anywhere in the world—e-mail is usually the route of choice.

In fact, we typically turn to other communication channels only when we must: if in-person contact is essential, for example, or when the occasion demands more formality or even faster speed.

What could happen in a given company if everyone wrote good, clear, appropriate e-mails day in, day out? I am sure that efficiency and productivity would rise. Customers would buy more and behave more loyally. Relationships inside and outside would improve.

But more to the point, what will happen if *you* write strong e-mails each and every time? Your work life and career prospects will improve—perhaps dramatically. Supervisors, colleagues, and customers will find you capable, logical, credible, persuasive and professional, probably without knowing why.

You are what you write. The caliber of your e-mails adds up to create a total impression, and you have the power to make it a positive one. Not to mention, your e-mails will get the responses you want much more often, whether you're asking people to meet with you or supply resources or refer you to an employer or client.

The same principles apply if you're communicating for business purposes through other e-channels, including social media, so learning to write successful e-mails is time well spent. And the planning, writing and editing process is exactly the same as for major documents like proposals and business plans.

So here's how to write e-mails that work for you.

1. Commit the Time to Craft Your E-Mails Well

Do this without exception, because you can't know which messages are important. E-mail was the first medium with that most special and frightening feature: limitless forwardability. You may address a progress report to your immediate supervisor, but he or she might send it right on up the food chain. You may dash off a casual message to a buddy who ends up forwarding it to half his address list, or includes it as part of a long message thread to people unknown and inappropriate.

So never write anything you'd be embarrassed to find on the CEO's desk, a billboard, or the front page of a newspaper. Don't write anything you won't want dug up years from now, either, when you're up for CEO or running for office. E-mail has another special feature: It's indelible. It may sleep, but it never dies. Invest in planning, drafting, and revising every message so it reflects your best writing in every respect. What you *don't* write can matter as much as what you *do* write.

That said, I acknowledge there are occasions when timing counts more than quality. If your boss calls from China to say he's signing a contract and needs the research results e-mailed *now,* don't labor over your wording. But here's the good news: The practice you give yourself when less pressured makes handling emergencies a snap.

VIEW FROM THE FIELD: USE E-MAIL TO YOUR ADVANTAGE

E-mail is one of the principal ways you can distinguish yourself because you do it constantly. If you get a reputation for being able to write concise, to-the-point e-mail that says only what needs to be said, people will always open your message and read it. Showing that you have the ability to summarize and wrap up is a fantastic way to show what a capable person you are. It should be a top skill for a person entering the business world to master.

—Leila Zogby, president of Leila Zogby Business Writer, Inc. (www.leilazogby.com)

---

2. Know When an E-Mail Is the Right Medium—and When It's Not

While "traditional" advice says to use e-mail for short messages and stick to one idea, in fact no one follows such rules. However, never forget that many people don't really like reading long documents on screen and resist scrolling. They tend to skim e-mails and will rarely print them out. Moreover, most people today read e-mails on their smartphones or other mini devices. So complicated messages full of ideas or instructions don't work well. Of course, you can attach a complex document—provided you're pretty sure the recipient will open it. Or you can link to online materials to provide backup detail.

Look for a communication channel other than e-mail when,

- The occasion calls for more formal documentation, with a potential legal aspect or a need to go on record. There are times you should protect yourself with a print document, such as when you're signing a contract, making a complaint, filing a claim or delivering a performance review.
- You're asking for something personally: a donation to a good cause or a reference, for example. Depending on your audience, e-mail may be fine, but in other instances a letter or phone call is better. Whatever written form you choose, craft the message to represent your best writing. E-mail may be easier to send—but that doesn't mean it's easier to write it well.

- The person you're addressing is e-mail averse. It's important to consider, for example, that many wealthy investors and donors to charitable causes are over 65 and, especially if they no longer work in office situations, may use e-mail minimally at best. Important audiences need to be addressed in their own terms. At the other end of the scale, many young people would prefer to sidestep e-mail in favor of texting or Facebook.
- The message should be delivered privately or in person. Don't criticize or fire someone by e-mail, send anything you don't want shared, or use it to break off a relationship. It's not only cruel and cowardly but apt to backfire on you in major ways.

SUCCESS TIP

SOME "ALMOST NEVERS"

Your business e-mails should almost never convey emotions, negative feelings, sarcasm and cute stuff.

Never send an e-mail when you're angry. It's something people won't forget or forgive and is guaranteed to bite you back. Take special care if you're writing to someone you dislike— you might ask a friend to check your message. Sarcasm, irony, and most humor don't belong in e-mails. Write nothing that can be misinterpreted. And unless you absolutely know your reader will relate to them, put the emojis or emoticons way back on the shelf when you want to look professional and be clearly understood. Limit exclamation points, though their use is common in texting and e-mail now because these channels offer few ways to express enthusiasm.

In general, don't make e-mail a substitute for in-person contact. It's not a great relationship or team-building tool as compared to face-to-face interaction or even telephone calls. Like all written communication, it doesn't come with clues to meaning like facial expression, tone of voice, and body language. So never negotiate by e-mail or use it to engage in give-and-take situations. The medium's impersonality is leading some companies to mandate weekly e-mail-free days, or daily e-mail blackouts, forcing employees to pick up the phone or walk down the hall.

E-mail use is "exploding".... Not only are workers wading through more clogged in-boxes, they're also checking frequently, an average of 74 times a day....

—Professor Gloria Mark, quoted in the *Wall Street Journal* ("A Company Without Email?")

3. Shape Your Message Based on Your Own Response Patterns

Are you impatient with meandering e-mails of dim purpose or those that require time to decipher? So is everyone. This tells you that relevance, conciseness and clarity count.

And all the human interaction factors do, too: sincerity, honesty and courtesy. We're the same people in the work setting as we are outside of it. Most of us want to feel included, respected and appreciated—liked, and maybe even cared about.

You've probably noticed that even the briefest work memo can convey subtle emotions when you're on the receiving end. Every message you send includes such a subtext, intended or not. Practice awareness of what you communicate in the emotional dimension. Think "golden rule" and you'll accomplish your goals and build good relationships far more easily.

4. Plan the Subject Line and Lead Paragraph Well

Crafting a strong opener is especially important for e-mail. Each message is a fight to keep the reader's finger from clicking Delete and her eye from moving back to its in-box scan. Write concise, to-the-point subject lines that clearly identify what the message is about. Puzzle out a way to put the important words on the left so they're not cut off in the in-box window. Here are a few successful subject lines I found in my e-mail box today:

USB DVD Drive $26.99

Reader Favorites: Content marketing . . .

Deal Alert! Michaels.com

And here are a few that didn't get me to open the message:

> *Simple English is no one's mother tongue. It has to be worked for.*
>
> —Jacques Barzun in
> *Teacher in America*

Last Chance to Register for . . .

Event of the Year! 30% Off . . .

Shocking News!

The first lines or paragraph of the message should go right to the bottom line and focus on why you're writing as well as answer the unspoken question: Why should the person care?

USE THE STRUCTURED PLANNING SYSTEM: GOAL, AUDIENCE AND TONE

To write successful e-mails—as with every written communication—approach the task systematically. This process will become second nature with surprisingly little practice. The process is explained in detail in Chapters 2 and 3. Here's how it applies to e-mail:

1. Define your *goal* as closely as you can, and consider your *audience* and its *characteristics.*

2. Figure out what *substance* will accomplish that goal with that particular audience, and put the elements in a logical order.

3. Decide what *tone* is appropriate to the reader, taking account of the person's status, personality, your relationship with him or her and the nature of your goal.

4. Based on the first three steps, figure out a direct, clear *opening.* For e-mail, that's the subject line, salutation, and first one or two sentences.

5. Follow through with the *middle,* which typically contains technical information, backup for your request, and the reasoning if you aim to persuade.

6. *End* strongly, making it clear what follow-up you want.

7. *Review, edit, and tighten:* Business e-mails (and I would say all your e-mails) must be concise and error-free with correct spelling, punctuation, and basic grammar. Poor writing interferes with comprehension and makes you look incompetent and uncaring.

Now let's apply this framework to a workaday e-mail.

You notice that you're not included in a flow of reports relating to a major department project, one you're not directly involved in but would like to be.

Here's how you should plan your message, preferably writing down the answer to each question as I do in this example.

Goal? Immediately, to be added to the distribution list. Long range, to be better positioned for interesting work that's important to the organization.

Audience? Primary: Your supervisor. Secondary: Possible higher-echelon executives who may make the decision.

Audience characteristics? What do you know about these people? You're writing for a range of personalities, but since they are all managers, you can safely assume they have a few things in common: self-interest in "getting the job done" and, one might hope, grooming new talent.

Tone? Must be very respectful. Even if your manager is a pal, you're asking for something, and his or her bosses may not even know you. But you don't want to sound artificially formal.

Substance? The question to always ask: What can I say that will make my case with this audience? Why should my targeted readers care?

VIEW FROM THE FIELD: TRY TO HIT THE E-MAIL MARK

It annoys me when an e-mail goes on and on, especially when it's a solicitation—getting a long complicated e-mail from someone I don't know and am not engaged with is a fast way to make me hit the delete button. So keep it simple. If you need to elaborate, send an attachment or have a conversation. Once in a while I get an e-mail that's fast, right to the point, doesn't include a lot of rhetoric or misspell my name, or approaches me in some way the person knows will be relevant to me. That shows they did their homework and figured out what's in it for the audience.

—Laurie Bloom, director of Marketing &
Communications, Rivkin Radler LLP

Looking at the situation through the other persons' eyes always provides your best clues. *If you were the supervisors, why should you grant the request?* Don't write an e-mail asking for something until you have an answer, because that's essential to deciding what to include and what to leave out.

Knowing the company also tells you whether your request is a hard sell or not. Is information flow generally good, or is there a knowledge-is-power mentality? Are there rigid guidelines on pecking order entitlements, or flexible ones?

If you assume your request is an easy sell, you could simply say,

Dear Jack,

I'll appreciate having my name added to the Carter Project distribution list. I'm interested in seeing how it goes.

Thanks,

Jane

But this would be a mistake. You can't really predict whether the recipients will see the change as insignificant or as a departure from protocol. So you need to make a case. Think about possible advantages to the other parties. For example,

- The information will help you with your current work.
- You possess some special background or experience that means you might make a contribution.
- You hope to be involved in similar projects down the line and this will help you prepare for that.

Draft 1

Subject: Request to be added to Carter Project distribution list

Jack:

I'd like to ask if I can be added to the information distribution list for the Carter Project.

Since I'm currently working on several smaller-scale but similar projects, seeing how the challenges are handled will be helpful and could save me significant time. Also, the chance to review the materials will enable me to sharpen my thinking so I am better prepared to handle future large-scale initiatives.

As you know, I have a background in the medical imaging industry, so I might possibly have some useful thoughts to offer on Carter.

Thanks so much.

Jane

This brings us to Step 7, editing and revising. Here's how I'd rewrite my own draft after reviewing and thinking about it.

Draft 2

Subject: Information request, Carter Project

Dear Jack:

I'd appreciate it very much if I can be added to the Carter Project distribution list.

I'm working on several similar smaller-scale projects right now, and seeing how the challenges are handled will be a big help. Also, reviewing the materials will help prepare me for future large-scale projects when those opportunities arise.

Thanks so much for considering this request.

Jane

Is this version better? Why did I make these changes? Here's the reasoning, step-by-step, along with guidelines that apply to all e-mails.

Subject line: *Focus them tightly or your recipient may trash your message without reading it.* The subject line in Draft 1 is long and wordy—only part of it will probably show up on the reader's screen. It needs to be tighter and more direct. Also, a good subject line enables you or the recipient to easily retrieve an e-mail in the future, which can be very valuable.

Salutation: *Pay attention to tone in salutations.* In Draft 1, using the name alone is abrupt, not appropriate to a request, especially when you're addressing a superior.

The lead: *The first sentence in large part determines whether your message will succeed. Take time with it.* Draft 1 begins okay in that it gets right to the point, which, almost always, you want to do. But it's a little obsequious, asking for permission to make a request. So I took out "I'd like to ask" and substituted words that set an appreciative tone.

Message substance: *Always aim for just the right amount of content to make your point—not too much and not too little.* Draft 1's substance works reasonably for the purpose but on more careful consideration—which is easy once you have the draft in front of you—Paragraph 3, offering to help on the project, seems a bit arrogant. So I cut it, though should a conversation result from the e-mail, it's a good point to hold in reserve.

The close: *End strongly by underlining your request—or whatever other purpose motivates your message, as specifically as possible.* In Draft 1, the very general ending doesn't really close the natural circle of your message. In this case, you're asking for a response to a request; at other times, your close might say, "Let me know when you're available to meet with me" or "I look forward to hearing when the new system will be ready."

Writing style: *Aim for simple, direct, conversational language that moves naturally to pull the reader through.* Draft 1 overall sounds rather stilted and clumsy. To instantly discover where the language needs attention, read the message aloud. Wherever it's hard to read smoothly and rapidly, look for ways to reword.

You can also find wording that interferes with speed by searching out repetitions—for example, there are two phrases using *to* in the first sentence. Paragraph 2 also fails to meet the reading-aloud test and sounds "hedgy." You may notice the word *help* appears twice, but that's okay, because that's your subject—asking for help.

Do you write telegraphic e-mails, leaving out words and relying heavily on abbreviations? Break the habit! You'll get better results with cohesive messages that don't require readers to fill in what's missing or figure out what you mean.

Tightening the message: *A major goal of editing is to make complicated sentences simple.* So always look for alternative ways to say the same thing more directly and plainly, eliminate unnecessary words, and rephrase the thoughts. I did this with Draft 1, sentence by sentence, and ended up cutting about 25% in the process. Notice that once you cut words back, it becomes obvious that they aren't needed. You can always check your editing this way: If eliminating words or thoughts makes a message read less well or seem less convincing, don't do the cut or look for another way to say what you mean.

Review Chapters 4 and 5 for a full rundown on almost-grammar-free editing techniques that enable you to improve your own writing.

Half my life is an act of revision.

—John Irving, novelist

Review the total message for the big picture—what's coming across? In the case of our example, is Draft 2 respectful and polite? Have any negative feelings crept in? Does the content appear to make the case with clarity and logic? Does the message as a whole seem to proceed logically? Are the transitions good? Can anything be interpreted against the writer's interests?

Also important is this: Does the message read quickly and easily? The faster your writing reads, the better it works and the more convincing it becomes. Contemporary means short: words, paragraphs, sentences, and documents.

Compare Drafts 1 and 2 to see how much faster the second one flows, how much more convincing it seems, and how it projects a professional image for the writer while being very respectful.

Are you reluctant to take time for the kind of planning and editing I recommend? Know that if you can achieve what you want with your first draft you're unique: Professional writers don't expect to and nor should you. There's an old adage that writers like: "A writer isn't someone who writes but someone who rewrites."

And know that if you don't invest the energy, you're gambling against your own success.

The good news is that just a little practice will put you way out in front of the field—and once you've built the habit of writing it right, you'll find it doesn't take much time at all.

Build in the Right Tone

Here's a kind of challenge you may face whatever your career field, and it's not unlike the challenges you deal with when doing group projects in school.

As project coordinator, it's your job to pull together a team report. The group consists of your peers and a few subordinates, and each has been working on a different section. The deadline is approaching, and you need to be sure the pieces come in on schedule.

Here are two possible ways of writing the e-mail.

Version 1

Subject: Assignments due!

Everyone on Martin Proposal Team:

As you know, I expect you to deliver your assigned part of the Martin proposal on Wednesday, April 3, by 2:00 p.m. via e-mail. Unless I hear otherwise from you, I'll expect you all to meet the deadline. Thanks.

John

Version 2

Subject: Due April 3: Martin Proposal Sections

Hi team—

I look forward to having all sections of the Martin Proposal on my desk by Wednesday at 2.

An e-mail attachment will be fine. If you're having any last-minute problems pulling your part together, give me a call ASAP.

The plan calls for me to review everything by the end of the week, so please be available to answer questions. Marian needs all the pieces in hand by Monday so she can edit the full proposal and make it cohesive in time to meet the client's April 12 deadline.

I know we'll have a great proposal and a good chance of landing this contract. Thank you, Mark, Jane, Eric, and Marie, for all your hard work on this.

Sincerely,

John

Which version would you rather get? I assume it's the second one, so let's analyze why.

There's nothing wrong with Version 1 technically. The spelling and grammar are correct, and it's clear and to the point.

The glaring difference from Version 2 is in the tone and its probable effect on the recipients.

The subject line in Version 1 is vague and at the same time threatening. It makes the writer sound like a teacher calling for essays and expecting the worst. The negative voice sustains throughout.

Version 2, on the other hand, takes the trouble to project a positive attitude and a team spirit. It gives a context for the proposal process, so the deadline doesn't seem arbitrary. It offers help with problems—better to find out any hitches now rather than later, no? It conveys enthusiasm for the result; reminds everyone that something important is at stake; and extends appreciation to each team member as an individual, treating everyone equally.

If you think the difference is trivial, consider: Which writer would you rather work for? Which would you work harder for: on this and future projects? Based on the messages, which person would you want to team with again?

Yes, it's essential to structure your messages well and use your editing and proofing tools to craft your language. But achieving the right tone is equally critical. *The complaint that employers most often make about how younger staff members write is failure to adopt the right tone.* So let's explore where tone comes from and how to control it.

Thanks to text messaging and the modern business tempo, with a boost from Twitter, many people have learned to get to the point quickly with the least possible number of words. But what can get lost in this minimizing is tone. Most noticeably, both respect and warmth are often glaringly absent.

Getting the tone right starts with how you think through your content.

In our e-mail example, Version 2's writer obviously thought not only about what she wanted but her recipients' needs and reactions. If I were in their shoes, she asked, what might I want to know? If I'm having a problem, what should I do? What would inspire me to a last final best effort? Can I feel that all my overtime work is appreciated?

As every good manager knows, there's everything to gain by making people feel included and important. Taking the time to write the thoughtful message is an excellent investment.

Many managers have trouble projecting warmth. But if you begin by looking at the situation from the other person's viewpoint, it will usually happen naturally. Consideration shows. But you may also have to consciously think about how to frame the message from the other person's point of view. For example, writing, "If you don't send your work in by Friday, you'll mess up the whole team project and it will be late" is very different from "Please send your work in by Sept. 5 so we can fit it into the final project and meet the deadline."

You can also choose language that reinforces the positive tone. What helps establish a friendly, persuasive, and even motivating tone? Writing tactics such as:

- Saying "please" and "thank you"
- Using polite salutations and closing words
- Using contractions ("I'm happy" vs. "I am happy")
- Using the word *you* a lot—cutting back on *I*
- Adopting a consistent "you" perspective, the "what's in it for me" (WIIFM)
- Using positive language and avoiding negatives
- Using names in the message body
- Generally conveying enthusiasm and confidence

Suppose you're sending a report to a client and must write a cover note for it. You might say,

Frank—here's the January progress report that you wanted. Regards, Ben

This short message sounds abrupt, barely courteous, and inappropriate to the relationship. It uses a "buddy voice" at best. What would work better? Perhaps the following:

Dear Frank,

I'm pleased to provide the attached report for January. If you have any questions, I'll be happy to answer them and can also provide more details if helpful.

Best regards,

Ben

Is Version 2 unnecessarily long and wordy? True, it doesn't contain much "real" information. Nevertheless, circumstances call for it. It sounds like the writer took the time to craft the short message carefully, which in itself shows respect, and it seems thoughtful. It is the tone a client expects from a supplier and, particularly, from someone who's not at the top of the pecking order.

In all honesty, a recipient might not actually notice your careful e-mail—but he or she will definitely notice one that's careless, breezy and blunt. Keep in mind that many clients are probably much older than your own age cohort and more formal to some degree in their lifestyle and expectations. Even if they are young, clients typically want the respect the relationship demands—and by the way, the same is true of many young bosses.

Let's look at one more example, a thank you note—famously difficult to write well—and how sentence structure affects the impact.

Dear Joan—thanks for inviting me to the networking event. I had a good time. Also I met a client prospect!—Regards, Ned

Not very convincing, is it? Here, we can fault the writing style. Ned's sentences are choppy and stilted, reminding us of a fourth-grade textbook. He forgot the sentence rhythm technique of alternating short sentences with long ones (see Chapter 3). He could have written,

Hello Joan,

I want to thank you for inviting me to the Celex networking event. It was great to meet so many new people who are part of our industry, and I even have a prospective client to follow up with. Thanks again for thinking of me. I very much appreciate it.

Sincerely,

Ned

An even better way to voice appreciation is to be very specific. Here's an e-mail I was happy to get from a business client.

I just wanted to say thank you for inviting me to the luncheon today. I really enjoyed the group. The presentation was interesting, but the highlight was one of the better question-and-answer sessions on the subject I have heard at any session. And I am extremely grateful for your introduction to numerous people, making sure that they knew what I did. You do go out of your way to help, and it was appreciated. Thanks.

Best regards,

Lewis

HANDLE E-MAILS ADDRESSED TO GROUPS

Marketing Campaigns

Marketers see e-mail as the most cost-effective way to reach their audiences: It costs virtually nothing and has a high rate of return when done well. It's a major tool for "in-bound marketing" that aims to draw people to websites or other locations for more information or to execute a sale. Politicians use this potential too. Many regard Barack Obama's e-mail campaigns, created by top copywriters, as a decisive factor in both his elections.

This book is concerned with everyday business communication rather than marketing campaigns, but here are some guidelines for e-mail promotion.

- Use clear, benefit-oriented subject lines, and convey a sense of urgency as appropriate:
  - Your Exclusive Promo Code Inside—Expires Today!
  - Announcing: How to Sell Without Selling (Special Offer)
  - 5 Top Social Media Dashboard Tools to Manage Your Social Account
- Keep messages short (under 100 words) and simple.
- Write in a friendly, casual style.
- Make the message visually accessible with white space and graphics.
- Frame the message in terms of *you* rather than *we*.
- Personalize by using first names.
- Employ power marketing words, such as *freebie, discover, surprise, proven,* and *thank you.*

See the section on persuasive writing for many more ideas that apply. You'll find e-mail marketing a well-covered subject on the Internet, so a quick search will turn up more than you need to know.

E-Mail Newsletters

Sending an e-mail newsletter is another significant use of the medium. Many bloggers find it an effective way to distribute their blogs, either in whole or in part: as a "teaser" to lure readers to the full blog itself. Newsletters can be more complex and contain news, announcements, and multiple articles. This book's advice on blogging, media releases and storytelling particularly relate to newsletter creation.

E-Mail and Customer Relations

Big and small organizations alike rely on e-mail to collect input, solve problems and maintain customer engagement. Whether they use it well is another story.

If a client has a problem with a service, he is likely to e-mail, since trying to get help by telephone is daunting. But customer service via e-mail only works for both parties if you

- provide an e-mail address, and preferably, a name, easily findable on the website or product;
- respond within 24 or at most 48 hours;
- answer each complaint or question directly—not with a form letter or by referring the writer to your FAQs;
- practice the utmost courtesy and consideration; and
- take responsibility for helping the customer and turning anger into satisfaction, a bad experience into a good one.

Think through what will turn the situation around: Technical help? A refund? A coupon for a future purchase? Use your writing strategies to convey empathy, an apology, explanation, and suggestion as appropriate.

SUCCESS TIP

E-MAIL KNOWS NO BOUNDARIES

Because e-mail (and all electronic media) leaps oceans and crosses national borders so readily, we forget that we're communicating cross-culturally. This can be a problem because even in its more formal moments, the American style tends to sound brusque and discourteous to people whose primary language is not English. So be scrupulously polite and considerate. Be aware of other countries' individual cultural norms—for example, whether requests are best made directly or indirectly and whether it's in order to express personal interest in your recipient.

To internationalize what you write,

- use short common words and short declarative sentences,

- cut the jargon and idioms,
- use lists when appropriate,
- phrase everything as straightforwardly as you can,
- avoid passive structures and those with *get* and *have*,
- don't pile up long strings of nouns, but
- write more formally though not in ways that sound unnatural in ordinary English (though the messages will often feel rather stark).

Remember that most businesses today must also consider internal audiences whose native language is not English, so the guidelines often apply.

CREATE E-MAILS TO NETWORK MORE EFFECTIVELY

E-mail can help you score opportunities and develop relationships and is especially important when you're looking for career opportunities. So let's apply the ideas to this situation.

Suppose you want to tap your school's alumni network for advice on your career path and perhaps even some direct job leads.

Your goals are clear, so think first about audience. Why might a graduate of your school take the time to talk to you? Here are a few reasons:

- Graduating from the same school gives you common ground and experiences.
- Many people like "giving back."
- A request for advice is flattering and reinforces people's view of their own accomplishments, especially if they're relatively recent graduates.
- Some people appreciate building goodwill—you never know if someone might prove a good contact in the future.

Tone: Your tone should be respectful and appreciative. You are, after all, asking for a favor you're unlikely to return.

Content: Remind the recipient of your common bond. Bring it alive in some way. Make yourself sound worth helping because you'll likely be successful as well as a person who'd be good to know.

Here are two examples that someone I know received from fellow alumni requesting informational interviews, reproduced essentially as received. Which works better?

Sample 1

Subject: White University career network

Dear Ms. Lewis:

I'm a senior at White, majoring in science and anthropology. I was hoping you could tell me a little about your job—what does an average day entail and how did you get to where you are today? Im interested in what working for a non profit is like.

Thank you and I hope to hear from you soon.

Sally

Sample 2

Subject: Requesting an informational interview

Dear Ms. Lewis,

My name is Jessica, and I too graduated from White. I obtained your name and contact information from the university's Career Network.

I am writing to request an informational interview. I am very interested in pursuing a career in high-level research and analysis—I hope on an international level. As a result, I would very much like to learn more about the work you do for FLU and your prior professional experiences.

Just to let you know a little bit about myself, while working on my degree, I was president of the International Club and active with the Speaker Committee. I spent a full year as an undergraduate in Dubai and interned at the National Association for Freedom.

I am ready to utilize my international background, and as I am brand new to this career path, any advice will be greatly appreciated.

I will be in your area on Thursday and Friday, July 27 and 28. If you are available either of these days and willing to meet with me for 15 minutes, I will be most grateful.

Thank you for your time, and I hope to speak with you soon.

Sincerely,

Jessica

Which e-mail would you probably respond to? If you agree that Jessica's e-mail is better than Sally's, think about why.

To begin with, Sally didn't take the trouble to carefully draft or proofread what she wrote. It comes across as off the top of her head and a bit illiterate, suggesting she is (1) not so smart, (2) not respectful, (3) not really appreciative, or (4) all of the above. Further, her note is very unspecific, so it's hard to understand what she wants to know. She shows also that she didn't trouble to make a good match between herself and her hoped-for information source.

Jessica, on the other hand, clearly thought the connection through and made the relevance of Ms. Lewis's experience to her own goals plain. Her gratitude is expressly stated, and a few significant details about her background are referenced.

Most important, Jessica sounds like a winner: a person who'd be interesting to talk to for half an hour—by phone if not in person—and worth your time. You'd even assume she'd present well to any contact you referred her to.

All this achieved by a solid, planned-out message that says the person did her homework and knows how to interact? Absolutely.

For good networking, follow through and always write to say thank you—few people do, and you'll stand out. If you find an opportunity through your contact, or accept one anywhere, write to let him or her know.

Use the same strategies to connect with people you meet or hear about from other sources as well—the woman you sit next to on an airplane, the man who mentions a colleague you should meet, someone you meet at a workshop. Savvy networkers follow through even years later by writing thoughtful, planned e-mails that trigger positive memories and positive responses. Or as appropriate, of course, use social media to maintain or revive contact.

The power of digital communication is there for you when you trouble to do it well.

SOME E-MAIL Q&A

Abbreviations: Y Not? Many people are unaccustomed to the abbreviations that are second nature to frequent texters and instant messaging. They may fail to fully understand your message, misinterpret it, disregard it, or read it resentfully. None of these outcomes is good.

An additional large number of people understand the abbreviations fine but do not like to see them in another medium—even e-mail.

Together, both groups probably include a lot of people important to you, such as clients, future employers and supervisors. Therefore, it's sensible to avoid abbreviating in general.

Attachments: When? Concern for computer viruses is one reason a fair number of people make it a rule not to open attachments. But when you have a lot to say, it's challenging to write a short e-mail. In the case of a report or other lengthy document, it can be impossible.

The best solution is to know your audience. Ask if necessary whether your recipient will open an attachment and prefers it. If the answer is no, then incorporate the material in the body of the e-mail, but use formatting to distinguish it from the e-mail message—for example, draw a line between the message and report, and give the report a clear headline. And make the rest of the document as readable as possible with subheads, some white space and so on.

Readers on the Go: How to Accommodate? Your e-mail may be read on a tiny screen while the reader is online at a checkout, taxiing to an appointment, or eating lunch. Your best strategy is nevertheless to write in complete sentences, not fragments, and avoid abbreviating. But use your awareness of smartphone readers to keep messages short and tight.

ETIQUETTE, SHMETIQUETTE—AN E-MAIL CHECKLIST

Do:

- Answer in a timely way—24 hours or less. People expect this with a medium geared for speed.
- Send only necessary messages. You need not have the last word, especially if it's just "got the message"; people appreciate hearing less rather than more.
- Include only what's needed, and write short messages. Speed readers may miss the point when you bury it.
- Use accurate subject lines to identify your message, change it when the discussion shifts, and make it audience directed and findable. Use "must-read" elements when justified—for example, "DATE CHANGE, Miller meeting."
- Use a strong opening line—bottom line on top.
- Build in a clear close, circling back to what you hope to accomplish.
- Use graphic devices to support clarity and stay organized: numbers, bullets, sub-heads, and so on.
- Use an easy-to-read typeface in a substantial size—12 point as a rule.
- Use the signature to your advantage: Cite your most important contact points, such as your website, blog, and social media addresses—limit the length.

Do Not:

- Betray emotion: You will instantly be seen as unprofessional, and your viewpoint or ideas will be disregarded.
- Say anything ambiguous that could be interpreted against your interests.
- Employ sarcasm, irony, and humor in general, always open to misinterpretation.
- Include anything you'd cringe to see on the front page of the *New York Times,* your boss's desk, or your competitor's e-mail in-box.
- Say anything you'd be embarrassed to have forwarded to anyone.
- Use jargon and abbreviations beyond the minimal.
- Include philosophical ponderings: This is not the place.

And Never

- Write whole messages in italic, bold, or capitals.
- Use smiley faces or other emojis or emoticons unless it's a good friend.
- Forget to edit and proofread.
- Forget to take a big picture view of how your message will (or might) strike a reader and make him feel.

PRACTICE OPPORTUNITIES

I. Request an Informational Interview

1. Write an e-mail requesting telephone or in-person time with a friend's relative who works in your chosen career, to ask for advice and possible job leads.

2. Exchange your draft with a classmate for reviewing and editing. Discuss results with each other, and revise if you agree with the suggestions.

3. Expect to be evaluated on both the quality of your own e-mail and the quality of written input you provide to your classmate.

II. Ask for a Special Favor

Write to a specific person to ask for a reference, connect you with someone she knows, or request a special assignment on the job. Then assume your request is granted, and write her a thank you note.

III. Group Work: Plan And Write a Communications Policy

1. Together, brainstorm how workplace supervisors should communicate in writing with younger employees: E-mail? Texting? Social media? Intranet? Other?

2. Draft an e-mail presenting your recommendations and reasoning to an older supervisor one of you works for—or once worked for. Begin by profiling the supervisor through asking questions of the group member who knows the person.

IV. Making a Request

Pair up. Student 1 acts as supervisor and Student 2 as a staff member who wants to attend an expensive conference. Student 2: Write an e-mail to "Supervisor" requesting authorization. Supervisor articulates his or her reaction to the e-mail—what worked and what didn't work. Together, rewrite the e-mail.

Then take on new roles. Student 1 becomes the requestor, and Student 2 assumes the role of a client prospect. Student 1 writes an e-mail asking for an appointment to demonstrate a product. Again, discuss the results and revise the e-mail.

Be prepared to present your thinking and ultimate written results to the class.

V. Write an E-Mail to a Friend Who Writes Poor E-Mails

Explain to your friend why he or she should take more care with e-mail, and share the most important points you learned from this chapter about how to write them well.

VI. Questions for Discussion

1. How do you think written communications like e-mails should take account of generational differences? Who has had a problem that relates to this? What did you learn?

2. What words do you typically use to communicate with a friend by e-mail that would be inappropriate when writing to your professor? A supervisor? A client?

3. How can you project a feeling of respect in an e-mail when the situation calls for it? Warmth?

4. In what e-mail situations is it suitable to "be yourself"—with little thought to content, wording, grammar, and punctuation?

5. Do grammar and punctuation matter anymore? Why or why not?

6. Should emojis or emoticons have a place in business communication? Debate: Half the group should argue for; the other half should speak against their use.

Chapter 7

APPLYING FOR JOBS

Résumés, Cover Letters and Networking

LEARN HOW TO . . .

- Plan a résumé that showcases your own skills
- Customize cover letters to the job
- Use good writing to connect with employers and networks

There is nothing to writing. All you do is sit down at a typewriter and bleed.

—Ernest Hemingway

WHERE TO START: KNOW YOURSELF—AND NETWORK

Not long ago, job applicants reached prospective employers by responding to ads, or through agencies, which act as intermediaries. Today, both employers and job seekers can connect directly on the Internet. One way of looking at it: The whole World Wide Web is your résumé. And it's totally public. Your degree of writing skill is more obvious and important than ever to employers, and therefore, you. So beyond presenting a carefully wrought résumé or letter—yes, you still need both—understand that your profiles and posts are read by those who want to know who you are.

Given how competitive most industries are today, you need to stand out. This is true whether you're just entering the career place or already possess solid credentials and experience. Added to the fact that you will probably hold a number of jobs during your career, you'll need résumés at many points. So make it part of your life to craft a strong résumé and keep it alive.

I don't recall ever knowing anyone who liked writing résumés. Why must the process be so hard?

A good résumé demands that you truly understand where you've been, what you're ready for and how to prove it. This requires you to think analytically about your life thus far and generalize about your experiences and skills.

Everything is relevant: work, education, specific training, part-time jobs, internships, sport and hobby interests, accomplishments, volunteer work, personal qualities, and what you did on your summer vacations. Also, the kind of people you relate to, the work atmosphere you prefer, the assignments that make you happiest and the ones that make you miserable. (Why put all that effort into getting an opportunity you'll hate?)

Consider all the elements of your personal history that have made you who you are.

Equally helpful: Have an idea of where you want to be next year—and in five years—even though your direction may change radically.

None of this means that you can't toss off an okay résumé over the course of a few days and score some hits or win the job you want. But there's a big bonus to crafting an outstanding résumé: The process sharpens your career planning, helps you recognize good opportunities, and convinces you that you're equipped for the job—which prepares you to ace the interviews.

VIEW FROM THE FIELD: USE YOUR WRITING SKILLS AND BE A KEEPER-IN-TOUCH

Communication has always been one of the top skills employers say they look for, and now it is much easier for them to get a sense of someone's abilities before reading a cover letter or meeting for an interview. Leverage various social media platforms to give people a sense of your capabilities before they even see your résumé.

Your LinkedIn profile, Facebook page, Twitter posts, and/or blog give employers a real sense of your communication skills and style. You are evaluated by what you put "out there" on the Internet, so build your brand by connecting with industry and sharing, posting, or tweeting about topics you are passionate about and relevant to the field you want to go into. Be mindful of what you put out there, as it can be easier to get discounted, but even more importantly it helps you to connect with industry.

It's a lot easier to build relationships with industry, and vice versa today. You need to have a clear idea of your personal brand and what you want prospective employers to know about

(Continued)

(Continued)

you. This doesn't mean you necessarily have to know what you'll do the rest of your life, but know your values, interests, motivators: What are you passionate about?

Be really aware that the relationships you build today will be very important in developing your career. Whatever the industry, you must be able to maintain your relationships even when there's no job attached to the conversation. Be a keeper-in-touch rather than a job seeker. Ask yourself: How can I achieve multiple touch points so people know who I am and what I offer? How do I get on people's radar so they can reach out to me if opportunities arise?

Don't worry about building relationships with important senior people. Engage with people who've been in your shoes recently, know what it's like, and will think of you when the opportunities come up. Reach out to individuals. Choose the social media platforms that make sense to you, use your alumni network, and find common denominators to build relationships. Let people know what you're involved in reading, attending, and writing about. People often connect based on personal interests—nothing to do with the job—so don't be too narrowly focused.

It's predicted that those now beginning their careers will hold over 20 different jobs in various industries throughout their professional life. Keep growing by doing an outstanding job wherever you are. Identify internal opportunities, take risks and volunteer for projects, and take on additional responsibilities that will give you more visibility in your own organization. Your hard work and dedication will pay off: Most people follow their managers, bosses, colleagues from organization to organization, so even though you might be in a role for a few years, your reputation and professional brand will be remembered as others in your network learn of opportunities or look to hire.

—Jeannie Liakaris, director of NYU Wasserman Center
for Career Development, School of Professional Studies

PLANNING YOUR RÉSUMÉ AND PRESENTATION FORMAT

Just as with every other writing format, plan your document based on the twin concepts of goal and audience.

Consider your goal: Do you think it's to win you a job? Actually not—the goal is more modest: to win you an interview so you can make your case in person. That may not change the content of your résumé, but it may mean giving it a different slant. It needs to work as a self-contained document and position you as worth interviewing so you survive the initial filtering process.

Consider your audience: Defining those who will view your résumé as "audience" reminds you of the following:

- You should bring to bear everything you know or can ferret out about the organization. As always, the more you understand the recipient, the better you can gauge your message.

- Your application, if successful, will be read by a series of reviewers on different levels so your message of qualification must be clear to all.
- The typical reader sees the review assignment as tedious and probably overwhelming; he or she will happily trash your effort on the least provocation—typos, poor writing, poor appearance, content not on target, maybe even because it's boring.

Remember: You may get less than six seconds of a reader's time to make the cut.

What Do You Mean, Traditional?

When an employer requests a résumé, whether e-mailed, snail-mailed or delivered in person, assume a traditional format is in order. That means presenting your skills, experience, education, and related background in a standard order on a piece of paper—real or virtual—using a reverse chronology (most recent first).

The ground rule applies even if you're trying for a creative position. Someone hiring a staff art director, for example, wants to see a portfolio but still wants to know about a candidate's experience, track record, education, reliability, and so on. The trick for creative people is to demonstrate their originality within the restrictive standard format: a writer, for example, through terrific writing, and a designer by making the document look great.

The biggest exception to this rule of thumb is the social media résumé, which exploits online capabilities to deliver a multidimensional impression of a person. This usually involves creating a website and using video, podcasts and social media links to showcase multiple aspects of your abilities and personality. When is this a good idea? It depends on your skills, the type of job involved, the company, who will review your qualifications, and many other factors.

VIEW FROM THE FIELD: A RECRUITER'S DOS AND DON'TS

A great résumé has flow, a presence. It captures the targeted industry. Its purpose is not to get the job but the interview, giving you the opportunity to sell yourself. So see it as a teaser and keep it down to one to two pages. Aim to speak about yourself with subtle confidence.

Based on my own peeves and what I hear from colleagues and employers, my advice is

1. Don't change the standard format: Keep it simple and chronological.

2. Put it in an easy-to-e-mail format like Word.

(Continued)

(Continued)

3. No typos! That's the biggest complaint we get from employers, and it amazes me.

4. Don't clutter the layout, change fonts and vary the type size—keep it clean and easy for that 20-second capture, which is the most time you have to make an impression.

5. Use the industry's keywords throughout but omit words that aren't searchable, like abbreviations.

If you have time gaps, definitely mention and address them—otherwise it's a red flag. And everything is so easy to check on now by Googling someone's name. Remember that the Internet is also your résumé and an employer can immediately find out if you're part of any dark side of the world. Use the Internet to your benefit, and build a sub-résumé on sites like LinkedIn or Spoke.com, which people look at when hiring.

—Tina Ruark-Baker, senior vice president of
strategic staffing at Access Staffing (accessstaffing.com)

Even with traditional résumés, you can take some liberties. The point is to present you at your best, so look for ways to adapt the format to what works. For example:

- To soften your job chronology if you jumped around a lot in a short period of time, or there are many gaps in your work history, put the dates of employment at the end of job descriptions rather than more prominently in a column on the left.
- Group brief jobs and generalize about them so they don't clutter up your landscape and make you look scattershot. Part-time or summer jobs, for example, can be grouped as such with a clear heading rather than listed separately:

Retail Sales Experience, Summers of 2010, 2011, and 2012

Salesperson for Macy's, Ben & Jerry Ice Cream, March Gift Shop.

Intensive customer interaction and problem-solving experiences. On-the-job training in customer relations, inventory management, large and small store operations.

- If a personal interest or pastime is relevant to the job and helps you stand out, find a way to cover it early on.
- If you're jumping careers or don't have a relevant job history for any reason, focus on "Skills" up front and make it clear why you can transfer them from whatever experience you do have.

Presentation: Formatting and Categories

Your goal is to present your information in a way that looks simple and accessible and is easy to absorb. Creativity is usually not called for, but use fonts, layout and white space to produce an inviting document. Usually it's best to use a standard format, such as the one on the next page, and adapt it to what shows you off best.

This is also true with choosing the categories to include.

The usual essentials after your masthead, contact information and overview are experience, education, professional organizations, and awards. "Skills" is another useful category. If you're at an early career stage, you may want to lead with this section. If you're experienced, you may want to put "Skills" at the bottom if not already covered—factors such as technical capabilities, software expertise, public speaking, foreign languages and so on.

But exercise some imagination to incorporate sections that let you include your strong points. Here are some to consider:

- Awards and recognition
- Strengths
- Social networks
- Technical training
- Clubs and associations
- Certifications
- Pro bono work
- Community service (better than volunteer activities)
- Catchall categories such as Additional Data, Related Experience, Special Qualifications or Career Highlights

Another good category is "Favorite Accomplishments," or something similar. If you've jumped around a lot, or want to highlight points of pride in a former job because it's more relevant to the one you want now than your current position, this is a good way to do that. (See the sample format on the next page.)

Do not waste space on the obvious, such as "References available on request" or "Available for interviews." And do not open with your job objective. Employers don't care about what you want. They care about what you can do for them. This is true even if you're applying for your first career job.

Vary the sample format based on your career status and industry. If you will be entering the job market with an MBA and a few years or more of work experience, then put the experience first because it will be of more interest to employers. If you're a business school student looking for a first or second job, or an internship, list education first.

The narrative "summary of experience" is in my opinion the most valuable part of a good résumé, but whether you need it "depends." You might prefer to include an overview of who you are and what you can do in your cover letter. But if the employer doesn't want a cover letter, the résumé should carry the summary.

Name
Address (City & State is sufficient)
Telephone, e-mail, website if you have one—perhaps LinkedIn profile or personal blog

Summary of Qualifications

Three to five lines putting your qualifications/experience in perspective

Employment

Dates, job title, name of company, location

Big-picture overview of your role and capsule description of the company

Bullet points representing accomplishments, up to six

For previous jobs, most recent first: Same format as current one but less detail (unless the earlier job shows especially relevant experience)

Career Highlights

Community service, special training, capabilities not covered by job descriptions, publications, speaking

Education

Starting with most recent:

Degree, name of school, location

For graduate work and college, any honors and strong focus

Any technical or professional training that relates to your career path

Include dates (unless you don't want to indicate age)

Distinctions

All awards, honors, recognition—including any given for character or time given to a good cause as well as academic achievement (if not covered under Education)

Skills

Technical, language, social media, certifications

Interests

Hobbies, community service (if not already covered), activities

Also, industries vary in their expectations. If you apply for a communications job, the summary is mandatory, but this is not true in the case of many business jobs. Where does a marketing or technical job fall? Use your judgment.

Definitely provide a summary of experience if you are changing careers or need to explain a break from the workforce.

Guidelines for creating summaries are given later in this chapter.

Opinions on whether to include activities and testimonials in the body of the résumé vary. Take into account also that a professional recruiter's viewpoint can differ from that of a human resources (HR) specialist or department head. Consider all the advice and apply what works best for you—always remembering goal and audience.

WRITING STRATEGIES TO OUTSHINE THE COMPETITION

A résumé must be crystal clear, concise, instantly understood and fast to read. It should be concrete, built on short words and sentences, and scrupulously edited. In other words, follow all the guidelines I've already set down for business writing in general. Don't shortchange the proofing process; borrow another set of eyes to double-check because one bad typo and poof! There goes your credibility no matter what kind of job you're applying for.

Do you need full sentences? No—you don't have room for that. Résumé real estate is at a premium. You can reduce some of the *I*'s and *a*'s and *the*'s, for example. But don't distill statements to fragments that may mislead or make you look illiterate.

For example, you needn't say,

I completed all the requirements for my Executive MBA in 18 months.

Nor should you say,

Exec. MBA, completed 18 mos.

Better:

Completed Executive MBA in 18 months

Do you need keywords? Yes! Many employers assign the preliminary review to people who have no idea what your experience means and depend on keywords, scanned for by eye or machine. Professional recruiters do the same. So build in the terms that characterize the industry and that denote required skills. Almost always you can glean these from the job posting and some online research, backed by your knowledge of the industry.

Do you need action verbs? Absolutely. Good résumés hinge on action verbs. If you want to come across as an active rather than passive person, someone who is outstanding rather than just capable and brings initiative and spark, make every verb zing. This is also how to take credit for your accomplishments. To find hundreds of great possibilities, just Google "action verbs" and scout out those that will work for you. (You might find this a good way to jump-start your résumé-think.)

For example, here are some strong verbs for describing management capabilities.

- Accelerated
- Consolidated
- Generated
- Piloted
- Secured
- Reorganized
- Steered
- Streamlined
- Strengthened
- Originated

- Launched
- Oversaw
- Instituted
- Rejuvenated
- Shepherded
- Mobilized
- Navigated
- Systematized
- Redirected
- Designed

You are entitled to use such words to convey a big-picture view of your work product. For example, don't say "I entered information into the database." It's better to say, "I managed the customer database and upgrade system."

Notice the different tone action verbs set, as opposed to when you depend on over-used and unconvincing words like experienced, dynamic and enthusiastic. Adopt the "show don't tell" mantra and your résumé will take you a lot further.

Do you need bullets? Yes, bullets are an excellent way to list skills or achievements in a short amount of space. But depending on bullets totally may not serve you well. Good narrative statements make sense of what otherwise come across as laundry lists, a disconnected collection of statements. This kind of disjointed rundown violates a fundamental principle—that it's the writer's responsibility to interpret the message, rather than letting readers draw their own conclusions.

If you choose to go the all-bullet route, be sure you compose strong statements that are easily absorbed and uniform in style. Remember that more than about six bullets makes readers sleepy.

Do you need to customize your résumé for every job application? Yes.

Writing successful cover letters is addressed later in this chapter. Review that section for more ideas on presenting yourself in writing.

Writing the Summary of Experience

It's very helpful to write a summary of experience even if you don't use it on your résumé, because it forces you to articulate who you are and what you're ready for.

You can begin with a clear definition of who you are professionally. At an early career stage, you have less to work with, so keep it simple. For example, if you're a recent graduate applying to a leadership training program at a multinational organization:

> Business Honor Society graduate with BS focused on marketing and leadership. Related internship experiences with three global organizations. Four years part-time work in retail sales with progressive responsibility, culminating in position of Team Leader. Excellent writing and in-person communication skills, proven analytic abilities, fluent Spanish.

This statement puts the writer's assets right up front and establishes a set of competitive advantages. Scour your own background: If your degree is from a prestigious school, work that in. If you edited the newspaper, graduated in the top 10%, were honored as a volunteer, helped a professor with an impressive project, won three scholarships, earned your way through college, created a business while still in school, lived part of your life in another country—all such factors set you apart.

A Business Communications Example

In her original résumé draft, this writer began with an objective:

> To obtain a challenging position in internal corporate communications that utilizes my prior experience in employee communications, internal web writing/editing, and executive communications/correspondence

Persuaded to begin with a summary of experience instead, she developed the following:

> Employee Communications Specialist: Strong track record originating and directing programs to engage employees, build morale and generate a positive

work environment. Four years multinational Fortune 500 experience producing publications, video features, online material and executive speeches. Adept in balancing, print, digital and social media channels to achieve company goals. Written and oral communication skills enhanced by advanced training.

Notice that with more experience to work with, this writer is able to follow up the "who I am" first statement with a very broad view of what her work achieves: NOT her specific job responsibilities. Then she moves to her major credentials and some specific work products and ends up referencing some differentiating skills. This is a useful pattern to try, but shape your summary so it shows off *your* best selling points.

Here's an alternative format you may prefer for your summary. It combines a short opening overview statement with a bulleted list of skills.

Profile

Hands-on, collaborative communications leader. Strategic thinker with a passion for helping organizations shape customer and employee perception to grow a healthy business. Recognized for:

- **Exceptional communications skills:** Can effectively simplify the complex to deliver clear, concise, and compelling communications
- **Trusted communications counsel to executives:** Have helped CEOs effectively develop and deliver their messages to multiple audiences
- **Equally strong left brain/right brain:** Ability to think creatively and execute effectively. Strong project management and analytical skills
- **High performance team-builder:** Track record of execution through teams, driven by a genuine desire to help others succeed

Your goal with the summary profile is to bridge between what you have done in the past and what you can do for a new employer. To simply list responsibilities qualifies you for the job you already have, and what's the point of that? *In the summary statement, and the rest of the résumé too, try to avoid phrases like "responsible for" and "duties include." Think about proven capabilities instead.*

An opening profile gives you a writing advantage: It tells you what content to focus on in the rest of the résumé. Everything you include should back up the summary with convincing detail.

Presenting Your Work Experience

Start with your most recent job, and follow with the rest in reverse chronological order. Logically, a current job merits the most description—but what if it's a diversion from your career path or you've only held it briefly? Then say as much as it's worth, and use fuller descriptions for one or more of your earlier jobs.

Try for a short narrative paragraph generalizing about the position and/or employer. For example:

2009–Present   JFL Inc., Seattle, WA

Increasingly responsible marketing roles for Fortune 1000 firm, second-largest distributor of home repair supplies on West Coast, employing 7,000 people. Skills range from market research to program planning, project management, presentation writing and design, and customer relations.

The reason for describing the company is that either the reader (1) won't readily know what it is or (2) may recognize the firm's name but probably won't know its scope. In both cases, positioning the company—especially as significant in some way in size or standing—makes your experience look all the better.

Following up in the same pattern, name each position in reverse chronological order with a short narrative and three to six bullet points for each.

VIEW FROM THE FIELD: WHAT A HUMAN RESOURCES MANAGER WANTS

When I hire for a position like marketing, I get easily seven or eight hundred résumés. Realistically, you have 5 or 10 seconds. So don't tell me—sell me.

You don't have to include everything you've done, but put it in a way that makes sense. For example, one résumé I reviewed said, "Managed a variety of integrated marketing programs." I asked her to explain and she redefined it to, "Launched 1.5 million person direct mail piece with a response rate exceeding 20%." Similarly, a line that read "Managed creative and production processes to ensure budget delivery" is better as, "Created new internal budgeting process that kept more than $700,000 worth of production under budget."

So write less, be more accurate and to the point. Try using the STAR approach: situation-task-action-result—to make a sentence or brief paragraph.

—Doug Silverman, general manager of human resources at Nikon Inc.; former president of Society of Human Resource Managers/Long Island

To Stand Out From the Crowd

Here are some strategies that can give you the edge.

Cite accomplishments, not responsibilities. A list of responsibilities you've carried out is a lot less interesting than evidence that you performed this work in an outstanding way. Employers want to know how you made a difference to the organization.

To understand how to do this, note the contrast between A and B in each of the following.

Statement A

Manage, write and budget enterprise-wide employee contest for two company intranet sites.

Statement B

Invent ideas for employee pop culture contests to engage a diverse workforce, regularly drawing 2,000 to 3,000 entries per month and contributing to a positive culture aligned with the entertainment industry.

Statement A

Responsible for managing and improving inventory process and supplying regular reports to team leaders

Statement B

Revamped company's inventory process and introduced new controls that reduced shrinkage 17% and saved 24% in staff costs, earning a department commendation

Statement A

Redesigned a warehouse

Statement B

Transformed a disorganized warehouse into an efficient operation by totally redesigning the layout, saving an estimated $50,000 annually in recovered stock

Notice in particular that the *B* statements

1. Use the industries' power words and action verbs to frame the work and energize the writing.

2. Relate *either* to major ongoing aspects of the position or to a project. Because project work has a beginning and end, think through projects you've handled to identify accomplishments worth citing.

3. Quantify accomplishments in terms of time or money saved, efficiency achieved, or other contribution to company goals—all music to every prospective employer's ears.

Numbers are magical and talk the bottom-line language of all business, so quantify everything you possibly can. This is challenging but well worth the effort. When you can't quantify, think about how to suggest a positive outcome in other terms. For example,

> Launched knowledge management processes to promote better use of resources companywide, introducing new tools such as orientation tool kits and e-newsletters.

> Created new process to streamline online purchasing, now being adopted organization-wide.

Another good technique for bringing your résumé alive is to look past the glib-type generalizations we tend to include and find the concrete facts behind them—what we do can be much more interesting than the generalizations. For example, I recently questioned a young woman whose résumé contained lines like

> I monitor executive e-mail shadowboxes and manage the executive correspondence processes.

What did she mean? On a weekly basis, she scans about 300 e-mails in the Fortune 100 company's general in-box, assesses their importance, responds according to her judgment, and prepares a trend report.

This might be phrased something like

> Monitor public input: Review hundreds of e-mails weekly, evaluate their importance, frame answers and report on trends to top management

Highlight promotions. Does your work history overall, or with a major job, demonstrate a steady advance in title or responsibility? Or fast progress? Make the most of it up front in your overview profile and in the way you detail the job. Recruiters will assume that impressing one employer means you're a good bet for their firms.

Cover personal attributes. Your "soft skills" can be very important to an employer: for example, leadership or facilitation abilities, good teaming, fast learning, consistent willingness to go above and beyond, ability to inspire others and so on. Are you unflappable under pressure? Good at training new staff members or mentoring? Able to handle multiple projects and deliver on tight deadlines? Play your strong suits but be specific and cite evidence as possible.

Use endorsements. Let others say it for you. This can be terrific if you're switching careers or are relatively new to the job market. Have a former boss or even coworker state how valuable you were to the team, how hard you worked and took initiative, how reliable you were. Endorsements need not come from employers. Your mother's word might not hold much weight, but a colleague's might, or the head of an organization for which you've done volunteer work. When including an endorsement, use quotation marks, italics, and a full attribution—the person's name, title, and affiliation. Put it at the top of your résumé or better, the bottom.

Include pro bono work. Especially in tough times, people on every level find themselves out of work and choose to give time on a nonpaid basis to a worthy cause or an organization they can learn from. Don't shrink from saying so—it demonstrates a mind-set that many recruiters will appreciate.

Include teaching and presenting. If you've taught anything that's career related—even remotely—use it. If you've given lectures, mentored others, coached a team, or taught a course even at your local high school, say so. Being able to teach shows mastery of the subject or at the least, a great sharing attitude. Presentation skills are highly valued in most fields.

Include your own business? Even if you didn't succeed with it, starting and running a business testifies to your initiative, courage, and big-picture thinking. Include it, and say what you learned from the experience. But be prepared to convince the recruiter that you're not looking for an opportunity to go back to entrepreneurial life anytime soon.

Create better job titles? If your official title is inaccurate, vague or unimpressive, take the liberty of generic titling, but keep it lowercase to be honest. For example, if you are Third Assistant Manager for Procurement Support, use a more descriptive title to set the stage—such as procurement specialist for recycled metals.

Play the social media card. In most industries, the people in charge recognize that social media is critical to their marketing, customer relations and employee communications. If you are adept with social media and your online presence bears this out, say so.

Mention other skills and talents? If you've raised championship bulldogs, grew up on a farm, lived in another country, won dance contests or chess tournaments, play in the community orchestra, captained the college soccer team—whatever:

It may or may not be worth mentioning in your résumé. A growing number of employers value social consciousness, so evidence of your commitment to something bigger than yourself may give you a plus. You must judge the value according to the job you're targeting. Always be aware of other people's sensibilities: Mentioning that you work for a particular political party or collect guns will probably not help your cause in some circles.

Make it look great. Take trouble with your layout; enlist the help of an artistic friend if you need to. Stick to one highly readable typeface and make it at least 11 point. Resist the temptation to make margins narrower than one inch. Make judicious use of bold, capitals and italics. Build in enough white space, even if this means cutting a bullet or two.

Use good paper if supplying hard copies. Don't depend on color for appearance or emphasis when you deliver a résumé online. The document will probably be printed out in stark black on white. And don't rely on special effects. One recruiter told me that when he prints out some résumés, graphic techniques like a shadowed font may not print at all—and if it's used for the heading, there goes your name.

VIEW FROM THE FIELD: Q&A WITH A RÉSUMÉ CONSULTANT

What are the most common mistakes you see in business résumés?

Three things come up in any industry, no matter how senior the people are.

1. Listing responsibilities rather than impact. You need both: You managed a budget, but what did you do with it? Manage it within a 2% variance? Save money? Use the situation-action-result method: State what you were responsible for, the problem, the result. For example, I increased X by 23%.

2. Including laundry lists of everything you've done instead of everything that's relevant to the job you're looking for. Just use related things or interesting ones, to build a focus.

3. Too much jargon. MBA graduates and career changers especially tend to be saturated with jargon from their old world that people in the new world might not understand. If you're applying for a marketing job, discount the real estate jargon. If you're changing careers, you need to translate so readers will understand—you can't expect them to on their own.

(Continued)

(Continued)

Which should you present first, experience or education?

If you've been in the workforce for years, place education at the bottom. But if by chance you're applying for jobs using your business school network, or for a posting you found on the alumni job board, you might want to keep it at the top because that is the point of connection you're leveraging.

Should you include personal information?

Yes, but it has to be interesting. Use something that's a hook with an interviewer, something you're passionate about, but it should be specific. For example, don't just say "traveling," but "travel in Mongolia." Think about what conversation could lead from it: "I love games" isn't as good as "I love Scrabble." It's something to talk about and puts the interviewer at ease, too.

How long should a résumé be?

Keep it to one page unless you have 10 to 15 years' experience that's related to the job. If you have that much experience but it's not related to the role you're applying for, it's best to be concise and not include detail. For a two-page résumé, be sure to include your name in the header or footer on page 2, because the pages can easily get separated.

—Stephanie Shambroom Boms, consultant for
strategy, leadership development, and recruitment

SUCCESS TIP

IS A SOCIAL MEDIA RÉSUMÉ RIGHT FOR YOU?

An online social media résumé may be a great way to showcase who you are and what you can do. It presents you as a multidimensional individual who can be seen and heard. But, to pull it off, you need the creative skills to produce a website or blog (preferably with HTML know-how and some design talent), produce your own videos and/or podcasts and, preferably, blog regularly. And need I mention, this all takes good writing skills. As with all online media, you must be committed to constantly updating your material so it doesn't grow stale.

A social media résumé also can instantly connect your audience with some or all of your online "lives," such as Facebook, LinkedIn, YouTube, Twitter, and so on. But be sure these sites show you to good advantage. Understand and exercise your privacy options, but don't count on them to protect you. Assume that if you put it online—they will come.

COVER LETTERS: GUIDELINES AND CREATIVE OPTIONS

Creating good cover letters is one of the biggest writing challenges for many people.

In business, you may need cover letters not only to apply for a job but also to accompany proposals, forms, questionnaires and a host of other documents.

There are times when a cover letter must carry the whole weight of introducing you as a job candidate—a résumé may not be desired or appropriate. Always send a cover letter with a résumé or job application unless the posting specifically says not to. It may be presented as optional, but it's not.

Adopt the Right Attitude

Producing a very correct letter is important, and I'll give you the guidelines for doing so, but don't lose sight of the big picture—how you want to be perceived.

Your cover letter should feel totally positive and upbeat. This is not the place to voice reservations about your qualifications or personality. Aim to show enthusiasm, even passion, for the work you want to do, the field or profession, and the specific job opening, as appropriate.

Harder to accomplish: Don't be a bore. It's probable that every job you apply for will be highly competitive, and the organization will receive far more applications than the screeners really want to read. A creative element will gain you favor.

These days, very few employers are looking solely for technical skills, unless they intend to plant you in some hidden back office. The "soft skills"—relating to people, teaming, leading, and communicating well—are almost universally valued. Prospective employers want to know who you are, how you'll fit. The cover letter is your chance to tell them.

Remember that the people you're writing to are focused on their own problems and challenges. They work hard to explain what they want. It's your job to match yourself to those needs. If you're doing a "cold" job hunt—writing letters in the hope of unearthing an unadvertised opportunity—you need to figure out what problem the firm might have, and present yourself as a solution.

In both cases, a generalized letter that simply says,

I'm applying for the position of ABC at your firm . . . my qualifications are great . . . my résumé is attached . . .

doesn't stand much of a chance.

Plan for Success

Never dash off a cover letter at the last minute. Most of your competitors spend excruciating weeks on polishing their résumés and then write sloppy, ill-crafted, thought-free cover letters. Or—maybe worse—they don't include cover letters at all. Either way, probably no one will ever read those painstakingly produced résumés. Everything the audience needs to know is right up front, in the form of a badly written letter—or absence of any at all. Invest the necessary time to plan, brainstorm, draft and revise a strong letter.

Remember your goal. A cover letter should introduce you in a more personal, targeted way than a résumé. It need not give a comprehensive overview of your career and qualifications—that's what the résumé is for (if enclosed)—but should aim to

- present an insight about you that the résumé format doesn't accommodate;
- highlight your most relevant experience or credential and add a little detail;
- suggest some personality, or personal attributes, relevant to the job;
- set the stage for the reader to review your résumé as you would like; and
- show why you are the most qualified person for the job.

Always, the last point on the list is the most critical: *A strong application demands that you **know** why you are the person that the company should hire.* Have a good answer to "why me," and the cover letter will reflect your conviction and include the facts to back it up. And so will the interview.

How to dodge the salary question? Even when a job ad asks for your salary requirements, it's perfectly fine to say "My salary requirements remain open and flexible, as I need to learn more about the responsibilities of this position."

—Doug Silverman, general manager of human resources at Nikon Inc.; former president of Society of Human Resource Managers/Long Island

Absorb the organization's philosophy and priorities. If you're answering a posting, read it 20 times; it's full of clues about what the advertiser wants and what's important to the company. Look at the company's website and whatever other materials you can access—talk to people who know the firm if you can. Especially if you're sending a cold-call query . . . try to figure out "what keeps them up at night."

Name that connection. If you have a personal link of any kind to the recipient or organization, say so up front. Name-dropping can work wonders: Who wouldn't rather hire somebody who comes vouched for, even a little bit? So don't be shy if you can come up with anything relevant—for example, that

- someone the recipient knows suggested you write—a colleague, former employer, professor, friend;
- you share a mutual acquaintance;
- you saw the person speak at a conference;
- you went to the same school; and
- your father or cousin worked there.

The list is in descending order of usefulness.

It's not just about you: Say something nice about the person you're writing to, and/or compliment the organization. Few people do this, and it can be magical. Here are some examples:

- I know you're a leader in your field because . . .
- I read your book (or article) on X and was fascinated by . . .
- I've followed your career with interest because . . .
- I admire the strategic marketing tactics you introduced . . .
- As someone who follows the business press, I know that Y is the leading company in its market . . .
- I'm impressed by how Y Inc. has created breakthrough products in only five years . . .
- Z told me that working for you was the best experience he ever had.

But don't follow this advice without doing your homework. If you write to Apple, admiring their innovative spirit will get you sleepy sneers. If you want to compliment an organization's ethics, make sure the leaders haven't been indicted lately. Take the time to know what you're talking about, and be able to cite some detail—what makes the firm outstanding, what the CEO has a right to be proud of, and what her book is about. Find a truly good reason why you want to work there.

Use the language, style and keywords of your audience. Cover letters, like résumés, are partial exceptions to the "no buzzwords" rule. Aim to reflect the company's style, and focus and get your message across in terms these readers will relate to. This is especially important because many reviewers will scan your letter rather than read it and may do this digitally. That said, people often don't like to read the way they write themselves or don't like the biz speak that job ads provoke, so a conversational (but courteous) style is still best. And be wary of adding any jargon of your own to theirs.

Use the space to communicate more personal factors. Aim to get across why you're a good fit for the opportunity, and be original to the extent that it applies to the job. Bring in an anecdote if it relates. And this may be the best place to tell your "inside" story. For example, if you're leaving a bank job to follow a career with nonprofits, share your reasons for doing that. If your résumé isn't linear and one or more gaps are evident, explain to the degree that seems called for.

Consider using a testimonial. It can be incorporated into the body of your letter or added as a "pullout," carefully placed on the page with the name, position and affiliation of the person you're quoting. A testimonial can speak to your technical qualifications but at least equally well to your personal qualities—perseverance, for example, or hard-work habits, people skills, fast learning, taking initiative, and so on. This is particularly effective if you don't yet have a lot of work experience to your credit. A professor who likes you is a great source.

Take the initiative for follow-up. Don't tell the reader when to call you—almost always it's better to say that you will call in a few days to schedule the interview. But use common sense: If the job posting says, "Don't call us, we'll call you," or a phone number seems deliberately hard to track down, don't try to call.

VIEW FROM THE FIELD: COVER LETTERS FROM HELL

Never underestimate the staying power of terrible cover letters. Bob Killian of Killian Branding reviews hundreds of applicant letters for creative jobs at his Chicago advertising agency. From these he culls "Cover Letters from Hell." Posted on the company website (killianbranding .com), these letters draw an immense and amused audience.

But it's not funny to be the person gaining such recognition. How to avoid it? Killian says, "Make it efficient, clear, don't bury the lead—most of the things are commonsensical. Many people use biz speak—the bafflegab of the clichés we make fun of—that's a smokescreen but rarely advances the cause of the writer."

Other mistakes: "Believing that my ideas and intense wonderfulness will come through no matter how I say it. Not recognizing the value of asking someone else to read it before you send it out. Not proofreading and spell checking.

"Young people tend not to hear the sound of what they're writing—always a mistake."

See the company's website for more advice along with this encouraging statement: "Good news: An error-free letter is now so freakin' rare that the minimal care required to send a letter with zero defects, combined with a few crisply written simple declarative sentences, will, alone, guarantee a respectful reading of a résumé. Maybe even secure an interview."

Nine Technical Tips

1. Keep the letter to one-page maximum. Less is better. If you're writing a cover letter that will be e-mailed, keep it even shorter—like three brief paragraphs. Needing to be brief is one reason not to waste space on stock phrases, stilted language and obvious statements (like "It is herewith my pleasure to provide you with . . . in response to your recent posting for . . .").

2. Don't send letters that look mass-produced. If you're mailing an inquiry to 500 prospective employers, personalize and tailor each and every one and include at least something that demonstrates your interest in that specific company.

3. Use people's names. Addressing letters "To whom it may concern," "Sir" or "Madam" or "Dear Marketing VP" doesn't cut it. Take the trouble to find out who holds the position—now, not five years ago.

4. Use a formal and respectful salutation. For men, Dear Mr. Wise is appropriate; for women, use Ms., unless you have reason to think the person prefers another form of address (as when, for example, a communication you're responding to is signed "Mrs. Ann Green"). If you're unsure of the person's gender, use the full name—"Dear W. Sutton."

5. Specify the job posting you're applying for. Write the name of the position in the upper right-hand corner or before the salutation (so you don't have to waste space on that in the actual letter and can write a more engaging lead).

6. Use all the good writing techniques you've been practicing: short, comfortable words; short, clear sentences; short paragraphs; concise language with good transitions; and lively verbs. This is one of the most impatient audiences you'll have. A good lead for your letter is crucial for keeping your résumé out of the trash.

7. Remember the serial audience. Expect your cover letter to be screened by somebody in the hiring office, a department head, the CFO's assistant, or the new intern—or the CEO. Fortunately, the letters I'm preparing you to write will work at every level.

8. Close respectfully and traditionally. *Sincerely* is generally best.

9. Make it look good. If your cover letter is accompanying a print résumé, use good quality paper, generous margins and white space, and a clear typeface like Times New Roman in 11 point or bigger. Match the heading and style to that of your résumé for a uniform impression. Keep in mind that when you e-mail your application, fancy formatting and fonts may get lost in cyberspace.

SUCCESS TIP

NETWORK IN PERSON

Many professional associations welcome newcomers to their events, and members go out of their way to make young people welcome and give them active support. Find the local associations that relate to your field of interest, and check out the national and international associations, too. Many have local chapters and some even offer student memberships. Show up at meetings and for the cost of a meal, you'll typically learn about industry trends or participate in a professional development workshop. Introduce yourself to people (use your elevator speech—see Chapter 13), and you'll quickly connect with key influencers. Present yourself well and job leads may materialize. Even more, volunteer for a committee to earn huge points and work alongside valuable people.

How to Craft Custom Cover Letters

Since this book's objective is to equip you to write your own first-rate, customized documents, don't look here for cookie-cutter samples to follow. You'll find plenty online—but you'll also find that most are not very good.

To get you thinking along productive lines, let's look at a specific job announcement. This is a slightly abbreviated version of how a Fortune 500 company (which we'll rename "JA") describes its MBA Human Resources Leadership Program.

> . . . an intensive two-year program consisting of three, eight-month rotational assignments in the human resources functions of a JA business. The program combines job assignments with focused training and leadership opportunities . . . .

> Candidate criteria: basically two years related work experience, MBA, GPA of at least 3.0 and geographically mobile

That's not much to go on, but the company website also provides several short videos to inspire candidates. One hints at the general attributes the company wants for all of its competitive leadership training programs: *ambition, a natural disposition to work hard, dedication to making a difference, team skills* and *global outlook.*

There's also a video specifically about the HR program. Current participants are featured talking about their work *bridging communication gaps, getting into the hearts and minds of people, interacting with people worldwide, being a talent champion* and *being willing to move out of comfort zones.*

How would you present your case to compete for this opportunity?

First, brainstorm all your obvious matching points. Make a list. This might, for example, include

- your MBA with a focus on talent management,
- 3.5 grade point average,
- three years' experience that can be interpreted as related work, and
- yes, you're willing to go anywhere.

Okay, you meet the formal criteria, but clearly that's not enough. So . . .

Second, ask yourself, What in my background speaks to the skills that are specified—and just as important, the skills that are implied? Your list might include:

- Ambition
- Hard-work ethic
- Making-a-difference orientation
- Good teaming
- Leadership potential
- Relating well to people
- Global viewpoint
- Flexibility
- Enthusiasm for HR work
- Ability to take initiative

Also, the company no doubt wants assurance that you'll really appreciate this opportunity, are prepared to make the most of it, and will welcome challenge.

You must come up with concrete facts and evidence to show you possess the desired skills and attitude. If the opportunity is any kind of a match for your credentials and personality, you can definitely do this. If you find it hard, try a version of the visualization technique described in Chapter 2. Imagine you're being interviewed for the job and imagine the questions you'd be asked. Or role-play the situation with a friend asking the questions. Write down all your possible answers—the "talking points" approach can help (Chapter 14).

Three, now study your list and check off your best selling points and evidence. Mull these over and do some freethinking to find ideas for the lead—and don't rule out any that seem nontraditional or far-fetched.

Before I offer some creative approaches, let's say that a simple "classic" lead will often serve you fine. Straightforward and "correct" may alone help you stand out. So you might lead your letter to "JA" like this, with variation to taste:

I'm writing to apply for a position in your MBA Human Resources Leadership Program, which I was extremely interested to discover on your website. I believe my work experience as xxx, forthcoming MBA from White, and personal qualities equip me to make the most of this outstanding opportunity.

However, when you face a lot of competition, it's often worth taking pain to stand out from the field. Imaginative presentation can make the difference. This is also true when you're trying for a job that's a stretch.

Here are a few different approaches to the "JA" ad to demonstrate how to think through your strategy. *The examples will suggest some useful language, even if you don't like the overall pitch or find them inappropriate.* Note that in some ways these general-type job postings are hardest to do. When the employer gives you a lot of information, you can key your response off the specs.

An engaging lead requires hard thinking. But when you settle on one, the rest of the letter begins to fall into place. If a résumé is attached, you don't need more than a few paragraphs. If you're applying without a résumé, you'll have to compose a middle section—a few paragraphs—that summarizes your top matching points with the job you want. But try to keep a readable style rather than listing 20 bullet points or condensing your whole life into a page.

Example A

When I was 9, I sold more Girl Scout cookies than anyone in the county. When I was 15, I talked 30 classmates into a waterfront cleanup program. In college, I founded an International Studies Club and while earning my MBA, created a Speaker Program that drew the region's business leaders to our doorstep.

In my two years in the Talent Management department of a leading regional manufacturer, I was twice commended for improvements in the recruitment system.

Now I'm ready to work harder than ever and learn from the best in human resources, the profession that fits my nature, experience, and education.

I know that JA is leading the way toward new models in talent management and economic development worldwide. I look forward to learning more about your Leadership Development Program in Human Resources but am already sure that it's my ideal opportunity: a chance to grow, meet new challenges, and contribute to the profession that creates the meeting point between global business and individuals.

I hope you will invite me to talk about the program with you.

Example B (Note Testimonial at End)

Your description of JA's Leadership Program for MBAs inspired me to speak with three White Business School alumni who have joined your staff. What they told me resonates with my highest career hopes: to learn from the field's best people while building my leadership skills, interacting globally, and practicing out-of-the-box thinking to solve tough problems.

My career to date has prepared me to make the most of this opportunity. Beyond my intensive MBA and undergraduate studies in management and psychology, I have:

Developed my communication skills through elective programs in writing, speaking and presentation

Chaired a student advisory board to help MBA program directors align academics with shifting workplace models

Handled four HR-related internships in three years, giving me field experience in a range of global industries

In my advanced marketing seminar, I routinely counted on John Black to introduce interesting angles for discussion . . . .

—Professor Jane Umber, White Business School

Example C

When I was 14, my father lost the job he'd held for 24 years because the company closed down his department. It could have been tragic for my family, but a company HR manager helped him: He spent hours with my dad, talking through his work history, qualifications, and old aspirations. The bottom line—my father agreed to obtain some specialized training, and the company rehired him in a new capacity.

So while other people cite a great doctor or entrepreneur as an inspiration, I've always remembered how a good HR manager made a big difference in my family's lives by doing his job well . . .

Example D

As an enthusiastic reader of many human capital journals, I know how challenging today's global business environment is and how much the human resources profession can contribute. It is the HR specialist who is called on to manage the people side of complex multinational organizations, find and retain the right talent, prepare workers for a new world, and anticipate needs that won't exist until tomorrow.

I consider HR the most exciting profession of all, and my goal is to contribute to it.

Example E

In my Talent Management class last year, as a first-year MBA student at White, I was assigned a case study on handling human resource issues on the international level. The subject was JA's challenge in establishing an operation in Beijing. I was so impressed with the innovative strategies developed by the team that I decided right then that JA was the company I wanted to work for . . .

These examples may not suit your personal style, goals, or experience but may prompt some ideas. Ideally, a cover letter makes readers want to know more and leads them to notice the "evidence" that prove your claims when they read the résumé. Learning to tell your personal story can go a long way in a cover letter and during interviews—see Chapter 13.

One more point: In all your written messages and application materials, don't show off! Overstating your awesomenesss can be laughable: Don't cross that line. And resist the temptation to demonstrate that you are more clever, knowledgeable, or superior in any way to the employer. One of the worst examples that's come to my attention was this response to a standard question on an application form:

"My salary history is not included because it is irrelevant and requesting that information goes against your mission. As a company committed to alleviating poverty, you should be aware of the current socioeconomic situation . . . ."

The writer went on to lecture on better hiring practices and the impact of poverty, ending with, "So why am I still applying? I see misdirection, but also potential." This candidate offered excellent credentials, but wrote herself out of consideration.

SUCCESS TIP

IMPRESS INTERVIEWERS WITH GOOD QUESTIONS

Employers generally don't hire based on paper qualification; they want to see you. Appearance, personality and "likability" count heavily. In most cases, those hiring prefer candidates who fit into the organizational culture, so check that culture out in advance through research or talking with someone already on board.

Come prepared to answer every question you can anticipate—a good technique is to prepare talking points (see Chapter 14). And prepare good questions to ask. What you hear will help you judge whether the match is a good one for you. Just as important, your questions are part of how you are evaluated.

You don't earn points for acting like a passive applicant who wants just any job and hasn't done her homework on the particular opportunity. And you don't get points for asking questions you can answer yourself by scanning the website.

Take a big-picture view of company challenges, the industry, and the role you want to play. Consider the role of your interviewer—a department head has different concerns than an HR manager, for example. Review any previous conversations you've had with a company representative. Then frame relevant questions.

Here are some generic questions that may work in many situations.

- How will I be contributing to the company's goals?
- I know the job entails xxx. Can you tell me more about that and the expectations?

- How will I know I'm succeeding?
- What attributes do successful people at this company have in common?
- What opportunities can I take advantage of to learn and grow?
- Why do you like working here?
- Do you have any concerns about whether I'm a good fit for this job?

Good preparation enables you to think on your feet and come up both with good answers and more questions. Good interaction spells success, even if you don't get the job—the interviewer may rightly judge that it's not in fact a good match.

If post-interview you think of things you should have said—as we all do—include those points in your thank you note. And yes, you must always write one if you want the job.

PRACTICE OPPORTUNITIES

I. New Job Planning

Expect to look for a new job, internship or summer associate position this year? If so, do the following:

1. Define—in writing—your set of goals, with detail. In addition to stating the job you'd like to have, specify what you want to gain from it.

2. Write the most complete profile you can of your audience—the people who'll review your application at the organization where you want to work.

3. In the framework of your answers to the first two tasks, brainstorm the content of your résumé. What should you include about your experience and personal qualifications?

II. Write a Posting for the Job You Want

Put yourself in your prospective employer's shoes and figure out how she would advertise your ideal job. Write a detailed posting that covers all relevant aspects. Then evaluate your qualifications against the posting. Are you well qualified? If so, does your résumé demonstrate that? Does this give you any ideas about how to improve your résumé?

III. Question for Discussion

How would the content of a résumé for a summer job or an internship differ from one for your next career job? Compare notes with other class members. Keep track of ideas you hadn't thought of, and consider how to use them in your next job search.

IV. Write Your Summary

Draft the strongest summary of experience you can with a specific job goal in mind.

V. Review Your Current Résumé

Evaluate how well it works in terms of what you've learned in this chapter and the book as a whole, and decide how to improve it. Turn at least three of the responsibilities you describe into accomplishments and try to quantify them.

VI. Write a Letter for Your Dream Job

Find a posting that at this point represents your dream job. Though you may not be ready to apply, draft the strongest cover letter you can think of to make your case. Be sure to

- brainstorm your history, experience, and all qualifications that might relate;
- analyze and interpret the job description and other employer material;
- figure out what you'd bring to the job beyond the bare essentials;
- know why you are the best possible candidate and why the organization should hire you; and
- come up with some imaginative leads and evaluate whether they are appropriate.

VII. Compare Job Application With Personal Intros

Scan entries on a dating site such as Match.com, or any app where people describe themselves in order to connect with individuals. Review what people say about themselves, how they describe the person they want to meet and how they say it. What insights do people provide (usually inadvertently) about who they are through their writing? What do you discern about their values and priorities? Are they presenting the right information—the content—to engage the kind of person they want to know? What ideas does your analysis suggest that relate to presenting yourself as a job candidate? Write 300 words or more about what you learned, citing examples.

VIII. Group Activity

Exchange your résumé and dream job cover letter with a classmate. Give each other constructive criticism, adopting the viewpoint of a hiring manager.

Chapter 8

LETTERS AND MEMOS

They Still Count

LEARN HOW TO . . .

- Plan, write, and format letters to achieve goals
- Strategize specific letters
- Write in-house memos that build relationships

I consider it a good rule for letter writing to leave unmentioned what the recipient already knows, and instead tell him something new.

—Sigmund Freud

WHEN AND HOW TO WRITE LETTERS

While you may not routinely write letters to friends and relatives—and might be surprised at how common a practice it was before digital communication—the art is still essential to many business venues.

Cover letters are usually essential to job applications and proposal submissions as well. You may also need to write letters to connect with clients, customers, government agencies, suppliers and many other people and organizations.

By "letter," I don't necessarily mean a printed document delivered by the post office. A letter can be e-mailed. But when you're writing for a formal purpose, you must thoughtfully craft and edit the message to meet more formal demands, whatever the delivery system.

Although you may be able to use some "standard" prefabricated pieces in some letters, for the most part, every letter you write must be individual and specific to your purpose. Therefore, we'll focus on how to apply the structured thinking process.

If you find yourself struggling with a particular kind of letter, Google the category (e.g., "letter of introduction") and batches of examples will come up. You can pick up useful ideas and language from these samples, but be cautious:

- Don't bypass the thinking process that starts with "goal" and "audience."
- Don't adopt the old-fashioned, stilted wording and tone of many online samples.
- Don't be tempted to use a premade cookie-cutter letter; it shows and will fail to accomplish your goal.

Characteristics of Successful Letters

Unlike e-mails and very unlike text messages, letters are natural relationship-building tools. They carry more weight than casual, spontaneous-seeming e-mail. Always treat them as a way to make a good impression or risk accomplishing the reverse.

So it is particularly important to write clear, concise letters that come to the point quickly and move fast. Don't visualize your reader as putting her feet up on the desk and perusing your letter in a relaxed, contemplative manner. Businesspeople don't have those moments anymore. Visualize an overburdened, stressed executive who needs to solve problems and find answers. Write to that person.

Make what's-in-it-for-the-reader loud and clear. Apply all the principles of economy—use short, immediately understood words (mostly one and two syllables), short sentences (14 to 18 words average), and short paragraphs (three or four sentences *on average*). Keep each paragraph to one idea.

A conversational tone is generally desirable, but many letters need to be somewhat more formal than e-mails. This may move your writing toward a more stilted pattern. Try to counter this by simplifying the language and thinking of concise ways to say things.

Always consider the relationships carefully. Invariably build in respect and courtesy. This isn't always easy: Figuring out how to frame some messages courteously can take some effort. When a client, for example, has repeatedly ignored your request for a conversation, focus on your most important goal: You want the information, sure, but you need to keep the client.

Letters should strike readers as well thought out and constructed. This means making them logically organized, carefully edited and visually effective—neat, clean, enough white space, very readable font, graphic balance. Letters must feel personal. Even if you're sending out a mass-audience letter to 100 prospective employers, for example, you must take the trouble to address each one individually.

Always write to an individual. It's off-putting to a human resources director to be addressed by his job title, for example, and if you write a letter that says "Dear CEO," don't expect an answer. Almost always a little research will give you the name—or you can even call the firm and ask for it.

The lead, generally the first paragraph, is critical—and should immediately engage the reader by stating what the letter is about and why he or she should be interested, although you won't say it that way. Throughout, use words that tell readers what to especially notice—for example, "the main idea," "more important to consider," "my most significant qualification," and so on.

The guidelines we followed in earlier chapters for determining your goal, audience, tone, structure and content will see you through every letter, no matter how challenging. We'll concentrate in this chapter on letters for career-building purposes, plus a few general business letter examples to help you apply the ideas.

VIEW FROM THE FIELD: LETTER-WRITING TIPS FROM AN EXPERT

Carol C. Weeks, a corporate training specialist who's taught hundreds of government employees and executive assistants to write better business letters, offers these tips.

1. Always start by putting the reader in the picture. So much material begins with *I*, and that's not nearly as effective as finding a way to start with *you*. For example, rather than saying, "I appreciated your taking the time to speak with me," say, "Your taking the time to speak with me is appreciated" or "Thank you for taking the time to speak with me."

   "You will see my schedule attached" is better than "I'm attaching. . . " And "Your presentation was excellent" is better than "I enjoyed your presentation very much."
   This approach may mean using the passive voice, which you're told generally to avoid, but it gives you a better opening. You can use *I* and avoid the passive in the rest of the letter.

2. Don't use all the jargon that makes so much writing meaningless. "Feel free to call me" says nothing—of course the person feels free to call you. "As per your instructions" is so stilted; "as we discussed" is better. Don't say "Call me at your earliest convenience." It's never convenient. Be specific: "Please let me know by December 15."

3. Take care not to sound condescending. When we reviewed letters written at an urban housing agency, we often saw language like "We will not tolerate people sneaking into the facility." There's never a reason to write like that. It's better to sandwich a negative between two positive statements. For example, "We're pleased to count you as a tenant. Please note that the recreation facility is not open after 10:00 p.m. Thank you for keeping this in mind."

Format: Keep It Simple

The same basic format will serve for just about every purpose. Use a letterhead or build a serviceable one for yourself at the top of the page, with your name, address, and contact information. It doesn't have to be fancy, but if you can print in color, using a sharp color for your name can present nicely. For the sake of personal branding, the letterhead should resemble your résumé's heading.

If you choose not to use a letterhead, then type in your name and address, flush left.

The rest of the document should also run flush left. Start with the date. Then skip a few lines, and put in the full name, company, and address of the person to whom you're writing. If you don't know the name of the person you're writing to, find out! Skip a few more lines, and write your salutation, generally "Dear Ms. X" or "Dear Jane," ending with a colon or comma.

Skip a few lines, and start your message in block paragraphs, flush left. Single space the body copy, but skip a line between paragraphs rather than indenting.

When your message is complete, sign off—for example, *Sincerely*—and be sure there's space for your signature underneath. You can type your name and contact information under the signature space (if the letterhead didn't take care of that) and/or social media information and direct phone line. If you're writing on behalf of an organization, type your name under the signature space and your title under that.

That's about it. When you're done, take a minute to center the letter on the page vertically so it looks balanced. If it's a long message, begin page 2 with a line that says something like, "Mr. Bob White/August 3, 2012/page 2." Use boldface to set it off. The heading ensures the continuation won't get separated and lost. If additional material is enclosed or attached, say so at page bottom: "Enclosed: Résumé, three work samples."

The major exception to the style described here is when creative license is called for. Note the solicitation letters that many savvy charitable causes send out these days. They use color, pull quotes, "handwritten" messages in the margins, subheads, images, and whatever else they can come up with to engage attention and get at least part of the letter read.

Some Frenchman—possibly Mon-taigne—says: I never think except when I sit down to write.

—Edgar Allan Poe

You can take a similar tack in a low-key way to ensure that those who skim rather than read business letters—which is just about everybody today—are pulled along and absorb the most important points. Your tools for this include subheads, bold lead-ins, numbered and bulleted lists of key points, summaries, pull quotes and underlining.

Use your judgment about deploying graphic techniques: A job application letter should be conservative (unless you're trying to demonstrate creativity); a sales letter, on the other hand, needs to capitalize on techniques that attract and direct attention.

In general, keep letters to one page. If your message is longer and essentially a report or proposal, it's smart to at least work in headings so readers can identify what's important.

What about letters delivered online, such as cover letters for résumés? Usually, it's best to use the same basic format as for print letters. When an occasion calls for a letter, then your document should look like a letter, not an e-mail message.

CRAFTING LETTERS TO THE SITUATION

Thank You Very Much . . .

Good thank you letters are hard to write: Just ask a communications specialist who works for a nonprofit. Coming up with credible ways to say "thanks for giving" is a constant challenge, especially since the important donors give periodically and gratitude must be expressed differently each time. But every organization knows that future contributions depend on effective thank you letters.

Thank you letters are equally important to you. They're in order when someone interviews you for a job, introduces you virtually, suggests a good contact, recommends you, and a host of other situations where an in-person or telephone thank you is inappropriate or impractical.

To work out the characteristics of a good written thank-you, consider what you'd like to receive from a charitable cause to which you sent a substantial check. No doubt, you'd prefer it to be:

- Sincere: conveying a genuine sense of appreciation
- Personal: appearing to be addressed to you, not a mass audience
- Specific: describing how your contribution will help the cause
- Timely: reinforcing a good deed is most effective done quickly

Suppose now that you're in the recipient's shoes. You've asked friends and relatives for money to build a library in a Nicaraguan village and received a good response. What could you write in appreciation? Here's one approach, which I'll use at the same time to demonstrate the basic format recommended.

JACOB SLATER

135 Rodeway Place
Washington, D.C. 01234
202–123–5678

November 14, 2015

Mr. Joe Constant
246 River Road
Washington, D.C. 10235

Dear Joe:

Thank you so very much for your contribution to Library Build. Your support for a cause I believe in so deeply means a lot to me.

As you know, when I visited Nicaragua as part of the school's student aid group last year, I was struck by how happy the children were—and adults, too—with the few Spanish books we had thought to bring. They shared them with such wonder that we wished we'd brought more. In talking about the trip later, we decided that starting a small library for the village would truly be a gift that would keep giving.

Your contribution is helping to make the idea real for a whole village. We're collecting books right now, and a group of us will travel to Perdita in the spring to help construct a simple building. Your contribution is helping us buy the supplies we need.

So, Joe, from all the people of Perdita, and from me, thank you for your generosity. I look forward to sharing pictures of the construction with you soon.

Sincerely,
Jake
Jacob Slater
Volunteer Director
Books for Perdita

Does the letter come across as sincere, personal and specific? Do you find it a bit effusive? Would you write it differently? Remember, put yourself in the other person's framework and think about how you'd feel receiving the message.

Don't overlook the advantage of creating handwritten thank you notes for many situations. They come across as much more personal and appreciative. I often notice that people post them in their offices, so their staying power is phenomenal.

VIEW FROM THE FIELD: PSYCHOLOGISTS SAY WRITING "THANK YOU" MATTERS

A number of studies show that thanking people makes us feel good and improves relationships. But recently a pair of psychologists (Adam M. Grant and Francesca Gino) studied the effects on individuals who are being thanked. Interestingly for us, the example they chose was to ask people to help a fictitious student named Eric with a job application cover letter. Half the people got an e-mailed thank you back, the rest got a neutral response.

When "Eric" then asked for more help, 66% of the thanked people agreed to give it, while just 32% of those who had not been thanked were willing. The investigators followed up by sending an e-mail from a second invented student, "Steven," asking for similar help. Among the group whom Eric had failed to thank, 25% offered to help Steven; by contrast, 55% of the group that had been thanked was willing.

The lesson: Expressing appreciation not only works to get you more help should you need it, but contributes to how people respond to others asking for help in the future.

—"A Little Thanks Goes a Long Way: Explaining Why
Gratitude Expressions Motivate Prosocial Behavior"
appeared in the *Journal of Personality and Social Psychology*

The same principle of expressing appreciation applies to many office and networking situations. If someone you work with does you a favor or helps you look good, if a subordinate goes to extra lengths so you can meet that deadline, or if a supervisor gives you a special opportunity or a client refers you to a prospect, it's smart to say thank you. And a written message tends to resonate even more than a spoken one.

Be sure to make your response timely. In fact, if someone connects you with a person you want to meet, it's best to thank the go-between before the meeting happens. You owe appreciation whether the event goes well or not. It's a good idea to write again to report on the meeting itself—or telephone. Better yet, take your matchmaker to lunch.

What if the meeting doesn't actually go well? This raises some interesting questions about what to put in writing. Here's an example:

Sam virtually introduced Angela to a former employer with a job opening in Angela's field. After the meeting, Angela wrote:

Dear Sam—Thanks so much for making it possible for me to meet with Mark White. I saw him yesterday. He was very nice to me, and the job sounds great. Unfortunately, I totally blew the interview. By the time we met at 4:00 p.m., I'd had a really bad day, and on top of that, I was unprepared for questions about the gap in my résumé from a few years back. I apologize for letting you down but no one could feel worse about it than me.

I promise to do better next time.—Angela

What do you think Angela's chances are of seeing a "next time"?

Of course, it's always awful to flub an opportunity, especially when someone else has put himself on the line by recommending you. But it happens. When it does, write yourself out of the worst scenario by focusing on your goal and desired outcome: Here you want to inform Sam that the interview wasn't perfect, sure, but you need to maintain his confidence in you as much as possible. This means there's no point in telling your benefactor that you disgraced yourself and took him with you.

Here's one solution:

Dear Sam—Thanks so much for making it possible for me to meet with Mark White. I saw him yesterday.

He was very nice to me and obviously thinks very highly of you. Mark generously spent more than an hour with me and gave me a very good understanding of the open position. At this point, I don't know if he considers me a good match for it, but I'll be very happy if he does.

In any case, I learned a lot about the industry from our conversation and I got some new ideas about how to position myself more effectively for the right opportunities.

So again, thanks so very much for introducing me to Mark and enabling me to have this valuable experience.—Angela

Do you think it's dishonest to send such a message?

Consider that (1) Angela can't know that Mark was as critical of her as she is of herself and (2) she's not made any false statements. The letter puts things in a way that encourages Sam to feel good about himself, which is only fair. It's clear that Angela values the experience whatever the specific outcome. While she might worry that Mark will tell Sam that she messed up, this is not likely. At worst, he's more apt to say something like "Thanks, but it wasn't a good match," so as not to insult Sam's judgment.

> *Never send a letter or a memo on the day you write it. Read it aloud the next morning—and then edit it.*
>
> —David Ogilvy, the "father of advertising"

Letters That Make Requests

Many of the ideas for writing thank-yous apply to request letters. Suppose you're Jacob Slater, who wrote the sample thank you letter in the preceding section, and you're writing to friends and acquaintances to ask for a contribution to your personal charity. Here too, you want to come across as sincere, personal, and specific.

A good way to start is to tell readers why you're writing and why it matters—to you. Here's an example:

Dear Jean,

I'm writing to ask you to support a special cause that means a lot to me.

When I visited Nicaragua last year with my school's student aid group, I was struck by . . .

The key to a request letter is figuring out *why* the person or group should give you what you want. When you're asking, in effect, for a personal favor from people who know you, they will be motivated by their feelings for you. So tell them why your request matters to you. Of course, unlike my example, don't write the same letter to thank them if they do give.

What if you're writing to strangers? They are much less likely to respond to the same strategy. In such cases, you need to find a reason for them to care about the cause or relate to it. This is easier if you already have reason to believe the audience is interested in your project. For example, if they're members of a literacy or library support group, you might begin:

Dear Mr. Black,

There's a village in Nicaragua where the children have never seen a book.

When my school group visited Perdita last year, the children were awestruck to even touch the few books we brought. . . .

A $25 contribution will enable us to bring 10 books . . . .

Solicitation letters from established charities are among the most sophisticated communications created today and are often written by PR agencies or direct mail specialists. Pay attention to the techniques they use to engage your interest and make you care. The most effective: telling a story about a single individual.

Nine-year-old Manuela is an alert and curious girl eager to learn. But she had never seen a book. When we unwrapped the four children's books we had added to our luggage at the last minute, Manuela was afraid to touch them . . . .

If you're writing letters for everyday career purposes—like securing an appointment or a reference—the process is similar. Figure out why the reader should agree to your request using the basic what's-in-it-for-me (WIIFM) thinking process explained in Chapter 2. Go light on communicating how supremely important the favor is to you. Rather than telling them how much you will gain, look for a reason they will empathize with or even better, offer an advantage to them, even if you don't make the point overtly.

Can you tap into the "giving back" way of thinking that motivates many successful people? Will granting your request make the person feel good about themselves or look good to other people? Will they have reason to feel satisfaction in granting your request? Can you offer anything in return, however intangible?

Above all, write thoughtfully and carefully. Edit thoroughly. In such situations, you are exactly what you write—no more, no less. People are willing to extend a helping hand to an amazing degree provided you demonstrate respect for their time, are appreciative, and likely to reflect credit on them.

For more ideas on how-to-ask communications, see the e-mail examples in Chapter 6.

After the Job Interview

Should you always write a thank-you to the person who interviewed you for a job? Well, only if you're seriously interested in the job, the company, future opportunities or your career. In other words, just about always. It's plain dumb not to give yourself the edge that courtesy and a well-written letter can produce. It's another chance to outdistance the competition and showcase your abilities.

Suppose you've just been interviewed by the assistant manager of a large multinational for a spot in the marketing department. This thank you letter is more complicated to create than those we've been talking about and should be based on the structure we've practiced with e-mails. Here's how it might work.

Your goal: To advance your candidacy for a highly competitive job

Your audience: An individual you spent time with and observed—so you know the person's age and something about personality, communication style, company status and so on. That's all relevant, *but*—because this is a highly structured interaction between a prospective employer's representative and you, a candidate, plan this way:

Your tone: Formal and businesslike. And just as for a charity's thank-you, the letter must feel very sincere.

Content: What will work? One approach:

- A paragraph expressing appreciation
- A paragraph expressing enthusiasm and confidence in your ability to perform
- A good close confirming your availability for further interviews, or to start the job
- And—if at all possible, new information about how exceptionally qualified you are

This is where to draw on your personal impressions: Replay the conversation, visualize the person, and figure out ways to distinguish yourself that the interviewer, and/or the company, will value. It's also the time to think through any points in your favor that you forgot to make in person.

Here's a simple example.

Dear Ms. Royal:

Thank you so much for speaking with me Thursday about the Marketing Associate position at Brandon Inc. I enjoyed our conversation and appreciate your taking the time to tell me about the company and the job.

Your description of the work convinced me more than ever that it is the right opportunity for me and that my background is an excellent fit with your needs. Thanks to my three years of experience with Malibu Inc., I'll bring a solid grounding in retail marketing practice backed by my course work in White University's MBA Program.

I'd also like to share that over the past five years, I've found additional opportunities to build the communications skills I believe are so important. I serve as managing editor of White's management newsletter, developing my writing skills, and have actively participated in Toastmasters International for two years. Recently, I helped win a regional debating competition for my program.

Again, thank you for encouraging my application, and I look forward to the next step.

Sincerely,

You've no doubt written letters like this already and won't be surprised that even a straightforward one takes plenty of time and thought. The more advanced your credentials or experience, the more difficult these letters are to write—and the more important. If you're applying for a creative job, you must really work to show off your originality.

Rejection Letters

If you haven't yet been in the position of having to write a rejection letter, you may not believe it, but these are famously tough to write, too. Let's see how the systematic process applies to an entirely different goal.

We haven't lost romance in the digital age, but we may be neglecting it. In doing so, antiquated art forms are taking on new importance. The power of a handwritten letter is greater than ever. It's personal and deliberate and means more than an e-mail or text ever will.

—Ashton Kutcher, actor

Suppose you're in charge of the internship program at your organization and must tell several candidates that the decision has gone against them. The goal here is to write a letter that considers their feelings but unequivocally delivers the bad news. This is important: Beyond the fact that any rejection deserves careful attention—we've all been on that receiving end and the experience stays with us—maintaining the candidate's goodwill toward the company is high priority.

In line with the concept of delivering the bad news immediately, crafting a lead is not very hard:

Dear _____:

Your interest in working as an intern for the Ivy Company this summer is greatly appreciated. Unfortunately, we will not be able to offer you a place.

The hard part comes next: What reason can you give? Try brainstorming the possibilities. Here are a few:

We had a large number of outstanding candidates this year and had to make a tough decision.

More than 100 people applied and we only have room for three.

We needed to coordinate different skill sets to build a balanced team.

We recognize that you are highly qualified, but other candidates had specific experience we need.

If any of these rationales strike echoes from the past, it's because colleges as well as businesses use similar terminology—and not lightly: How to word rejection letters can keep admissions officers up at night, and the results don't always succeed in spreading goodwill.

Especially if you're writing to a particular individual, you should also brainstorm any ways to soften the blow or even to be directly helpful. Such an element might give you a good closing. Here are a few examples:

We invite you to apply again next summer.

We'd be happy to talk with you when you graduate should a full-time position be open.

I suggest you talk to X at Y Company, which has a larger associate program than ours.

If it's not appropriate or honest to say any of these things, and you can't come up with an alternative, then you might close with simply a "good luck" statement.

Problem-Fixing Letters

In the business environment, letters can be critical to maintaining good relationships with clients, vendors, collaborators, investors and more. Here, tone is really critical: How friendly should a message be, or how formal? How personal should you get? It depends on the situation and the relationship and on your specific goal. Often it takes some thinking to settle on the right voice.

For example, suppose you head a department and you've learned that a supplier has been overcharging for "fabrications." It's your role to rectify this. A letter is called for.

Your audience: Bob Brown, your contact at the supplier, who has always been pleasant. The relationship is cordial but not personal. Until now, Bob's firm has been reliable, provided good quality products at good prices and accommodated you in difficult scheduling situations.

Your goal: You want the error acknowledged and restitution made. But you must also consider the longer-range goals. Your options include:

1. Fire the supplier immediately—maybe even sue for the overcharge.

2. Let Bob know you're angry and demand an apology.

3. Get the error acknowledged, ensure you are not charged more than you've agreed to again, and maintain the good working relationship.

If you review your options dispassionately—which the structure we're practicing is designed to help you do—you'll see that Option 1 is clearly against your interests. You'd need to find a new equivalent supplier and build a new relationship. Your response should take into account how much trouble that would be. At the least, the effort will be time-consuming, plus you'll end up with an untested supplier.

Option 2 is tempting; it's always nice to vent—but never productive. And you should consider that you don't actually know whether the error was deliberate or a billing mistake. So why not act as if the supplier is honest, which may be the case, and be satisfied with ensuring that it doesn't happen again?

That leads you to embrace Option 3 as your goal.

Tone: The occasion calls for fairly formal business style with a no-nonsense, non-judgmental, very matter-of-fact atmosphere.

Structuring the message: The principles we've established tell us to lead with strength and immediately engage the reader with the subject, organize our points in the simplest way, and end with a confirmation or call to action.

Here's one way the situation can be handled.

Dear Bob:

I've learned that your invoice #5742A of July 7 is in error.

The price of #12 fabrications is calculated at $34 per thousand. However, the correct price according to our most recent contract is $31. Thus, on our order for 3,000 boxes, it appears we've been billed $9,000 too much.

Of course, we'd like this corrected immediately. Please confirm that you'll send a corrected invoice.

Acme and Ideal have been working together a long time, Bob, and I hope this matter can be quickly resolved so we can continue to do so.

Sincerely,

Joan

In general, be on the alert for situations that call for thoughtful, letter-type communication and accord them the planning they merit. For a sophisticated way to use the format to advantage, see View From the Field: Letter in Your Pocket.

VIEW FROM THE FIELD: LETTER IN YOUR POCKET—A TAKE-CHARGE STRATEGY

Instead of writing a follow-up memo after an important meeting or interview, I often prepare a one-page document in advance and present it on the spot when the meeting is over. This may look like a magic trick, but it comes from doing your homework and being very well prepared.

A meeting is a "purposeful activity" and usually follows a predictable pattern. If there's a good agenda, you know in advance what the discussion will cover and can probably anticipate the outcome. Sometimes knowing the target audience and the outcome you want is all you need. Or you can anticipate the questions that will come up, or the next steps that need to be addressed. Having a general idea of where the conversation will go is often enough for you to take one of these approaches.

Your one-pager can take the form of a letter, a memo, a set of talking points, an infographic. It can be formal or informal in tone depending on the situation.

This is a versatile technique. It's effective for sales calls and works very well for job interviews. Instead of writing later, prepare the document in advance with the main points you want to make. Just like a follow-up thank you note, this gives you the chance to communicate points in your favor that may not come up during the interview, as well as reinforce those that do.

Always use your judgment. Sometimes it helps to pull the memo out during the meeting to move the discussion along. Or it may turn out not to be prudent to pull the memo out at all—so keep it in your pocket. In any case it's an excellent way to prepare. Writing forces you to think better, and the one-pager requires you to anticipate. You have to know in advance: What do I want? What do "they" want? Where are things likely to go? What are the alternatives?

Present a memo-in-your-pocket carefully so you don't put people off: Say "this is what we talked about," not "this is what was decided." If you're using it in a sales call, review it together with the other person "to make sure everything important was covered and understood."

What if you're wrong about what you thought would happen? Keep the memo. At times when I was unsure of the outcome, I've gone into meetings with two different memos in my briefcase.

The leave-behind technique gives you the opportunity to frame the issues in the way you find most favorable. In the right circumstances it can be electrifying, an attention getter, a differentiator. It demonstrates confidence and sophistication. And shows that you've done your homework.

—Peter Winslow, Temple University professor;
president of the nonprofit Evolve Foundation, Inc.;
and founding director of a business consulting firm

WRITING INTERNAL MEMOS

A substantial percentage of your on-the-job writing will be addressed to coworkers and supervisors. Oddly, this activity is increasing because so many workers are "virtual" and often don't occupy offices next door to each other and may be in another building—or country. Moreover, many organizations encourage employees to communicate by memo even when they sit side by side. This is unfortunate—there's no substitute for face-to-face interaction—but you may need to work with it.

Internal memos in many organizations are an important way to create a "paper trail." It may be necessary to document a difficult employee situation or ensure that timely notice is given for an event, process, and so on. And many an in-house memo is in the CYA category: You want to be sure a supervisor is aware of an action or need.

But most internal memos will deal with practical matters. They may ask someone for an appointment or to attend a meeting, announce a policy or procedure change, deliver or request information, or solicit input. Such messages may seem to call for a less thoughtful and careful approach than those directed to customers, clients, donors or the media, but writing carelessly within your own organization is a mistake. Succeeding in any job depends on relationships. Building good ones requires close attention to how you interact with peers, how superiors perceive you, and how you deal with those who report to you.

Even a big company resembles a small village in this way: "Word gets around." Written communication is easily shared and rarely forgotten, especially when the impact is negative. Use all your best planning, drafting, and editing techniques for every message. If you have a long-range *written plan* for your career, as recommended in Chapter 2, you'll easily write all your messages within that framework. A plan enables you to identify bonds you want to forge, opportunities and promotions to aim for, or connections to your next career move.

Interoffice communication may be done via e-mail, an Intranet, or an in-house distribution system. Memos may even be posted on a bulletin board if they relate to everyone. Many organizations still use some sort of "memo" format. In a new position, investigate the preferred style and pay particular attention to the tone commonly employed. Formal? Impersonal? Or warm and friendly? In general, use an objective, factual tone—never an emotional, critical, or complaining one.

If you need to devise your own format, it's simple. Begin at the top with:

Date:

To:

From:

Re: (or Subject:)

Or juggle the order. You may also want to add a "CC" line so recipients know who else is receiving the memo.

All the advice about e-mails in Chapter 6 relates to internal memos, and there are specific examples for a variety of situations. For in-house communication it's especially important to check the following:

How will the person receiving the message react to it? *How will it make him or her feel?*

How does the writer—meaning you—come across: efficient, resourceful, respectful, friendly, "nice"? Or abrupt, disinterested, careless?

Is the style and content appropriate to your relationships with the person or group?

Is the message's purpose clear, and does it get to the point instantly?

Is the whole message specific and totally unambiguous?

Is the bottom line clear—what you're asking the reader to do?

Is the message as concise as it can be without missing essential information? Any irrelevant ideas and unnecessary words?

Is the message short enough? Does it read fast?

Is the memo necessary at all? Is the subject better dealt with by phone or in person, because it's sensitive or timely, or just a good opportunity for in-person contact?

Messages that add nothing to the conversation are better left unwritten and unsent. Who doesn't resent inefficient, ambiguous, time-wasting, wordy messages?

Here is one more important point: If your memo asks the reader to do something—and virtually every memo does—it's usually smart to tell the person *why.* Abrupt commands, like show up at 1:45 or change the process from A to B, are far less successful than "Getting together will give us a chance to share . . . " or "We've changed the CCC process because we need to comply with . . . "

Here are some examples of bad memos to illustrate these points.

Negative Example 1:

To:	All Professional Staff
From:	Carla Bond, VP for Training & Advancement
Subject:	Skills Development Day, Tuesday, March 5, 20xx
Date:	January 25, 20xx

Tuesday, March 5, 20xx is Skills Development Day. This year's theme is "Improving Technical Skills," a most relevant topic. The day begins at 8 a.m. with coffee and conversation in the cafeteria. The program will begin at 9:15 a.m. with introductions, greetings, a short presentation and an opportunity to participate in fifteen concurrent breakout sessions. These breakout sessions have been selected to offer a wide choice of subject areas and it is possible to attend two.

The planned program promises to be relevant, timely, and important to your professional growth as well as the advancement of this organization. I'm sure you will agree that the day promises to be interesting and rewarding. I look forward to seeing you there. Should you have any specific program questions, please contact Burma Black, Assistant VP for Human Development, who along with a diverse committee, is responsible for planning and organizing the day.

Analysis:

If you got this message, I doubt you'd look forward to this event. Technically it's passable. But the memo overlooks the critical importance of audience reaction. It's a "mark your calendar" notice, with no attempt to generate any enthusiasm for participating. It communicates that a committee assembled an event as a rote task without real regard for making it either interesting or relevant.

What Would Work Better?

- An enthusiastic tone rather than a bored one, because tone is highly contagious
- More specific description of content, preferably including a few sessions with exciting titles
- A clear indication of how attendees will benefit: They might gain insight on company direction, a first look at major new systems, tips on how to handle a common problem, new technology to support their various roles, and so on.

The problem is that the event itself must justify a more effective communication. If the day proves to be boring as it sounds, a jazzed-up memo is dishonest and pointless.

SUCCESS TIP

USE COMMUNICATION AS A REALITY CHECK

If you plan an event or initiative of any kind, or are part of a planning group, think about how you would write or speak about it to the target audience at an early stage. If this description seems off target, unnecessarily boring or inadequate in any way, go back to the drawing plan and improve the plan itself. Note that professional communicators find it hard or even impossible to promote ill-planned events or programs. In a broader perspective, it's challenging to create good communications for organizations that lack a clear sense of mission. Writing spotlights the gaps in thinking, just as it does with everyday writing.

Negative Example 2:

To:	Mark L.
From:	Jessica B.
CC:	Jack G., Anne T., Jerry F.
Date:	Oct. 6
Subject:	Where were you????

Mark—The department meeting was held this morning—without you. You never showed up. When I checked, I found you hadn't come to work at all. This is highly irresponsible. I expected you to take notes and had to do it myself! I need someone I can depend on. If that person isn't you, perhaps someone else would better appreciate the opportunity.

Jessica

Analysis:

Jessica writes a huffy, peevish memo to a subordinate that only serves to vent her anger. She overlooks the all-important question: What do I want to achieve? If her goal is to move Mark to look for another job, she succeeds, especially because she sends the memo to three other staff members. But if her goal is to make Mark "shape up," she fails. Such a message will not help him become a better, more enthusiastic and loyal staff member. Worse yet, she exposes her poor management style to others in the organization, probably including her own supervisor.

What Would Work Better?

Probably a conversation. Jessica jumps to a conclusion about Mark's irresponsibility, but she doesn't know the reason for his absence. Better to know your facts rather than react to assumptions! If she must write rather than call or meet, she'd achieve more by sending a simple, low-key request for an explanation. This saves her from damaging the relationship, and losing points for poor supervisory skills in the eyes of her superiors.

Never write a memo—or anything else—when you're angry. Or at least, don't send it until after you cool down.

SUCCESS TIP

SHOW A GENEROUS SPIRIT

In the business world, even when you've got someone dead to rights on a failure, or can decimate their position on an issue or disprove their argument, it's often best to show generosity. Go out of your way to let the person save face and you'll probably be repaid many times over. If the relationship is important or the person is a boss or client, you may even want to let them off the hook with phrases such as "I know you've been too busy to read all the material on this . . ." or "Congratulations on concluding the X negotiation. I hope there's time now to turn to . . ." Or, "I've identified some additional information that has a bearing on . . ."

Negative Example 3:

To:	ALL EMPLOYEES
From:	Head Office
Date:	September 30, 20xx
Re:	Forthcoming: New E-mail Regulations

It has come to our attention that typical employees check their e-mail 74 times per day. We have 2,437 employees. That adds up to a staggering loss of productivity! Therefore, we have asked our Talent Resource Dept. to develop a set of mandatory guidelines. If you wish to provide any input for the department to consider do so by October 7th. We will be instituting the new rules by November 1, and all employees must adhere to them.

Analysis:

The goal seems to be to annoy the entire staff by forecasting an arbitrary set of rules to increase productivity, whatever that means. The stilted language and mean-spirited tone will reliably add to the general resentment. If there are still any water coolers out there (where office workers were presumed to gather and gossip), you can imagine the conversation.

What Would Work Better?

As with the Skills Development Day memo, the basic action needs to be rethought. A genuine invitation might be issued for employees to come up with ideas for stemming the e-mail tsunami that everyone struggles with—perhaps in groups.

This trouble is more than offset by achieving staff buy-in. An initial memo that makes it "our problem" generates both goodwill and quite possibly new ideas (like workshops on writing more efficient e-mails!).

Negative Example 4: Worst-Ever Internal Memo

All of the negative examples in this chapter are drawn from real communications, adapted to protect the guilty, but here is a verbatim memo to Microsoft employees from the vice president of a major company unit. It went viral on the Internet. The purpose was to announce the layoff of 12,500 employees:

> Hello there, Microsoft's strategy is focused on productivity and our desire to help people "do more." As the Microsoft Devices Group, our role is to light up this strategy for people. We are the team creating the hardware that showcases the finest of Microsoft's digital work and digital life experiences, and we will be the confluence of the best of Microsoft's applications, operating systems and cloud services.
>
> To align with Microsoft's strategy, we plan to focus our efforts . . . .
>
> *Seven l-o-n-g paragraphs follow about the company's plans for product development and marketing strategies. Around paragraph 9 comes this statement:*
>
> We plan to right-size our manufacturing operations to align to the new strategy and take advantage of integration opportunities.
>
> *And finally, in paragraph 11:*
>
> We plan that this would result in an estimated reduction of 12,500 factory direct and professional employees over the next year. These decisions are difficult for the team, and we plan to support departing team members' with severance benefits.
>
> *Three more paragraphs ramble on about where the company will focus with hints about which segments are affected. Here's the close:*
>
> Collectively, the clarity, focus and alignment across the company, and the opportunity to deliver the results of that work into the hands of people, will allow us to increase our success in the future.
>
> Regards,
>
> Stephen

Analysis:

Make your own list of what's wrong with this memo. Don't overlook the tone, use of language, poor grammar, and shockingly misguided sense of audience and appropriate content.

WRITING TECHNIQUES TO IMPROVE RELATIONSHIPS

The preceding memo illustrates how easily bad communication can destroy relationships. Imagine how the readers will react—both those about to lose their jobs and those whom the company wants to retain, not to mention the added bonus of untold thousands, including customers, who shared the memo on the Internet. The flip side is that thoughtful communication offers you a powerful tool for managing and even improving your relationships with coworkers and supervisors.

Depending on whether you're writing to a superior, a subordinate or a peer, a message's content may vary even when you're writing about the same subject because each needs different information and has different self-interest. The tone might also vary—but only somewhat.

It's always best to write with courtesy and consideration regardless of the hierarchy. Use your everyday communication flow to build trust, goodwill and credibility. Build in a "caring" spirit as appropriate. If you're writing to an individual, this may mean personalizing the message with a brief comment about a mutual interest, an important event in the other person's life, or anything else that's not out of line.

Every chapter of this book refers to the WIIFM principle, which requires you to look through the other person's eyes. The strategy is especially useful with internal communications, both written and spoken. Work to understand where the other person might be coming from—her pressures, worries, positioning in the company. Consider generational differences (Chapter 2) that might affect her expectations and behavior. Pre-Millennials tend to find many members of the younger generation impatient, condescending and disrespectful. Avoid giving that impression and your relationship building will escalate.

In any case, keep in mind that one of your ultimate job responsibilities is to help your boss perform well and look good to his or her superiors. Doing so will always work to your advantage. In fact, it's pretty much a universal that people respond well when you make them look good and/or feel good about themselves. As touchy-feely as that may sound, it's how you build alliances.

Take these ideas into account both in your face-to-face interaction and writing. I guarantee you some happy surprises.

PRACTICE OPPORTUNITIES

I. Networking Challenges

A. Request an Introduction

Think about a connection you'd particularly value if a former colleague, acquaintance, or professor could ease the way for you. Write a letter asking for a virtual introduction.

B. Thank the Introducer

The person made the introduction and you will shortly have a telephone conversation with the person you want to know. Write a letter expressing appreciation to the colleague, making your message sincere, personal and specific.

C. Thank the Contact

You've talked to the person you were introduced to and received some useful insights into the industry and his job responsibilities, but no specific leads to follow up. Write to thank the person for his time in a way that will make him feel good about giving it.

D. Make a Virtual Introduction

Think of two people you know who would gain something worthwhile from knowing each other, or just having a conversation. Write a joint introduction message to both of them.

II. Write a Letter for Bob

Take the role of "Bob," who represents the company that incorrectly billed its client in the situation described in this chapter. You've received the letter specifying the error and determined that a new accounting clerk had used the wrong price index. Write a letter to your customer, Joan.

Consider this: How would your letter differ if you discovered that your employee was deliberately overcharging and had found a way to siphon off the overcharge?

III. Respond to Rejection

You've applied for an associate job you wanted, at a company where you hoped to find a foothold, and just received a rejection letter. You're very disappointed but know it would be smart to send a response, because you're planning to try for a full-time job there after completing your degree. Write a complete letter.

IV. Write Your Own Rejection Letter

As described in this chapter, you're called on to write a rejection letter to internship candidates—what can you add to the list of possible reasons for rejecting those not chosen? Do you see more ways to soften the blow? Draft a complete letter rejecting an internship candidate. Produce a cohesive, thoughtful message with an effective closing statement. Try for a letter that would make you feel as good as possible if you were on the receiving end.

V. Group Discussion

What's the best rejection letter you ever got? What made it good? And what was the worst one? Where did it go wrong, and how did it make you feel?

Share with classmates. Collaborate on a list of bad rejection letter characteristics and a second list of characteristics that define good ones.

VI. Manage a Client

You're an accountant. A client has provided a carton of information and after sorting through it for hours, you find it doesn't contain some of the major items you asked for: tax returns for the past three years, documentation about technology expenses, and correspondence with the IRS about tax shortfalls. Write a letter to the client requesting these materials within three days.

VII. Write a Better Memo About Skills Development Day

Choose an industry and organization you've worked in or are otherwise familiar with, and aim to generate enthusiasm for the day. Feel free to invent programs and events that will interest recipients or serve a need they will agree on.

VIII. Draft a Letter About Writing Letters

Your department head has noticed that some embarrassing letters are going out to clients and prospects and wants to assemble a short how-to guide for everyone's reference. She's asked for staff input on guidelines to include. Consider what you've learned in this chapter and the preceding ones, and draft a letter presenting your best advice. Use graphic techniques to make your message clear and readable.

PART IV

CREATING PERSUASIVE MESSAGES, DOCUMENTS AND MATERIALS

Chapter 9

WRITING TO PERSUADE, PART 1

The Tools and Techniques

LEARN HOW TO . . .

- Understand the tools of persuasion and advocacy
- Use writing techniques that support persuasion
- Use storytelling
- Employ graphic tools

No matter what people tell you, words and ideas can change the world.

—Robin Williams

Your everyday writing enables you to demonstrate your professionalism and open doors. Of course, you also need to know how to handle opportunities once they're in hand. Among your likely challenges are creating "long-form" documents such as reports, proposals, presentations and business plans. This and the following chapter will show you how to apply the principles of good contemporary business writing to these materials.

Since every message you create intrinsically asks the reader for something, persuasion techniques strengthen everything you write. The approaches introduced for "short-form" communication such as e-mail and letters apply equally to long documents—and those covered here will help you with the everyday messages. But since the stakes are often higher with lengthier materials, they demand more planning, more thinking, more crafting.

Look at the world around you to see persuasive strategies at work. Ads, commercials, and solicitations of every sort bombard us in every medium. Cast an analytic eye and ear toward these sales pitches. Notice which ones engage your interest and how they do it. Read op-ed pieces critically, especially those you disagree with. Think about how the strategies can be adapted to your own writing.

In these two chapters, I'll focus on ways to write persuasively with a resource of practical ideas from professional specialists. The tools of persuasive writing are key to marketing, advocacy, speechwriting and more—and you will need them every time you're called on to present or defend what you believe.

USING THE TOOLS OF PERSUASION AND ADVOCACY

Nobody cares how much you know until they know how much you care.

—Theodore Roosevelt

The ability to advocate for a cause, whether it's a company's new service or a nonprofit's mission or your own enterprise, is a critical element of communication today. For a start, it involves psychology, negotiation and creative thinking just as much as technical skills.

First, here are some general principles to guide the substance of your message.

Believe it! If you want people to believe in something, first believe in it yourself. Ask a master salesperson, a public relations (PR) executive or an entrepreneur to name the one essential of persuasion, and they're likely to say it's personal conviction. To sell something you must believe in it. Many documents call for an objective tone, but it can be combined with passion if you avoid promotional words and tone. Proposals, for example, should feel objective and reasonable, rather than showing emotional investment in your recommendation. But even in such instances, a rock-solid conviction should shine through. And it's always right to project a passion for what you do when you aim to pull people into your orbit.

Know your document's story. Drill to the core so you don't get lost in the detail. Unless you focus on your central message and base content decisions upon it, you'll miss the mark. Challenge yourself to think like a scriptwriter pitching a producer— you've probably seen it done on film and television, and it often works that way: The pitch must boil down to a few sentences that distill the heart of the project—what it's about, who the main players are, why people will care. In fact, scriptwriters try— whatever the subject—to crystallize their theme in three words or less (e.g., "love redeems"; "crime doesn't pay"; or, in line with shifting mores, "smart crime pays").

Keep in mind that even a 50-page document is ultimately a message. Because it's an in-depth message meant to influence decision making, it may require a lot of backup detail and support material. Nevertheless, it must present your story in a cohesive, simple to follow, convincing way.

Know what you want. Be clear on the result you want the document to achieve, and set realistic goals. You're unlikely to change 100 years of tradition with one proposal, no matter how good. And be sure what you want or recommend is 100% clear—the action you endorse, the amount of money you need and your own bottom line.

Clarifying the goal makes content decisions easier throughout the planning process. If you want funding, bottom-line numbers and proof of your own capabilities are important. If you want to talk someone into a new customer relations strategy, you may need to explain its successful use elsewhere, what will improve, staff training needs, and more.

VIEW FROM THE FIELD: A NEGOTIATOR ON GAINING YOUR POINT

It's a scientific fact that the brain makes decisions in the emotional area 100% of the time. The business writer who understands that spends her time crafting words to create vision, which drives the decision the writer wants. The great negotiators of the world work hard at creating vision for the other party because people make decisions because they see something—"I see how that works and I'll do it." They may see the future and how a problem can be solved.

Here's the system for negotiating that I train people to use.

1. Create vision in an adversary's world based on mission and purpose.

2. Consider, what problems must we overcome to succeed in this negotiation?

3. What preconceived ideas do we have going in, good or bad, that encumber us? Emotions like excitement, for example, would hinder us.

4. Examine our assumptions about what the other side may be carrying in—for example, did we fail to deliver on time two quarters ago and are they still angry?

5. What do we want to accomplish from this negotiation? I always want a decision, even if it's a rejection.

6. What should we do next? In the case of a reader, what should the reader do next?

To me a writer is negotiating. It's about painting pictures with words to create vision—being conscious of the purpose of this paragraph, this sentence. A writer invests effort into bringing about agreement to what he's saying or delivering.

We often destroy vision by overloading the knowledge.

—Jim Camp, CEO/founder of Camp Negotiation Institute;
author of *Start With No* and *No: The Only
System of Negotiation You Need for Work and Home*

Know and understand your audience. See things through your readers' eyes—a letter, a proposal, business plan, or report succeeds when framed in *you* terms, not *I* or *we*. Business materials are not about you or even your company. They are about the reader's needs, problems and hopes. If you're responding to a request for proposal (RFP), mine it for clues—analyze the questions asked and the reasons behind them. If you're assembling an in-house proposal, center it on the problem your recommendation will solve.

Think, too, about where your primary readers' self-interest lies, what they know about your subject, how they are likely to feel about it, what elements they will resist, the arguments and evidence they will find convincing: Statistics? Anecdotes? Expert opinion? Historical context? Impact on the bottom line, or on people, or company image, or personal reputation?

Focus on benefits, not features. This is the mantra that drives marketing and advertising. A feature is a fact, such as a car's high horsepower engine, a skirt's A-line pleating, a customized training system. The benefit is what the feature will do for you—for example, the hot car will make you feel young and powerful; the skirt will help you look slim so you feel attractive and confident going to the party; the training program will teach your employees exactly what you want them to do without wasting their time and your money.

Effective marketing sells benefits, not features. Figuring out benefits takes some work. Look at your product from your customers' perspective, and ask the following questions: What will this feature do for me? Why would I want it? Why would I want to change the services I buy—or my opinion? Take account of this thought pattern in all your marketing messages.

Write with a sincere effort to inform and educate. Never patronize your readers or allow that sense to permeate your messages. Think about the reasons you hold a certain conviction and how you can share that reasoning with others. Provide information. Bringing readers along with you through the sequence that led you to a conclusion can open their minds. It's especially powerful to give people facts and ideas that lead them to draw their own conclusions. Stories can do this, which is one reason why great orators depend on them.

Keep in mind that it's hard to ask people to make huge leaps in new directions all at once. Good teachers are satisfied to move students along in increments. Start where your audiences are.

But give them a vision, too. We all want to believe that the future will be better, our problems solved, our hopes fulfilled. If what you offer in any way contributes to a better, easier, healthier, happier, more convenient, more productive, more interesting life, let people know. Give them the biggest picture that legitimately applies.

When you find something you read or hear inspirational, it's usually because you've been given a vision.

VIEW FROM THE FIELD: A PSYCHOLOGIST'S ADVICE ON ADVOCACY

To communicate your viewpoint or effect change, first listen and look for common ground. Make a genuine effort to understand the other person's point of view and identify things that you can appreciate. When people feel listened to and understood, they are more open to another's perspective. Then when you engage in a discussion about alternative possibilities, the person is more likely to be receptive to your perspective.

You must be genuinely respectful and authentic—people are very intuitive and will sense any effort to manipulate them. Be sensitive to their frames of reference and speak in a language they will understand. Talking to a technologically oriented person when you're a businessperson, for example, can be like speaking English to someone whose language is French. When you're advocating, it's up to you to adapt your language. You have to translate, put your proposal in a language that takes into account the other person's way of looking at the world.

Don't stop listening. Pay attention and don't make assumptions. If you get caught up in your own ideas and forget the other person, you lose your connection. Always show respect for the other person and don't focus so much on trying to sell your point of view that you forget to do this. Remember, people are more responsive to what you offer when they feel respected.

Concrete examples help, such as how well something worked for other people. But the examples must draw on something real and feel like something the person can see himself doing. Acknowledge your reader's concerns, and even when you seem far apart, thoughtful language can help bridge the gap: "I wonder if you've ruled out..." or "I understand that...but let's look at what might work."

—Susan H. Dowell, psychotherapist

Organize material in a logical, natural way. A poorly organized long document is less convincing than it should be, and may even go unread. You need an outline. If you're developing a business plan, you may not have to start from scratch, since sample templates are readily available. You can, for example, find sample business plans relating to various industries online at Bplans.com.

For business proposals and reports, however, you may not find helpful models because each is more or less unique. In such cases, take account of your goal and audience analysis—just as you practiced with e-mails and letters—and brainstorm what the document should include.

Begin by remembering your central message because everything must support it.

Assemble a list of sections. Then juggle your content list into a logical order, taking care to put what's important and interesting up front. The backup stuff most people find dull, like research data, should go in back so it's there for those who want it but it doesn't slow reading down to a crawl. But this depends on the audience: If you're preparing a document for a CFO, data and financial analysis should probably go up front.

Take special care with transitions. Connect every thought to what precedes and follows—good transitions are the binding that holds your piece together and reinforces the logic of your argument. Check the discussion in Chapter 5 for how to use transitions between sentences and paragraphs. Try building them into every sentence—you can always cut some later when you edit. The strategy will force you to make sure your thoughts do in fact proceed logically. The payoff is that your presentation will appear cohesive, your arguments logical, and your conclusions inevitable.

VIEW FROM THE FIELD: A METHOD FOR ORGANIZING LONG DOCUMENTS

You can solve organization problems with long documents the same way as for short ones. (See Dr. Haber's "View From the Field: An Easy Organization Technique" in Chapter 3.)

Create a map of what you'll write about by coming up with a sentence that represents your main point. Then, determine what your keyword is, which will help you identify the sections of your document. Each section will usually contain a singular example of your keyword. (Sometimes, your document might be so complex, that you may have several keywords.)

As an example of how this planning works, if you're writing a report or technical document that has a point of view—for example, the company should do X or Y—the body of the document must contain a keyword such as justifications or reasons. Get all the ideas down to prove that point. It's not sufficient just to enumerate the reasons—you need to come up with sufficient supporting details for each reason.

To take a different example, suppose your main point is, "We should give more breaks because it will improve productivity in various ways." You have to prove that. How will it improve productivity? Use the keyword "ways," and for each way, you need to thoroughly explain how that way will improve productivity. Good writers support their ideas by coming up with good supporting details. If you assume your audience is hostile, it forces you to come up with more supporting ideas.

Once you have the ideas, organize them and decide which to begin with, and how much information to include. Most managers complain that they either get too much or too little

(Continued)

(Continued)

information. Think of your audience, and you'll know how much detail they need, and which reason, if that is the keyword, is most important.

What if the document is very complicated and you can't come up with the keyword? Try starting the other way around—the "back-door" approach. Write down the topics you want to cover. Say you come up with three problems, and you have solutions for each. Then you know that your main point is, "I'm going to tell you about three problems and possible solutions for each."

—Dr. Mel Haber, president of Writing Development Associates

Create trust. When you're selling something through a piece of paper, whether print or digital, building trust is a challenge. One of the first rules of selling is to get in the door so you can connect in person and show that you are credible, knowledgeable, likeable, and so on. It's a chance to establish common ground through factors such as a mutual acquaintance, a shared sports interest, or where you live and went to school. Good salespeople pose the right questions and read the other person's responses, including body language, to gauge concerns and present their service or product as the solution.

But you can't do that with writing. A proposal, for example, must often stand on its own. So you must establish credibility and trust. Your techniques include supplying the right information, which might include credentials; related experience; examples of similar work; testimonials; and hard evidence of accomplishment proved by data, photographs, graphs and other visuals.

Trust is typically built over time. We like someone's blog, for example, and read more. Maybe we follow him on Twitter or other social media and find value. Then he promotes a book—and we're ready to buy it.

And, build trust by strong, accurate writing and good presentation. *A report or proposal in itself is important evidence of how you work.*

VIEW FROM THE FIELD: TECHNIQUES TO BUILD TRUST

The first step is always to start with your goal and work backward from there. Too often people in business skip that step and jump right into tactical or narrow-focus questions.

A lot of times companies will throw in a lot of spin—a cardinal mistake—and will try to cover five points. Whether you're writing an op-ed or speech, if you're trying to persuade an audience, make a single argument—know your core argument and then support it with evidence.

The most effective technique for business, politics, nonprofits, is credibility. Build trust with your readers by acknowledging valued points of the other side. This has disappeared from politics, which is why people are cynical and frustrated. It's much more successful to take account of an opponent's points or rebut them: "Yes, you have a good point per se, but here's why ultimately it's not convincing."

—Dan Gerstein, president/founder of Gotham Ghostwriters;
political strategist, analyst; and commentator

Acknowledge other viewpoints. It is much more credible to refer in an objective way to opposing ideas or approaches rather than disparage or omit them. You can absorb the other side into your argument if appropriate. For example,

As recently as last year, Strategy X was the standard way of doing things. But today, new technology empowers us to choose a more efficient, less expensive model.

Certainly, investing in Opportunity A offers some immediate advantages. Opportunity B, however, gives us a long-range potential in a new market and will ultimately pay bigger dividends.

Three other products are available to clean clay floors. However, Miracle Wax J is the first and only one to restore their original color.

Similarly, anticipate objections and speak to them. You'll disarm at least some resistors and deprive them of their counter-arguments.

"Show don't sell" is the business world's version of the fiction writer's show-don't-tell mantra. The point is to think creatively about what will bring your message alive and the elements that will help it work.

Incorporating stories and anecdotes is a major way. They're hard to pull out of the air on demand and need to be true. So collect them over time—from stories friends or colleagues tell you, articles, and your personal experience. You might even ask for ideas through your social media channels. Most useful are stories that center on people to illustrate a point; a success; a problem; or, best of all, a solution. Notice how good journalism presents big problems and trends through personal stories. Editors call this technique "storifying." See the end of this chapter for more on corporate storytelling.

Specific examples of every kind may help support your case. Concrete examples resonate and shore up abstractions. So tell readers how some other company made a strategy work, how a similar investment paid off, or how the recommended course of action is in line with another successful change. Graphs, charts, and relevant photographs are excellent "show me" pieces.

Remember: Most decision making is emotional. Good salespeople are born knowing this, and the advertising world has relied on the concept for generations. That's why you see ads that show cute babies to sell investment opportunities and car commercials with happy families enjoying the time of their lives.

Recent research supports this premise. Neuroscientists track how the brain functions during decision making, and the new field of behavioral economics studies buying behavior. *A main finding is that people generally make decisions based on emotions, often almost instantaneously, and then bolster them with reasoning.*

This suggests that whatever you're marketing, consider people's emotional attachments and anticipate reactions. This may mean identifying the problem that keeps them up at night and what frightens them, or at the other end of the emotional scale, linking to things that ring positive bells and trigger good associations.

Another corollary is that people buy more readily—and find arguments more persuasive—when they like the person delivering the message and feel they are on the same wavelength. The best salespeople work hard to encourage other people to talk and they listen carefully. They can then identify the problem the other person wants to solve and her personal triggers, and respond appropriately while building rapport.

The idea of emotionally based decision making is a big consideration in management thinking, communication practices, and fields from marketing to finance. When you aim to persuade, think about what your audience cares about and what elements you can incorporate that generate the emotions you want and are relevant.

Try, try, try not to bore. If you've done a project and are reporting on the results, or you're recommending an operational change, or asking for money to fund your start-up, the message isn't boring to you—and it must not bore your audience. Remember, when it comes to communication, we live in an opt-in world. To succeed, craft messages carefully.

Draw on all these techniques to determine the right substance. Then apply the techniques of good writing and good graphics to carry the message.

I leave out the parts people skip.

—Elmore Leonard, novelist

WRITING TIPS FOR MATERIAL THAT PERSUADES

It is all very well for you to write simply and the simpler the better. But do not start to think so damned simply. Know how complicated it is and then state it simply.

—Ernest Hemingway

Apply the Basics

1. **Write with a particular person in mind.** Just as this helps focus your everyday messages, it helps focus substantial documents. Pick someone you know who typifies the audience you're addressing. Visualize that person as you write, and you'll have a good sense of his or her level of knowledge, concerns, and probable questions. It's easier to gauge what might be clear to one individual than a sea of unknowns.

2. **Keep it simple.** As with all media, short concrete words, short sentences, and short paragraphs are best. Stay with basic sentence structures, though it's good to alternate between simple ones (I recommend we purchase the Model XYZ) and longer, more complex ones (However, should IT project a volume of more than 3 million, HJK will serve us better). There are additional reasons why the generic KISS rule (keep it simple, stupid) applies to documents meant to persuade. *Simplicity conveys authenticity and transparency.* The converse is true as well. If you employ $2 words when the nickel versions will do and write in difficult long sentences and dense paragraphs, what you present is less credible. Beyond giving people material that they're less likely to read, you create the impression that you're hiding facts—and that you don't understand your own story very well.

Remember, no matter how complicated your message is, it can and should be presented in simple, clear writing.

3. **Build for speed.** Your goal is to make your whole document read as fast as you can. Rhythm is important. Apply the "say-ability" test: Read what you write out loud and where you hear that sing-song sound, or stumble, look to rewrite and then retest. Connecting every thought to what precedes and follows is critical, so take care of transitions in your sentences, between paragraphs, and between sections. Transitions show people how things fit together.

4. **Cut ALL hyperbole.** Do not use empty, inflated descriptions of your product, company, or yourself. To say, "We are exceptionally sophisticated strategic innovators" or "We are noted for excellent teaming skills" or "We take pride in our

unique craftsmanship" says nothing to your busy skeptical readers. They want proof. To demonstrate innovation, cite some actual examples of how you solved problems. To talk about teaming, you might give examples of how your teams are assembled and the skill sets coordinated. To show craftsmanship, include images and show off your specialists. You can also bring in third-party testimonials from happy customers and other people you've worked with and for. Case histories are effective and engaging.

Ask, how can we prove our main points and qualifications to get this job or recommend a course of action?

The show-don't-sell concept also gives you interesting ways to spice up your language. *Painting pictures with words and providing familiar frames of reference* are among the fiction writer's best tools for bringing the abstract alive. You can use these techniques, too.

Similes are figures of speech that make comparisons using the words *like* or *as*:

Eliminating System A without replacing it would be like removing the pillars that hold up a bridge.

A metaphor is a more subtle comparison that doesn't use *like* or *as*:

The region is a crazy quilt of farmland, suburbs, and urban patches loosely knit together and, these days, fraying around the edges.

Analogies are also comparisons and can lend reality to an abstract idea or help explain something technically difficult. To express a key theme of this book, I could say this:

It's critical to write well, because although few people seem to notice when you fail to, they may nevertheless respond negatively.

or

Bad writing is like bad breath. People won't mention it, but they may keep their distance.

Communicating through visual ideas is especially convincing. A website that advocates against bottled water states,

Bottled water produces up to 1.5 million tons of plastic waste per year.

A television commercial for a water filtration system, on the other hand, says (paraphrased):

Americans drink enough bottled water every year that, laid end to end, the bottles could stretch around the world more than 100 times.

Whether the second statement is true or not—bloggers take issue with the math—it's certainly more powerful.

Writers work very hard to come up with original metaphors and images. While it's definitely not an easy task, the impact can be worth the effort when you're pitching something that matters.

Don't overlook the basics of vivid language and tight writing covered in Chapters 4 and 5. Use vigorous verbs to carry a feeling of action. Try to use the present tense as much as possible—"This tool performs a variety of functions" is better than "This tool will be able to perform a variety of functions." Cut back on all those extra words and phrases: "This system can be adapted to..." works much better as "This system adapts to..."

Keep away from trite wording and jargon. Edit ruthlessly, borrow extra eyes from friends or colleagues, and eliminate every error and misspelling.

Formal business documents are a good reason to explore a thesaurus for word choice. Find one you like in print or online—or simply Google the word and a ton of options will appear. (For example, to find alternatives for *simplicity*, just type *simplicity syn* in the search box, and a choice of instant resources comes up.)

Simplicity Rules

> *Perhaps the most common problem...is that a well-intentioned and informed writer simply fails to get the message across to an intelligent, interested reader. In that case, stilted jargon and complex constructions are usually the villains.*

—Warren E. Buffett, financier

Let's look at how Buffett, looked to as a model by most Wall Streeters for his writing as well as moneymaking ability, follows his own advice on both counts.

Here's an excerpt from his July 26, 2010, report to shareholders:

Charlie and I hope that the per-share earnings of our non-insurance businesses continue to increase at a decent rate. But the job gets tougher as the numbers get larger. We will need both good performance from our current businesses and more *major acquisitions*. We're prepared. Our elephant gun has been reloaded, and my trigger finger is itchy.

Buffett's simplicity shows the benefits of making it easy for the reader through sentence structure, word choice and folksy tone. Beyond being clear, the document is more enjoyable than you'd expect of an annual report letter. Moreover, it conveys that the message is sincere and heartfelt.

Buffett also sets a wide stage to good effect. Later, in the same letter, he presents a vision of the big picture that comforts and inspires:

No matter how serene today may be, tomorrow is *always* uncertain.

Throughout my lifetime, politicians and pundits have constantly moaned about terrifying problems facing America. Yet our citizens now live an astonishing six times better than when I was born. The prophets of doom have overlooked the all-important factor that *is* certain: Human potential is far from exhausted, and the American system for unleashing that potential—a system that has worked wonders for over two centuries despite frequent interruptions for recessions and even a Civil War—remains alive and effective.

We are not natively smarter than we were when our country was founded nor do we work harder. But look around you and see a world beyond the dreams of any colonial citizen. Now, as in 1776, 1861, 1932 and 1941, America's best days lie ahead.

The more concise, easy to read and lively you make your document, the better it will work. The more you bring information alive by communicating vision, telling stories and crafting vivid language, the more convincing it becomes. Like Warren Buffett—who I'm willing to bet plans and edits his writing obsessively— you can practice good writing strategies to communicate your message.

STORIES: FINDING, SHAPING, AND TELLING

Professional communicators have recently rediscovered storytelling for every conceivable purpose: marketing, branding, speech-giving, PR, advertising. Of course, storytelling is the heart of all the arts, as well as good salesmanship, since human time began. It's the true heart of business, too.

We all love stories. Why not? They're so much more fun than receiving mounds of data or long logic-based arguments about why we should do or buy something or change our minds about anything. They entertain us. Moreover, stories are persuasive and memorable. Unlike mere facts, they put things into perspective. And they reach right past our defensive reasoning to inspire, influence and motivate us.

Neuroscientists who watch the brain in process of reacting, thanks to new technology like fMRI (functional magnetic resonance imaging), report that when we hear or read about someone undergoing an emotionally charged experience, our brains respond as if we were living that experience ourselves. This effect persists, too. And it's true of stories we hear and also see, as in TV and film, and stories we read.

Storytelling is enormously valuable to small and big enterprises alike because it can be the best way to present a product or service to customers or other target audiences and also, an ideal way to engage employees through a shared common mission and an embodied history.

Telling stories is also a terrific tool for an individual looking for a career foothold or advance and everyone who wants to sell a product or service or support a charitable cause.

Successful businesspeople I know use stories in a few basic ways:

1. To distill who they uniquely are, what they can do, and why they are an asset

2. To prove their own success (perhaps through the success of others they've helped)

3. To pitch for something they want in terms that the other person or group will relate to

On the organizational level, many corporations and nonprofits today try to define a central story that unifies and energizes all communication and provides a decision-making touchstone. If gifted with charismatic leaders, or founders with an interesting history, they may personify the enterprise through that person.

Others will tell the history as a tale of overcoming challenges, much like the personal storytelling process. In many cases, it's a matter of drilling down to an enterprise's core mission and specific characteristics: the "unique value proposition," as it is sometimes called. Ultimately, this can be expressed in one great phrase or tagline—and/or through a fully developed narrative.

An allied technique useful on a smaller scale is to focus a business story through people whom the product or service or individual has helped. Case histories, so useful for websites and marketing pieces, fall under this umbrella. So do stories that make the customer or service beneficiary the hero. What can be more persuasive than showing how someone's work or personal life was radically improved by the product, or process, or service? The client's success is the business's—a premise that clients relate to beautifully.

Unless you own a business or are at an advanced stage of your career, finding and developing your individual story is more important. This is covered in Chapter 13.

GRAPHIC GUIDELINES FOR PRESENTATION

It's tough to pull people through long-form documents. You need your full tool kit if you want to create documents that are readable, inviting and enticing. Your competition will certainly take trouble with appearance and so must you.

In some industries, extraordinary skill goes into the visual appearance of proposals. They devote whole creative teams to this effort.

Whatever your goal, represent yourself with a document that makes a good impression. Design a title sheet—simple is fine. Build in headlines for sections and subheads as well as lots of white space to rest the eye. Short paragraphs are especially helpful. Use a very readable typeface even if it's less slick and "modern" than one that's trendy.

VIEW FROM THE FIELD: A GRAPHIC DESIGNER'S ADVICE ON GOOD PRESENTATION

The general rule for just about all documents, in print and online, is keep it simple and keep it clean. Here are some guidelines.

About Typeface

The point is readability and accessibility. So...

- Consistency counts. Don't mix two different serif faces—those are the ones with the squiggles at the ends. Stick with one font. But you can mix a serif face with a sans serif (squiggle free) face. For example, Times New Roman or Garamond for body copy works well with Arial for heads and subheads.
- Sans serif can also be used for body copy if you don't have a lot of it or a pretty face counts, like in an advertisement.
- Size matters: In general, keep to the 10- to 12-point range.
- But size is subtle: Fonts have different "x heights"—meaning that the bottom part of a lowercase letter in one face will be higher than that of another. The higher one is more readable. For example, Helvetica has a higher x height than Berkeley. So if you're using a small type size—like 8 or 9 points—Helvetica is a better choice. You can check this effect visually.
- Caps and italics are hard to read, so use them only for emphasis or headlines. This is true for bold as well.
- Don't justify: Run copy for most purposes flush left and rag right—justifying forces text into unappealing letter spacing and makes readers feel uptight. Rag right is calming.

Break It Up

Use all the tools available for creating air and space.

- Let your lines breathe: Don't cram copy in so the lines run too close to each other. If your column is wide, try adding space between lines (if you have control over this, use at least 2 points between lines such as 9 on 11, or 10 on 12). On your computer, see how it looks for your purpose if you add 1.5 spaces between lines on documents rather than 1.
- Keep substantial margins on left, right, top and bottom—generally no less than an inch and, yes, even on résumés.
- Use bullets and indenting deliberately as a way to break up space.
- When using subheads, leave more space *above* the subhead to separate it from the body copy than the space left *after* the subhead; it offers a better visual break.
- Headlines: Be consistent in using caps or upper/lowercase and making them flush left or centered—don't alternate.

For Proposals and Other Big Documents

- Take the trouble to make proposals inviting. This will increase the likelihood of winning the bid.
- Be sure proposals reflect your brand identity. Use the colors associated with it.
- Choose fonts and arrange your pages for instant readability.
- Build in LOTS of white space and page breaks—wide margins, subheads, pullouts, indents, bullets, colored boxes, a rule element, images. Designers love white space because of what it says to the audience. People associate white space with higher value and quality, luxury, simplicity, sophistication, calmness, design savvy, concern with aesthetics, and thoughtful attention to their preferences.
- Use relevant graphics and keep to a single style: Don't mix and match cartoons and photographs, for example, and keep visuals in line with your graphic image.
- Clip art: Stay away from it! If you can't find an appropriate image resource, get your message across with color boxes and other variables.
- Spark up graphs and charts with color. Think about a more intriguing way to present them than plain and static. Try to build in a feeling of motion and action—see the difference between the "Boring" and "Not So Boring" examples.

—Tina Panos, president of Panos Graphic Services

CREATING INFOGRAPHICS

The infographic is a visual representation of information, data or knowledge intended to present complex information quickly and clearly. It can be as simple as a well-designed graph or pie chart or a substantial document that compares or aggregates an extensive amount of information based on a theme.

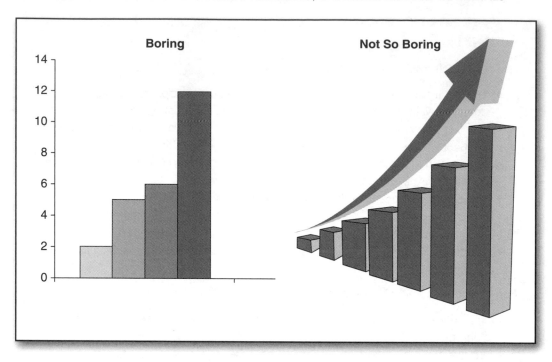

They are entertaining, memorable and popular, rather like stories—what's not to like? In fact, they are stories but visually told. They put things together into a perspective, which is a lot more fun than studying masses of data to figure out what, if anything, all the numbers and facts mean. They tempt Internet scanners to open posts and tweets, and people like sharing them, so they have good marketing value.

A good infographic can penetrate right past our logical defenses to persuade us to a viewpoint, making it a powerful tool for persuasion. But here are a few caveats: First, don't imagine you can create an infographic through "visual thinking." Words are how we think and how visual concepts are born. Second, generally speaking, creating an infographic is not a man-in-the street process that anyone can use to casually enhance a portfolio. People who create them professionally find them highly time consuming. They must be planned, researched, written. Images must be created or found. Graphic design must tie it all together.

That said, you'll find a growing number of good resources on the web—many of them free—to help you create charts and graphs, find and adapt photographs and other images, and assemble your visual story.

VIEW FROM THE FIELD: THE INFOGRAPHIC—A STORYTELLING TOOL

Infographics are visualizations. They resonate with readers because they put things in context and show relationships. Creating them is a way of predigesting the information for people and giving them the big picture.

First we come up with an idea to explore, usually at a client's request—for example, what apps are being created for mobile platforms, how are they used, what are the trends. Then we do the research, canvassing the existing data and sorting it out for relevance. Next it's a matter of interrogating the numbers and facts to find a narrative.

Infographics let you tell a more nuanced story. People read data in a hierarchical way and take numbers for granted. The infographic leads you to dig deeper and find the meaning of data and the relationship between things. It lets you unstick the dominant narrative and tell the bigger story, not just the one making headlines.

When we do a Google search, for example, we tend to assume only the top listings count. But that's not true. It's just the way the data is presented. If you research more of the listings to see how many clicks they get, you find for example that placing in the top six is worthwhile and a good value compared with what's needed to take the much more competitive first place.

So it can be a tool for marketing or strategizing. You can use it for your own purposes as well. If you're looking for a job, for example, finding the data and representing it visually can help you strategize the search and decide how to best invest your time.

Once you know your narrative, you already have a more powerful story than the one you started with. You now look for a way to visualize each component, because each may suggest a different kind of representation, and decide how each piece relates to the others. The graphics can be very simple—images, graph, charts. If you're working with an artist, at this point he can contribute ideas for more interesting visuals.

So the infographic is a way of thinking. Language makes it happen—you're creating a narrative and taking the next step to show people what something looks like. Graphic design is the supporting argument. The infographic is a form of storytelling, and like stories, a great way to bypass rational thinking and communicate an idea or persuade people.

—Jonathan Allen, president of L&T, a New York digital marketing consultancy firm (www.landt.co)

To see interesting examples of high-end infographics, just Google "Best Infographics of 2015" or another year, or just "best infographics."

In the next chapter, we'll move on to explore how to apply the principles of persuasion to the important business documents you may need to create for yourself or an employer.

PRACTICE OPPORTUNITIES

I. Analyze the Advertising Around You

Review three print ads, three television commercials, and three online ads. Answer the following questions, and write about your observations:

1. Who is the target audience (or audiences)?

2. What persuasive techniques can you identify?

3. How effective is each pitch?

4. What differences can you observe in the tactics used in the three media?

II. Discuss: How Decisions Are Made

Do you agree that people make decisions, from life choices to minor purchases, on an emotional rather than a reasoning basis?

Pick three decisions you've recently made, such as choosing a school, selecting a smartphone, making a donation to a specific cause, pursuing volunteer work, or making a major purchase like a car or computer. Carefully analyze the process you followed and assess what motivated your decision.

Does thinking this through lend support to the emotion-first concept? Does it affect your outlook on using persuasive techniques?

Research emotional decision making for a more in-depth view, and think about whether the concept makes sense to you and to what degree.

III. Read and Analyze Warren Buffett

Find and read at least three pieces of Buffett's writing, easily available online. Identify all the persuasion techniques you can identify, and try to add more not covered in this chapter. Share your findings with a small group of classmates and assemble one master list with examples.

IV. Questions for Discussion and Writing: Persuasion and Ethics

Here's a statement by Warren Buffett, part of a cover letter to his company's directors. It accompanied his letter to stockholders.

The priority is that all of us continue to zealously guard Berkshire's reputation. We can't be perfect but we can try to be. As I've said in these memos for more than 25 years: "We can afford to lose money—even a lot of money. But we can't afford to lose reputation—even a shred of reputation." We *must* continue to measure every act against not only what is legal but also what we would be happy to have written about on the front page of a national newspaper in an article written by an unfriendly but intelligent reporter.

Sometimes your associates will say, "Everybody else is doing it." This rationale is almost always a bad one if it is the main justification for a business action. It is totally unacceptable when evaluating a moral decision. Whenever somebody offers that phrase as a rationale, in effect they are saying that they can't come up with a *good* reason. If anyone gives this explanation, tell them to try using it with a reporter or a judge and see how far it gets them.

If you see anything whose propriety or legality causes you to hesitate, be sure to give me a call. However, it's very likely that if a given course of action evokes such hesitation, it's too close to the line and should be abandoned. There's plenty of money to be made in the center of the court.

1. Analyze: What do you think of Buffett's position? How would you feel if you received this message from your CEO? Does it feel like Buffett believes in what he's saying, rather than just giving lip service to a moral directive? How does the way he writes carry sincerity (or fail to)?

2. Note that not long after Buffett wrote this letter, one of his top executives (and probable successor), David Sokol, was accused of unethical behavior (buying substantial stock in a company that Berkshire Hathaway was about to acquire). Sokol resigned, but Buffett's initial response, which didn't express much outrage, was widely criticized. He later called the violation of the rules and company ethics "inexcusable." Does this set of events alter your view of Buffett's letter? What does it suggest about the relationship between written ideals and actions in business? Other spheres?

Research the events and statements this situation generated and write an opinion piece, in blog or op-ed style, about what the episode "means" or how it should be seen.

3. Do you see any dangers in using persuasive techniques to accomplish business purposes? What examples of unethical use come to mind in what you've observed or have read about?

4. Identify a specific example of unethical use of persuasion strategies you find interesting in any realm. Analyze why you believe the tactics were unethical. Then present your thinking to the class or group in three to five minutes. After hearing from all participants, collaborate with the group to draft a set of guidelines for the ethical use of persuasive techniques.

V. Write a Persuasive Letter or E-Mail

Select something you feel strongly about from your school, business, or personal life. It can be an idea, such as why companies need to enforce strong ethical guidelines or give new hires more access to leaders or why the person you're writing to should buy a different computer, take a particular course, read a book, build an aquarium—whatever. Write a persuasive memo to the relevant person using as many of the techniques covered in this chapter as you can, including the graphic guidelines. Then list the techniques you incorporated and identify the corresponding examples.

VI. Research and Report on a Corporate Story

Check out some of your favorite companies and identify one that tells its story in an effective way. Write a report that capsulizes the story, explains why it's successful, and how the company uses it.

VII. Word Choice Practice: Dump the Clutter

When we write An Important Document, the process seems to trigger our most old-fashioned instincts toward the formal and pretentious. Here are some phrases that are not only too wordy but interfere with the reader's ability to absorb the big picture or even get through the document. How would you replace the following?

At this point in time	Reach a conclusion
In consideration of	In view of the fact that
In a position to	It is important to note that

Notwithstanding the fact that

The manner in which

Following the conclusion of

In the event that

Contrary to the assumption that

In mitigation of

The purpose of this document

In a very real sense

Chapter 10

WRITING TO PERSUADE, PART 2

Creating Successful Business Documents

LEARN HOW TO . . .

- Write long-form business documents
- Create an executive summary (ES)
- Prepare a report
- Write formal and conversational proposals
- Write grant applications

When dealing with people, remember you are not dealing with creatures of logic, but with creatures of emotion.

—Dale Carnegie

Now or in the future you may work for yourself, a company, nonprofit, or government agency. It's probable that you'll move among these spheres during your career. Even if you keep to one domain, most communication tools are common to all.

Reports are universally needed because accountability matters on every level. As organizations become more geographically scattered and personal contact diminishes, they become even more important. Proposals and applications are not just for business owners—they're part of the day's work for many people. Staff members in many organizations must compete for assignments they want and make their best case for higher positions.

If you're entering the business world, here is some useful advice: Think and act like an entrepreneur. This means not just doing your job but doing it within the larger perspective of the organization's challenges and goals. Take personal responsibility to understand and advance company interests. Find opportunities to contribute and improve how things are done. Of course, use your top writing and speaking skills to let people know you're an active contributor and promote your ideas. Writing good proposals and reports will earn you support for your in-house projects and win outside contracts when that's part of your role.

All these materials must be persuasive, whatever the goal. To amplify the techniques of persuasion explained in Chapter 9, this chapter gives you a more specific resource of ideas to draw upon in writing major business documents. Each writing challenge is different, and only a handful can be covered here. But if you practice the thinking structure covered in earlier chapters and build up your repertoire of effective techniques, your business documents will help you stand out.

WRITING TIPS FOR BUSINESS DOCUMENTS

As different as the various business formats are, as well as their subject matter, the writing style is similar for all. These guidelines, which are detailed in previous sections, are important to business documents:

- Write crisp, simply constructed sentences that read fast.
- Use an objective third person tone and relatively formal language that is still accessible and clear.
- Choose short, vivid, concrete words, and avoid jargon and clichés.
- Choose action verbs rather than dull, passive-sounding ones.
- Maintain an upbeat, positive, "in charge" tone that communicates good judgment and conviction.
- Avoid hedgy words and statements (e.g., *about, we hope that, we'll aim to,* or *it's possible that*).
- Write a strong lead plus informational headlines and subheads to attract and retain the readers you want.

Check that the copy is sayable—read sections aloud and to friends. Some advisers suggest reading portions to a teenager to see how easily the document can be understood and what questions come up.

Expect to edit through a series of revision cycles. If your first draft (or two) is too long, as it probably will be, look for redundancies in thought and word. Cut empty phrases as well as unsubstantiated hyperbole to tighten the writing. Eagle-eye any vagueness and boilerplate-style material that is not completely customized to the occasion—readers find the one-size-fits-all approach insulting. Sharpen language. Polish, polish, polish. But don't edit the life out of it.

And don't allow the technical challenge of creating a major business document to overshadow your message. You must know what it is—be able to state it in a few sentences—and stick to it throughout. Everything included must support, prove, or demonstrate the truth and relevance of your message.

For best results, steep yourself in your own conviction and the excitement (or need) that drove you to prepare the document. Write from inside your own commitment. But at the same time, remember that it's not about you—especially with proposals, immersion in the audience perspective is a must. Invest in understanding your target readers and the problems they want to solve, whether you're preparing the document for your boss or a client or the public.

You cannot manipulate language to cover a lack of basic understanding or knowledge.

Logically examined, each project will suggest what to include. You might plan a long message similarly to a short one—shape a beginning (reason for the project, why the reader should care, definitions, orientation to the subject), middle (technical material, evidence, research, details), and end (a strong conclusion that brings the content and bottom-line recommendations home to the intended reader). A long document also requires a table of contents, ES, and, often, an appendix, where you can stash the backup without distracting readers from your story line.

SUCCESS TIP

USE A FOLDER SYSTEM TO JUMP-START BIG PROJECTS

When a major writing project looms, ease your path by collecting ideas, thoughts, and resources in file folders, either real or virtual—or both. (If you use paper folders, note that colorful ones are better than plain manila. You can color-code by subject.) If you're working on a business proposal and your outline has 10 sections, make up 10 folders. Then, as random useful thoughts come to you, write them up and put them in the applicable folders. Do the same with materials like financial statements.

If you've allowed reasonable time for the project, you'll end up with a batch of ideas and information for every topic. The writing will feel less formidable, and you'll have good material right at hand. The system also keeps you organized. Best of all, this simple collect-as-you-go method builds your thinking much more forcefully than if you sit down and try to create the document from scratch, all at once.

You can also use online systems to organize, such as Evernote or Scrivener.

THE EXECUTIVE SUMMARY: TECHNIQUES AND OPTIONS

The ES is a critical element for many kinds of business materials: business plans, proposals, white papers, reports, grant applications and more. The busier everyone gets, the more vital a role the summary plays. In many cases, it will be the only part of the document your key audiences read. If they like it, they may read the rest—or take action based on the ES alone.

So leave plenty of time to develop this piece. Don't pull out excerpts from the full document and tack them together. Use the ES to tell a complete, self-contained story. In some cases, its role is to fully present your idea and recommend a course of action, supported by evidence. In other cases, it must convince readers that they need the information and that it's relevant to their interests.

Touch on every element of the whole document to put the pieces in context, but give center stage to what matters most to the reader. If you're writing a business plan for a new venture, focus the ES on communicating your idea vividly as well as why it matters and why it's viable. A research report summary should concisely relate what you did, why, how, basic results, and perhaps next steps. A proposal summary should usually identify the problem and your solution.

Use the ES to put the whole document, and therefore your subject, in perspective. It's where you tell readers what the rest of the material means and why they should care. And aim to accomplish it all in one to two pages—rarely is a longer summary called for or welcome. The rule of thumb is to limit an ES to 5% to 10% of the full document.

Marshal your writing tool kit to make the ES as interesting as you can. This is the place to recreate your own excitement as an entrepreneur ready to seize the day or as the dedicated adviser prepared with a solid, innovative recommendation for a client or boss.

VIEW FROM THE FIELD: THE EXECUTIVE SUMMARY AS INTERNAL ADVOCACY

My goal in writing an Executive Summary is generally some form of advocacy: to get my point across, to influence, to make a compelling argument that can be fully trusted. Very often your audience has limited time so it needs brevity—but the Executive Summary should also show a solid organization and logic in respect to a business issue. The most successful Executive Summaries are self-contained. You may get approval based just on the summary.

(Continued)

(Continued)

It's good to show your audience that you know what came before and use it for context. Don't discredit it. And it's sometimes appropriate to make one recommendation but show other possibilities. This lends credibility, and people like to have a choice.

Move with gentle guidance into key findings or data points to support the recommendation, putting the most compelling ones on top. Know your audience: If you're appealing to the CFO, you may want to arrange your data points to address return on investment, cost saving and other financial aspects. Think of your audience's core responsibilities to help you plan your arguments and prioritize what you say.

Avoid flowery language and too many superlatives. I like to use language that shows an attempt at objectivity, focusing on the facts of the situation. The Executive Summary is not the time to put your heart on your sleeve. Err on the side of formality. Decision makers expect a level of seriousness when you ask for buy-in—chummy doesn't work. And accuracy is really important: It's a first impression thing. People will focus on a typo rather than your argument.

—Lisa Cuevas Shaw, vice president of Editorial and
Professional Learning for Corwin, a SAGE company

SAMPLE EXECUTIVE SUMMARY FOR A REPORT

Summaries are best written after the full version of the document is drafted, but you may find it helpful to draft a preliminary version first to guide you through the development process. Just expect to rewrite it later, when your own understanding is more complete.

At that point, you may feel like you're buried in a morass of material and have lost your story line. Ideally, step away from it for at least a day or two, and then think about what settles out as significant and important. Or try the tell-it-to-someone-else method.

Find a way to lead with the idea or viewpoint or need that rises to the top. You might think of the first few sentences as an elevator speech for the document.

Here is how Towers Watson (http://www.towerswatson.com), an international consulting firm that helps organizations improve performance, led off a report a few years ago on how communication and change management connect. The purposes appear to be multiple—to demonstrate thought leadership, serve clients, impress prospects and interest media. (Just as with short, everyday messages, goal and audience should be implicit.) Notice how explicit the headline and subhead are and how carefully the reasons for reading the report are stated.

Clear Direction in a Complex World
How Top Companies Create Clarity, Confidence, and Community to Build Sustainable Performance

Change and Communication ROI Study Report

Executive Summary

In a challenging and dynamic business world, success depends on establishing a clear path to navigate through complexity. Organizations and their leaders—wherever they are around the world and whatever business environment they face—must be able to chart the right course and deliver results.

Organizations that are doing this best have leaders, managers, communication and change practices that create:

Clarity: Conveying to employees the direction of the business along with ways they can contribute to the enterprise

Confidence: Supporting development of leaders and managers to better deliver confidence, and using a disciplined process to ensure effective use of change and communication resources

Community: Building a shared experience, a sense that employees and leaders are in it together—sharing both the challenges and rewards of working.

This report describes what the companies that communicate and manage change effectively are doing and how practices compare globally. Read on to find the steps you can take to create a clear direction for your organization.

The table of contents for the 30-page report lists Key Findings, Introduction, Defining Communication and Change Effectiveness, Assessing Effectiveness and Performance, Clarity, Confidence, Community. (In a shorter report, the ES and Introduction are more likely to be integrated.) The last section—Conclusion—comes full circle to the beginning:

As we noted in the introduction, internal change managers and communicators are like guides on a whitewater river. New technology and techniques can aid in the effort to shoot the rapids. But at the core, the best guides have mastered the art of reading human behavior and the skill of judging the best moves to make when the water is roughest.

Towers Watson began this series of studies in 2003, and we remain impressed with the innovative approaches of the most effective companies and strong advocates of those that continue striving to deliver more.

Outline-Style vs. Narrative Executive Summary

You can also use an outline style for your ES. Here is the beginning of a white paper on an environmental situation targeted to the media, government officials, and civic groups. (It is shown in abbreviated form—in the full version, each bulleted item is a paragraph long.)

Craven County's Brownfields

Analysis, Recommendations, and an Action Plan

The problem: Craven County is home to 5,450 *brownfields.* These contaminated parcels of land

- pose health and environmental hazards,
- put our undeveloped land at risk,
- prevent logical economic development,
- cost the county millions in lost taxes, and
- create suffering in disadvantaged communities.

How we got here—a complex set of interrelated problems must be faced:

- Bewildering state and federal laws and confusing local regulations
- Lack of leadership: Who takes the helm?
- Lack of centralized information
- Uncertainty that makes developers reluctant to invest.
- Community resistance to change

How the campaign will be managed: Craven County Citizens for Cleanup will take a leadership role to

- develop community understanding,
- build a database of sites and data,
- advocate for more effective laws and incentives,
- serve as a clearinghouse for information and ideas, and
- provide guidance and road maps for stakeholders.

Resource needs

- Government grants
- Bond issue potential
- Citizen contribution campaign

A narrative version for this paper might, by contrast, begin like this:

Craven County is home to 5,450 *brownfields*—contaminated parcels of land—twice the number of any other county in the state. They stand undeveloped or abandoned. Ranging from former dry cleaning shops and gas stations to industrial sites, they exist as eyesores in many communities but compel our attention for more serious reasons.

The rest of the summary follows in the same sequence as the bullet version but in narrative style with strong subheads.

Which approach is more effective? It depends on the nature of the project and audience. Technical subjects may present well with the outline format. But narrative style offers more potential to create emotional impact and tilt the reader in your direction. Here's how Warren Buffet sets the tone in his annual report to shareholders in two different years. In both, he starts a paragraph summarizing stock performance, so dear to his investors' hearts. Then:

2012:

A number of good things happened at Berkshire last year, but let's first get the bad news out of the way.

When the partnership I ran took control of Berkshire in 1965, I could never have dreamed that a year in which we had a gain of $24.1 billion would be subpar, in terms of the comparison we present on the facing page.

But subpar it was. . .

2013:

On the operating front, just about everything turned out well for us last year—in certain cases very well. Let me count the ways:

We completed two large acquisitions, spending almost $18 billion to purchase all of NV Energy and a major interest in H. J. Heinz. Both companies fit us well and will be prospering a century from now . . . .

WRITING WINNING PROPOSALS, IN FORMAL AND CONVERSATIONAL STYLES

Writing leads to wealth.

—Jeffrey Gitomer, chief executive salesman,
in *Little Green Book of Getting Your Way*

Whether you're pitching for a project, contract or grant, proposals must be first rate. There just aren't many huge piles of money sitting around without a horde of applicants buzzing around, vying for a share or the chance to do the job. Lean times tempt less qualified applicants to try for every opportunity, so in many fields, competition keeps rising.

Bear in mind that with adaptation, most of the concepts apply more or less to the corporate, nonprofit and government arenas. Consultants and independent contractors also draw on the same set of tools.

Business proposals aimed at securing work of any kind may need to be formal, informal, or anywhere along the line. In creating a proposal, judge carefully according to the circumstances and context. A large company or government agency may present a formidable set of instructions and even a form to fill out. But even when your presentation is dictated by a strict format, following good writing guidelines helps you succeed. This often takes some imagination. Here are some universals.

Know your audience. Can you tell who will read the document? That may determine the level of technical detail to include and the angle to take—a CEO and COO and CFO have different interests, not to mention an engineer or HR director. Usually, however, you should assume a variety of people will review it. This is not a problem if you write with relentless clarity and simplicity that everyone will welcome.

Know your goal. As with a résumé, you want the proposal to qualify you for the next step—usually an interview. Rarely is a group hired based solely on "paper."

Know the problem the organization wants to solve—and why it's important. Read the RFP 20 times if the problem isn't stated outright and look for clues. Is a tight deadline mentioned over and over again? Are there an unusual number of checkpoints that may suggest a prior bad experience? What skills and capabilities are stressed? Read between the lines, do research, and be aware of industry trends and challenges.

Know your story—the big picture message. Try writing a brief crystallization of what you'll say in person at the next stage if your proposal reaches the "call" pile. Why are you the best choice? Answer this basic question as a guideline for the full proposal. It may evolve into a good ES.

Give them the proof. Marshal the evidence of how well you'll handle the work and deploy it as appropriate. Proof may include previous jobs, results, client roster, client testimonials, team credentials, special expertise, graphics, photos and more. If there's an issue with deadlines, or coming in on budget, include factual proof of your consistent performance.

Don't get lost in detail. Provide what is asked for, but never lose sight of the message you want your audience to hear.

Remember that people hire people. Take opportunities to get across who you are and what you care about, how the team coordinates skills and works together, any special advantages you bring, and why you're nice to work with (perhaps via testimonials). Trust me, likability counts a lot. The more enthusiastic you sound about the prospect of the work, the more magnetic you are.

Building relationships in person, by phone or e-mail as opportunity allows is the way organizations successfully compete.

And throughout, write with clear, jargon-free language based on short words, sentences, and paragraphs. I've heard proposal advisers claim that a pitch for big money from a big company should be written in big language: a weighty, formal, impressive, fancy-word style commensurate (their word, not mine!) with the value of the prize. I believe that's absurd. Your substance must be solid, but aim to be a breath of fresh air in how you present. I don't promise you'll win all the time—just more often.

VIEW FROM THE FIELD: PROPOSALS FOR PRIVATE VS. GOVERNMENT SECTORS

It rings true in both the private and public sectors: Always know your audience! For business proposals, focus not on you so much as on the clients. You need to really know them, what they're thinking, and what their true objective is (besides revenue). Here's what I found works with engineering proposals, for example.

First, look at all the hot buttons mentioned in the RFP. Repeat them throughout, and incorporate them into the cover letter. If the RFP says, "Here are our goals and what we hope to achieve from this project," great. If not—dig a little, interview key stakeholders and research the project's history.

Establish a theme for the entire proposal. For example, if it's a redevelopment project and the main goal is to create jobs, our theme would be economic development and we would carry it through the captions, images, and photographs in addition to the cover letter and technical scope section.

The proposal must read well and easily flow between focus areas. Use an active voice, keep sentence length to 15 words or less, be positive, and remove unnecessary words. Write it so that someone outside of the "engineering world" can review it and understand it. Proposals are often reviewed by committees that include members of the broader community; therefore, they must be understood by the layman. Appealing graphics are an extremely important component of the proposal. Use them to engage the reader. Remember, the goal is to pass the first stage and get an interview!

For government grants, such as the National Science Foundation proposals I manage, it is the quality and promise of the proposed research that is the focal point and probably accounts for

(Continued)

(Continued)

80% of the scoring. The project summary is most important. It includes character limitations and requires details about the broad impact of the research—its intellectual merit and how it will affect the community and world at large. The emphasis is still on the story that appears in the form of a project description. A technical committee will review the proposal, but it must be understood by nontechnical people, since the award notices and the entire process are in the public domain.

—Christine M. Cesaria, director of grants/communications,
Department of Computer Science, Stony Brook University;
former marketing production manager for engineering firms

A COVER LETTER EXAMPLE

In the private sector, an individual, well-thought-out cover letter is very important. If it doesn't appeal to the clients, they won't go further. A guideline to follow is this: Restate the client's goals in the first paragraph so that from the beginning, it's not about "us," and you show your understanding. The second paragraph should introduce the team members, not just who they are, but why the client should care—have they worked with the company before? Have relevant experience? Then, take a look at the RFP and the evaluation criteria, show how you meet the criteria and how your team benefits the client. It's matching "our" story to "theirs."

Next refer to what is unique about your proposal—shortened timeline? Coming in under budget? Ideally, something that makes you special. And don't forget to include contractual matters, such as "This contract is good for 180 days . . ."

The cover letter should be clear, concise and one page when possible—two at the most. Here is the closing section of one written to compete for a major construction project:

". . . Unlike pure bike planning firms, our firm knows what it takes to get to construction and we will therefore help ABCDE find feasible solutions for the White River trails."

Enthusiasm and Dedication

We have a passion for bicycle projects. For us, they are not a side business; they are a stand-alone practice area. Furthermore, our team includes avid cyclists and bike advocates. Our enthusiasm translates into focused attention to quality and service, and we take special pride in and ownership of these assignments.

On behalf of the project team, thank you for this opportunity to present our qualifications for this interesting assignment. We hope to have the opportunity to discuss our experience and approach further. Please feel free to contact me at xxx-xxx-xxxx should you require any additional information.

—Courtesy of Christine M. Cesaria

How to Handle Rigid Formats

In private industry as well as the government sector, you often don't have the freedom to choose the shape you prefer for your presentation. An RFP may dictate a
standard set of categories and even set strict word limitations on each section.
Follow the guidelines scrupulously. Watch for the "do nots" as well as "dos." If the
RFP specifies, "do not write more than one paragraph" for a section, don't sneak in
a super-long paragraph. You will be disqualified. The thinking: If you can't follow
instructions for the proposal, why expect your performance to be better?

Still, apply ingenuity and find ways to incorporate the idea of an ES anyway.
Usually RFPs have a project overview section that lends itself to this use.
Predetermined formats can make it hard to maintain your story line, but you are
more likely to be rewarded when you do.

How to Write Informal, Conversation-Based Proposals

Especially for service providers who operate on their own or in small groups, writing a proposal is a formidable task. In response to this challenge, many people
produce generic boilerplate pitches that go on at length about their wonderfulness
and devote perhaps a few paragraphs to the work at hand. A much better alternative is the conversation-based proposal that zeros in on the job without spending
a ton of time on proposal writing.

Typically, a client has a problem to solve and hopes you will solve it. With a
little encouragement, she will gladly tell you exactly what that problem is, why it
matters, and what has already been tried. Resist the temptation to tout your qualifications! It may sound counterintuitive, but once you're in front of prospects,
most take your credentials for granted. They want to know you can do the job or
solve their problem.

Use the in-person conversation to find out as much as you can about that problem as well as the person and the organization. If you need to prime the conversation, try open-ended questions such as:

What do you want to gain? Why is that important?

What would you like to see different about_____?

How would that make your life better? Improve the organization?

What are you losing because of this (inefficiency/missed opportunity/waste/
lack of competitiveness, etc.)?

How have you tried to solve this problem so far?

Listen for below-the-surface clues. Often people are conscious of symptoms rather than underlying causes. Someone might tell you his website doesn't draw because it's not optimized well, for example; this may be true, but poor content may be a bigger factor.

From this point, you can develop a solution right on the spot, working collaboratively with the prospect. Or end the conversation, make a second appointment if possible, then draft your analysis and recommendation on your own time. Two pages are enough for a simple synopsis that spells out the problem and its importance, followed by your solution.

For example, if I'm selling e-mail-writing workshops to a company and have spoken in reasonable depth with the person in charge, by telephone, or in person, I could write in a simple letter format this way:

> Dear Anne:
> It was a pleasure to meet you and learn about the interesting work ABC does.
> I'm sure the Can-Write team can help you meet the challenge we discussed. Here is how I understand your need.
>
> - ABC's junior managers are alienating the firm's wealthy, elderly investors by sending abrupt e-mails perceived as rude.
> - These staff members also produce internal messages that are confusing and inefficient, creating dissension and time-wasting situations.
> - An estimated 14% of staff productivity is lost through these poor e-mail skills, costing the company an estimated $xxx annually.
>
> Etcetera. Three to seven points are usually enough. Then:
>
> We propose a set of customized workshops led by writing experts who are seasoned presenters and work frequently with busy professionals. A series of five three-hour interactive, lively learning experiences will train your staff members to build good relationships with customers in all their writing. Specifically, they will learn and practice how to:
>
> - Understand the needs and expectations of ABC's audiences.
> - Create messages that demonstrate respect and consideration.
> - Plan and strategize all messages to accomplish specific goals.
> - Write with clarity, brevity, and impact.
>
> . . . and so on.

An effective proposal can be built this way, along with a few more sections according to the occasion (see the example below). Notice the emphasis on what will be accomplished. Typically the *how*—the process used to perform the work—is secondary. Good proposals, whatever their length, give the reader a vision of how much better life (and profits) will be when the project is accomplished.

A proposal in this letter format can easily be converted to an agreement—just amend it based on your prospect's input, add any provisions needed, and specify space at the end for signatures and dates. If a more formal proposal is needed, it's easy to adapt the written pitch along these lines:

Proposed by Can-Write for ABC Inc.

A training program to improve e-mail communication company-wide and build customer relationships

The Problem—in narrative style with bullets

The Solution—narrative with bullets

How We'll Work—some detail on what you'll provide (e.g., content of the workshops)

How We'll Collaborate—e.g., interactive client process to sharpen goals and deliverables

Who We Are—a tight profile of you/your team showing why you're the best for the job and your excitement with the project

What We'll Accomplish—a tempting vision of the problem solved and the wonderful future that beckons

Mutual responsibilities (and perhaps deadlines, relevant logistics, etc.)

Fees (which should at some earlier point be discussed, but not before defining the problem's scope and importance)

The conversational approach automatically produces a you- rather than me-based way of selling your service and writing proposals. And except perhaps for celebrities who tire of reading about themselves, if there are any, this approach never bores the audience. Moreover, clients are often more receptive to your solution when you lead them to clarify the problem and give it a value, typically higher than they originally would have assigned.

Four more tips for a competitive advantage in all proposals:

Practice the art of omission. Adopt the attitude of the popular fiction writer Elmore Leonard, who said, "I try to leave out the parts that people skip." Do the same. A concise proposal is more apt to be read all the way through and hold reader interest. Leave out the boilerplate statements full of empty hyperbole that anyone, in any industry, could use, and everything that does not support your story.

Skip the tech-speak. Pile it in back as a separate section or appendix if you feel it's needed, but don't break the narrative flow with details your prospect will not understand or care about. A businessperson, for example, doesn't want to know what programs a web designer will use to build a site. What that new website will accomplish, however, is magnetic.

Go for speed. In today's hyperactive world, the faster your writing reads, the better your chances of reaching other people and persuading them to your viewpoint. This in large part translates as "write short"—words, sentences, paragraphs, sections.

Inject energy and enthusiasm. Above all, evidence your passion for what you do. You want the work or the project or the grant—don't be afraid to make that 100% clear. Enthusiasm coupled with thorough understanding of client needs is hard to resist, sometimes even when the price is higher than the competition's.

SUCCESS TIP

COLLABORATIVE WRITING PROJECTS

In both classwork and the business world, you're often called on to participate in collaborative writing projects. This is a challenge: People have different levels of capability, especially when it comes to writing. In many instances, good writers feel like they are holding a very big bag.

The best solution is to plan the project carefully, breaking out the tasks and distributing them as fairly as possible. The work may encompass planning, research, obtaining information through interview, collecting and analyzing statistics or other data, creating graphics for illustration and final design, perhaps preparing an oral presentation—and writing, editing, and proofing. Agree on a project leader or coordinator, who should be given extra recognition.

Each person can take responsibility for one or more of the functions, according to the team's size, so that everyone agrees the workload is fairly distributed. Set a timeline that specifies when each phase must be completed, allowing for the time needed to accomplish all subsequent phases. Also set parameters for completing each aspect of the project: in what form research, data, interview, and technical information must be delivered . . . what the finished project should look like . . . checkpoints for the coordinator to manage so he can field problems. The full group should maintain regular contact and review each member's progress.

Put the plan in writing and mark deadlines clearly.

Be sure to allow enough time for the individual or team responsible for final writing to produce a cohesive document that doesn't sound like it was written by a committee. And at least one other person should thoroughly proofread.

CREATING EFFECTIVE NONPROFIT GRANT APPLICATIONS

An application for funding or project support from a government agency, foundation or corporation shares the essentials of proposal writing with some additional requirements. Foremost: Take the grant-giving organization's mission seriously. Invariably, those that invest money in a good cause or project of any kind feel passionately about their mission. *Be sure you understand what that mission is, and dovetail your application so it directly relates to it.* The mission orientation is also one reason foundations prefer to fund projects rather than support "operational expenses."

Another guideline is don't be boring. *Besides getting to the point quickly and succinctly, tell your story.* This might cover how your organization was created; what it has accomplished, preferably told through people you've helped or goals achieved; and a vision of how much better the world will be if your application is funded.

Avoid repeating material more than necessary. In the case of grants, most reviewers will read the full document and you need not keep regrounding them in the same ideas. If necessary to repeat, find another way to say it.

Stick to your central message, what you'll accomplish with the funding. Organize the document to correspond to the RFP and specific format requirements, but have a clear idea of the message you want to deliver and build a cohesive narrative as best you can. Each answer should stand on its own, contribute new information and add up to a compelling story.

VIEW FROM THE FIELD: A GRANT REVIEWER ON WHAT LOSES, WHAT WINS

What annoys me most is that people just do not answer the questions. They talk around the issues and don't get to the heart of things, the core interest of a donor or funder: Why should we give money to you and not another organization that's doing similar work?

Many grant applications are particularly light on the organization's impact. One, for example, asked for more money to do more work in the same area. They talked about how horrible the problem is that they deal with but not the agency's impact. I asked about it: "You've been using the money for 15 years—what difference have you made?" They talked themselves out of the funding.

Don't just cite numbers to show success—saying "we trained 500 people" isn't going to make me invest in your organization. I want to know what happened to those people a year later. It can be hard to track results with figures but you can show them anecdotally.

(Continued)

(Continued)

I notice bad writing, I don't notice mediocre writing, and I do notice good writing—when you see something written well it has stars around it, sparkles. Good writing stands out.

Given that the application shows capacity and evidence that the organization can do the work, good writing gets the grant.

—Ann Marie Thigpen, director of Long Island
Center for Nonprofit Leadership at Adelphi University

Grant Application Strategies

Nothing is particularly hard if you divide it into small parts.

—Henry Ford

Get in touch. Talk to the grant administrators. Ask questions about the level of detail they'd like to see, data to include, and even whether a particular project is a good candidate. This enables you to perfect your pitch.

It is a rare funder that will mind hearing from you, as long as you speak with intelligence. Making awards is a grueling business for funders as well as for the applicants. They're happy to help you meet their needs. Moreover, the interaction works toward building a relationship. We choose to work with and invest in people we trust. If you must pose your questions in writing, do it well and carefully.

Define the problem and focus on outcomes. Show clearly that you understand the problems to be solved, and what will be accomplished should the money be awarded to you. Funders often complain that many grant applicants fail to provide enough information on outcomes, which must be meaningful: "We will train 50 farmers to use the new agricultural method" is a so-what statement. But this is not: "We will train 50 farmers and show them how to train their peers. Each will train an additional 25 per year and they in turn will share their training. Within two years, the program will reach half the co-op's farmers and yield a collective crop increase of 15 to 20%."

Connect to the action. Link outcomes to the activities and methods you believe will bring them about. For example, if a program's objective is to help failing students improve their math grades by 20%, and the application says only that this will be accomplished by presenting 15 workshops, you haven't said, What will the students learn, who will teach them, and what innovative strategies will be adopted? Show a track record for the methods if you can.

Demonstrate accomplishments and set the stage for future applications.
Understandably, many nonprofit organizations cannot afford expensive follow-up
studies to prove a program worked. When you're responsible for managing the
grant, look for tracking options at the very beginning and build them into the work.
For example, field workers can be asked to make note of clients' input on how they
were helped. In-person testimonials shot with a simple system, such as a smartphone, offer an excellent option for showing results in the human terms everyone
responds to.

And always, report project results to the funder in writing, whether that's a
formal requirement or not. Many requestors fail to do so and wonder why their
new applications fail.

VIEW FROM THE FIELD: PROPOSAL ADVICE FROM AN NGO PROGRAM DIRECTOR

We start with knowing the audience and the language it speaks. We aim with all our writing to
be very clear and direct. Saying it in simple terms is important. People often want to overexplain
things in a proposal but then the less clear it becomes. Thread in too much detail and you lose
directness and intensity. Put in too much mechanics and people start to get lost in the machinery.

There's an art to finding the most direct way to say something about a sophisticated idea in a
short amount of space. Usually we have 10 pages to explain what we'll do with millions of dollars.

The underlying structure we use:

- Rationale
- Political context
- Why it's important
- Why we're the best to do the work
- What the work will actually be
- Timing
- Results we expect

I recommend outlining what you're trying to do, so you go into a document with a road
map of how it all fits together. This tells you where questions will arise and what research you
have to do so you have a game plan. The document may not end up much longer than the
outline. This process helps people distill the ideas and concepts down to bullet points—then
they have the luxury of adding detail and can figure out the sequence people will understand.
An outline also lets us brainstorm with other people, who many times are overseas, so it's
easy for them to contribute and you build buy-in in advance.

Always, put the bottom line up front. If you're asking for something, whether in a letter or
proposal, come out with it right away. Be unambiguous. It gives the reader a unifying idea of
what the document is about.

(Continued)

(Continued)

This is important also because of another element, how you want readers to think of you. They learn about the team, and the project, by how the document is written. You want to be seen as straightforward, direct, easy to understand. You need them to trust you and feel they can get a very direct answer in a quick amount of time.

—Erin Mathews, director of Iraq Programs, the National Democratic Institute (an international development agency)

WRITING PROJECT REPORTS THAT WIN SUPPORT

Those who write reports often underestimate their value. If you hold a job that requires you to submit regular accounts of your own activities or your unit's to a supervisor or client, see them as opportunities rather than rote chores.

Pause to think before drafting a report to consider: Who's my audience? What do those readers want to know—need to know? What decisions may be based on what I say?

If the report goes to a supervisor, remember that he or she values staff reports not only as a way to hold people accountable but as information sources: They are probably her best access to knowing what's happening at ground level, degree of progress (or its lack), early-stage problems, activities to share or coordinate among different groups. A good report showcases your writing–thinking skills and often rewards you: with help if you need it, more responsibility, more interesting assignments, a promotion.

If you're a specialist who performs research and/or analysis for your client or your own organization, reports are how you tell a client what you've accomplished on her behalf. Reports are platforms for decision making. Many professionals with highly sophisticated technical skills fall into traps that undercut the value of their work. One way is to undersupply clear perspectives and bury readers in detail. This is a mistake because most readers care little about what you did to get your results or information and the data: They want to know what it means.

Delivering the message in an uninteresting, non-engaging manner is another mistake. Reports may not on the surface look like a source of entertainment. But in today's high-pressure environment, we all choose what we read and how much. This certainly applies to multitasking business leaders. Just because they want information doesn't mean they'll happily slog through a ton of lifeless material to find what they need and interpret it productively.

If you did the work well, the substance of a report isn't boring to you. So why bore the audience? Here are some techniques to make your reports at once more interesting, clear, readable, useful—and valued.

Stay Tuned to the Big Picture

Especially when massive amounts of data are involved, don't let readers get lost in the bog. People today don't want more information and data—we're all overburdened already. As always, it's the writer's job to predigest the information and develop a clear perspective based on what matters to that audience.

Journalists, the quintessential information gatherers, always ask themselves, "What's the story?" It can be far from obvious when a lot of research is involved, and the original concept may have evolved into something quite different. The reporter's mantra: Don't bury the lead. Identify what's important, interesting, and valuable about your message to the reader; lead with it; and organize the rest of your story (or document) to support it.

To uncover the message, try telling your story to someone else. This taps into your oral instincts, bypassing the more complicated way your brain works for writing. It also gives you more direct, simple language. Or ask yourself these questions: What is this really about? What did I find? Another route to true meaning is to frame the question your audience expects you to answer, such as: What does the evidence or analysis indicate to be the best decision? What are the alternative courses of action, and what are the risks and benefits for each?

Once you know your story, use the ES to highlight it. Offer a complete perspective on what's in the report, what's important, and your recommendations or conclusions. Usually the bottom line is your most captivating lead.

View the rest of the report as evidence and backup. You can cross-reference the sections within the ES so people can find the detail they prefer. But don't weigh those sections down with all your research and analysis. A report works best when relatively nontechnical readers can move through it quickly without becoming embroiled in too much data they probably won't understand or care about.

The bottom-line-on-top strategy works for all a report's sections. For each, first figure out the main import and put it in perspective. Don't slow down or interrupt the narrative flow with too many calculations, charts, graphs, or other "evidence." Most readers care about conclusions, not the process.

Use Action Heads and Subheads

Pull readers along with "action" headlines and subheads that say something, rather than labels.

Instead of writing, for example,

Pension Fund Forecast

Try

Pension Funding Inches Up

Or, use the label and add a headline:

Pension Fund Forecast: 14% Rise Seen for First Quarter

This technique automatically makes the material more interesting and captures reader attention. Being more specific helps people identify the must-read pieces, too—which is good. Today's reader, trained by the Internet, is active rather than passive and decides what to read based on the clues we present.

Use content-based headlines everywhere, including the ES. You can still use the label if preferred, but amplify it meaningfully. For example, "Executive Summary: Three Routes to Funding Pensions That Meet New Legal Guidelines."

Put the Backup in Back

Statistics, charts, graphs, and data batches are in general better placed in an appendix section, where they don't undermine your narrative flow, unless they're critical to your central message. Here's a quick formula for an effective technical report: ES/overview, main body spelling out major findings and implications, recommendations or conclusions, and a set of appendixes with all the data you find appropriate. The decision makers may well read just the summary, depending on the numbers people or tech specialists to vet the rest for problems.

VIEW FROM THE FIELD: WHY GOVERNMENT VALUES GOOD REPORTS

In international work, you need to communicate with people in different time zones, so writing is really the only way to do it. And we're the government, so we also need a documented paper trail for the record to show why we did something.

My job is to enable people to make good decisions, and to do it without my being present. We communicate a lot verbally, but not everyone is at the meetings. Even if they were, given the amount of information flow, they won't remember everything I say. So I need coherent, clearly written documents that give people everything they need to know.

Getting people to come together around a document to agree on major conclusions can, if it's concise and clear, generate the underlying decisions needed. For an internal audience, if I'm presenting research, I need the takeaway and justification for what I believe to be the case.

So writing is very important to me when I hire people. When I interview, I ask, "How would you explain this to our vice president who will make a decision about it? And how would you explain it to a group of curious students?" I walk them through different groups and it's quite telling to see how people would write for different audiences.

—Alicia Phillips Mandaville, managing director
of development policy at Millennium Challenge
Corporation (U.S. foreign aid agency)

WRITING PERSONAL REPORTS

The same techniques that work for research reports and funding applications will work for you when you report on your own activities. Even if you're filling out a form, think about what to say in the big-picture context. Start with an ES, not necessarily labelling it that.

Ask yourself all the questions about why the reader cares about the information, what it means, why it matters, what you need. Go for a proactive, upbeat tone and deliver the bottom line immediately. If you're writing about what you accomplished in January, for example, rather than beginning in a hum-drum just-doing-my-job fashion such as . . .

This month, I continued to work on the software issues for the project I'm assigned to. Twenty hours were spent on research. I analyzed 47 possibilities. I also made some telephone calls . . .

Try something more like this—more like Warren Buffett:

I'm happy to report that I will complete my analysis of software for the Zilch Project by January 17th. The good news is that we can accomplish all our goals and come in under budget. Here are some of the purchases I plan to recommend, which coordinate for efficiency and speed . . .

If you want help on the project, add something like this at the end of the summary: I can complete the report a week sooner if I can get some help with . . . .

Reports give you a major opportunity to demonstrate that you are a responsible, resourceful and capable individual who understands the organization and contributes to its bottom line, even if in a small way. Show that you're a problem-solver and that you're committed to your role.

SUCCESS TIP

HOW TO IDENTIFY CONTENT FOR REPORTS

When you have trouble establishing perspective on what you or your department accomplished during a given time period, or aren't sure what's worth sharing, ask yourself some of these questions.

What's important about the period's events in terms of company or department goals, immediately? Long-range?

What has changed or progressed?

What initiatives did you take? How did they turn out?

What challenges or problems did you encounter? How did you solve them?

Did you see new opportunities and act on them?

What surprised you?

Did anything occur that bears watching, or should be taken into account in planning?

Anything thought-provoking to share?

What (if appropriate) do you recommend based on recent events?

A WORD ON BUSINESS PLANS

Business plans are highly individualized documents that can take months or even years to evolve, because developing a new enterprise is tough. Writing the plan often pulls entrepreneurs through the grueling work of thinking out the idea and how the business will operate.

Develop the written document much like a proposal. You'll need sections explaining the mission—why the idea has value and why it's needed, who it will interest, how it will operate, and what it will produce. A business plan also needs a full marketing strategy, a convincing portrayal of a capable leader and team, and a detailed financial plan. All the techniques of persuasive writing apply to the presentation, including a great ES that shows off both your passion and practicality.

Asking for money is a serious business. There is help out there: the Small Business Administration, Small Business Development Centers, local business advisory groups, college programs, and many online sources of business plan formats and advice.

PRACTICE OPPORTUNITIES

I. Group Project: Invent and Propose a New Course

Collaborate in small groups on ideas for a new course that would add to your capabilities and qualifications. Pick one and brainstorm its benefits. Divide up the responsibilities, and collaboratively write an ES for a formal proposal to your school's director. It should explain what you recommend and why, using techniques of persuasion.

II. Group Project: Develop a Project Proposal

1. **Propose a cause.** Brainstorm in small groups to choose an idea for a new local charitable cause or a major project you agree would be of value to the community and is practical (e.g., cleaning up a park, collecting used clothing for a children's shelter, volunteering for an after-school tutoring service).

2. **Plan a proposal** to raise funds for the idea from local businesses or a civic group: Identify what needs to be done, set a timeline for each stage, and determine how to collaborate; each team member should assume an appropriate part of the work. Decide together on the central focus of your story, and be sure to include why the project is needed, who will benefit and how, the extent of demand, exactly what support you're asking for, activities and outcomes, and so on.

3. **Create the proposal in line with your plan.** Include an ES. Draw on the writing and persuasion techniques presented in this chapter and Chapter 9. Include appropriate graphics (or describe what they would consist of).

4. **Present the proposal.** The full class reviews all the proposals and votes on which to support, taking the role of a civic group or committee on corporate giving. If desired, the class can also conduct Q&A sessions with each group (which will highlight any missing information).

5. **Discuss results.** What characterized the most successful proposals? What persuasion strategies did you observe, and how well did they work? Were opportunities missed? And, how did the collaborative process turn out? Can a best practice set of directions be assembled for collaborative writing?

III. Write a Report

Create a written report on what you accomplished in this course during the past month. What did you learn, why does it matter, and how will you use it? What problems do you need to work on? How do you chart your progress? What recommendations can you give yourself for further improvement? Where do you need help, and how might you get it? For this, you (along with the professor) are your own audience.

IV. Class Discussion: When You Don't Agree With Your Employer. . .

In the business world, you may well be called on to write memos, letters, social media posts and endless other materials that speak to a viewpoint you disagree with or for which you have no natural empathy. This happens especially often in professional communications work. When should you voice your opinion? Where should you draw the line? Should personal values reconcile with job demands— and if so, how? Consider a concept public relations specialists espouse: There are many truths. Do you agree with that?

SELECTED RESOURCES FOR PART IV

A number of interesting websites and blogs connect psychology research to marketing and other persuasion needs. Here are a few I like. Notice that each site or blog has a tagline. Which do you think work best?

Changing Minds: "How we change how others think, feel, behave and do." Large resource of ideas about tactics of persuasion: (http://changingminds.org/techniques/general/overall/overall.htm).

Psyblog: "Understand your mind." Psychologist Jeremy Dean's website covers scientific research that relates to everyday life (www.spring.org.uk).

Psychotactics: "Why customers buy and why they don't." Sean D'Souuza on psycho-tactical strategies for small business (www.psychotactics.com).

Neuromarketing: "Where brain science and marketing meet." Roger Dooley blogs on this subject and recommends other current material. He is also the author of the book *Brainfluence: 100 Ways to Persuade and Convince Consumers With Neuromarketing* (www.neurosciencemarketing.com/blog).

Social Triggers: Derek's Halpern's take on applying psychology science to business (http://socialtriggers.com).

You Are Not So Smart: "A Celebration of Self Delusion." David McRaney's in-depth observations on the flawed perception and reasoning behind what happens in the world (http://youarenotsosmart.com).

The Web Psychologist: "Want to discover the science of online persuasion?" Nathalie Nahai applies persuasion techniques to online writing (www.thewebpsychologist.com).

Influence at Work: "Proven Science for Business Success." The website of Robert B. Cialdini, PhD, the leading researcher in the field and author of widely respected books including *Influence: The Psychology of Persuasion* (www .influenceatwork.com).

A Few More Books

Tell to Win: Connect, Persuade, and Triumph With the Hidden Power of Story, Peter Guber.

Illuminating and entertaining view of "the story" and how to use it in business by a Hollywood/sports/business power broker.

Fascinate, Your 7 Triggers to Persuasion and Captivation, Sally Hogshead.

How to fascinate people and influence decision making.

PART V

WRITING FOR THE INTERACTIVE WORLD

Chapter 11

WRITING FOR WEBSITES AND ONLINE READERS

Your Ticket to a Level Playing Field

LEARN HOW TO . . .

- Translate print writing into online writing
- Plan a basic website
- Create copy that works for websites and online media
- Plan a home page
- Brainstorm content ideas

I write my own website and I've taken a really long time doing it.... I want to make it just as clear and intuitive as I can. I'm absolutely convinced that clear writing makes my business succeed.

—Jason Fried, founder and president of the software firm Basecamp; coauthor of the best-selling book *Rework*

WEBSITE WRITING: WHAT'S DIFFERENT, WHAT'S NOT

Websites over the past few years have evolved from "one more marketing tool" for organizations to front and center in the marketing/communications/PR/branding mix. Along with blog platforms, which give smaller players the chance to operate sites with few technology barriers, websites are the core of the "Content Is King" premise.

For many people, websites are the first port of call for finding information, products, and services. Many marketers use social media primarily to drive connections to a website or blog, where the in-depth substance lives. Even paid advertising is used more and more as a conduit to a website. So writing for these media is important. Do you need to master a whole different skill set?

Basically, no. The principles for writing well online are the same as for older media. Earlier chapters show you that contemporary business writing works best when it's conversational, as opposed to the stilted, formal language that used to be the norm. Apply this principle to online writing, escalate it maybe 30%, and your writing works.

Like all practical writing, online material needs to be accessible, clear, friendly, and audience oriented. And, absolutely, it demands "correctness":

- Good spelling
- Good grammar—*with liberties*
- Good editing and proofing

It's critical to write correctly because anyone reading a website, blog or online article looks for clues to credibility, consciously or not. Since the digital world enables anyone to be a seller, author, critic or expert, the unspoken question is always, "Why should I trust you? Why should I accept this site as authoritative or even honest?"

Good writing signals that you're credible and can be taken seriously. Moreover, it's impossible to produce a good site without formulating your themes, mission, and structure—in words. And words remain the crux of viewer experience. Surprisingly, research shows that response to even this visual medium is text-based. People focus first on headlines and continue reading if they find the copy relevant. Generally, they are uninterested in images that don't relate to content directly.

If you need more incentive to write your best on the Internet, consider how public it is. Everything you put up has a limitless audience—a post may be viewed all over the world and may last forever even if you try to erase it. Your audience includes every employer you'll ever care about and people in your personal future, too.

Some Special Characteristics of Websites

There are some important differences between writing for print and digital media: with online media, writing is not just about writing anymore. It has:

1. **More dimensions.** A website, blog, or social media posting can embed or link to video, blogs, podcasts, articles and other sites. Think of it as the spider in the center of a complex web.

2. **More dependence on graphics.** Sites must support eye appeal and readability by using the full repertoire of techniques: headlines; subheads; sidebars; boxes; bullets; an inviting typeface; and, of course, images.

3. **Interactive thinking.** Traditional print media have a one-way direction—"here's the word from the author." Much online media aim to foster dialogue, along the lines, "Here's what I think. What do you think?"

4. **Nonlinear nature.** Print documents were traditionally conceived as linear information flows with a beginning, middle and end. On websites most viewers don't start at A and finish at Z. They search for specific information and may never see your home page. So pages should be self-explanatory and may need to repeat information.

5. **"Information packaging" outlook.** Because the digital world offers so much material, to draw and keep people engaged, writers must "chunk" material into short, digestible lumps; find alternate ways to attract attention; and develop interpretive visuals.

6. **Scannability.** Online writing must take account of scanners and divers and robots. We dive for what we need—for example, a product to fix a leaking pipe, a plumber, advice from people who solved a similar problem, or tips for dealing with plumbers. To be found by robots, pages must incorporate well-planned search terms. Once on screen, a page has about six seconds to show the visitor who's scanning it that it's got the goods. Copy must therefore get right to the point without fluff or empty verbiage.

7. **Changeability.** Traditional documents took a long time to prepare, print, and deliver. And then they were unchangeable. Producing a good online document requires time but not so much on the production end. It's highly mutable and can be instantly delivered. Because constant updating is possible, we expect it.

These shifts hold a lot of implications not just for writing but also for basic ideas about communication. One-way communication was the norm through most of history: Those with authority delivered their opinions and orders. Those with products to sell bought the biggest advertising packages they could afford and mass marketed them to us. Talking back to an employer, a company, or government office took enormous resources or pressure from masses of people. Unsurprisingly, individuals and small enterprises were not much heard from.

Websites Level the Playing Field

Today, the barriers to entering either the marketplace or global forum are down, given access to minimal technology. Anyone can be a player—express ideas, create a business, find a new market, organize a cause or a protest. Anyone can present as an authority and weigh in equally with trained journalists, academics and professionals. Millions of businesses are now strictly virtual: no buildings, no offices, no inventory, no on-premise staff. They thrive in proportion to their ability to serve a need, be found by customers, pitch effectively, and deliver—online.

Social critics call it democratization.

Is there a downside to this leveling? It depends on your vantage point. What's certain is that we humans haven't yet caught up with the impact of the digital world we inhabit. And since communication media keep evolving, we won't anytime soon.

So here's the bad news: There are no definitive guidelines to follow for using, and writing for, digital media. And the good news: The fundamental ideas about writing that you're practicing remain as valid as ever, with adaptation. Plus there's plenty of room to experiment with what works for your purposes.

More good news and bad news: Such a tsunami of written material vies for our online attention (including at least 160 million blogs last time I checked) that if you're writing for anyone beyond your mother or best buddy, what you write must be good.

VIEW FROM THE FIELD: HOW PEOPLE READ WEBSITES

Researchers study how people look at websites by tracking their eye movements across a page. They've found a common pattern that's roughly shaped like an *F*: Eyes fix first on the page's upper left area then move right, then scan across the second arm of the *F* and eventually down. Viewer attention wanes as the eye moves toward the bottom and everything "under the fold"—past what appears on the screen before scrolling—is less likely to be viewed. Many professional designers take these habits into account particularly when planning a home page and place the most important element in the upper left area.

More findings:

- Text is usually the reader's entry point, not photographs. Strong headlines draw the eye most effectively, especially when placed upper left.
- Headlines grab attention for less than a second—so the first few words are important. The same is true with sentences.

(Continued)

(Continued)

- People prefer straightforward headlines and single-column text.
- Short paragraphs (one to three sentences) draw twice the attention as long ones.
- Readers don't like generic stock images and images not related to content—they do like bigger images and those with people looking directly at them, but "real" people, not professional models.
- We read up to 25% more slowly on the web than on the printed page—and remember considerably less.

The research is most notably conducted by the Nielsen Norman Group (nngroup.com) and the Poynter Institute (poynter.org); check their sites for a wealth of useful information and updates.

HOW TO PLAN A WEBSITE

Whether you're developing your own website or participating in a team effort, remember that a site needs first to be strategized—in words. Many website developers move too quickly to the technical stage of design and production. Planning is the difference between a good site and an indifferent one. And to plan, use pretty much the same process you use for an e-mail, proposal, or report.

Think About Goals

First define what you want the site to accomplish. Most websites aim to accomplish a number of goals but they should be prioritized. If you have markedly different audiences or product lines one size may not fit all, so you may need more than one site. Many big companies may have different sites for consumers, business to business, or different operations, and more.

Websites accomplish or support a number of basic goals that were once the province of traditional venues. For example, they function to:

- Sell a product or service
- Provide customer support
- Build brand awareness and loyalty
- Attract new employees
- Announce news and build media relationships
- Communicate with investors, board members, government agencies and regulators
- Disseminate information
- Establish credibility

Websites also enable organizations to more easily accomplish goals that were once formidable, such as:

- Interact with and learn from customers
- Create an organizational personality
- Present a unified face to a complex multi-division, multi-location firm
- Unite geographically scattered staff
- Demonstrate social commitment
- Market an individual as an expert, a speaker, or a personality
- Educate relevant audiences

Nonprofit organizations, which must also function as businesses, typically share these goals and add a few—for example, to attract donations and volunteers, recognize these groups, support grant applications and humanize the organization.

You or your firm may have other goals than those listed and some that are more specific.

Put your goals in writing. Prioritize them. This gives you a basic touchstone for decision making through every stage of development. If the site represents a group or organization rather than one person, reach agreement on goals. Consider from the outset how to make at least some goals measurable so you can evaluate how well you're achieving them. Websites offer many more chances to quantify results than print media. You can access data on number of visitors and inquiries, length of visits, preferred pages, ultimate purchases, click-throughs and much more.

Think About Audience

Here's why you simply can't produce a good website without careful audience analysis: Online media work in ways radically different from "legacy media." It's like fishing. A print or television ad casts a wide net to catch all the fish within reach, so you can filter out the particular fish you want, let's say, mackerel. A website, on the other hand, empowers you to specifically attract mackerel and draw them neatly to your net. But this only works if you understand their eating preferences and offer them the right lure—in the case of websites, the right content.

Take account of all the audience analysis guidelines in Chapter 2. You want to decipher what your target audiences want, how you can meet those needs on many levels, the graphic look and tone they will respond to, what interests them, what problems you can solve for them, and how they search for what they want.

Break audiences into segments. For example, if you want to attract money from donors or investors, do you mean people under 35 or elderly millionaires? If you want more media coverage, are you aiming at the trade press, your local newspaper, the *Wall Street Journal,* the *Huffington Post* or industry bloggers?

A good website is not created as an isolated communication product. It should fully integrate with all the organization's other marketing efforts both in what it says and how it looks. Consistency is key to branding for individuals, companies and nonprofits. Whatever marketing channels you use—whether websites, print materials, blogs or social media—aim for a consistent graphic look and style. All should present you, or the organization, in similar ways.

Developing a website is such an intensive process that it often ends up reframing a company's messaging in all other media.

Think About Tone

Defining your goal and audience enables you to choose the appropriate tone of voice. Note that if you ask colleagues to identify the websites they like best, they will often mention idiosyncratic sites that stand out because of their humor, spontaneous feel and edginess. Such sites achieve an individualistic style that at best, embodies the business's nature. But this approach is unlikely to work for an insurance company.

Another caveat to planning an entertaining site: it's hard. It takes talent and usually enormous work over an extended period of time. Be cautious about creating a funny or witty site; it's smart to try it out on members of your intended audience and collect honest opinions.

Fortunately, a solid, effective site can be built with a straightforward tone. In fact, some sites formerly renowned for their cleverness now opt for simplicity. A good site has an objective, reporter-like tone and avoids promotional-sounding rhetoric. Avoid a formal, stilted, abstract spirit, and try instead for friendly, highly accessible, lively and concrete. Make a site welcoming and easy to understand at a glance. Visitors do not like to search a site for the part that interests them, so never force them to figure out how to find it.

Contemporary sites are experimenting with more visual approaches, especially on their home pages. Many product sites—for example, Zappos and Lululemon— feature images of the product categories and visitors click directly on them. This is appealing: Just be sure you have enough words to orient people and allow them to navigate easily.

SITE-BUILDING PRACTICALITIES

Ideally, the process is a push–pull enterprise with other specialists, such as designers and technology experts, whatever the size of your team. If you look at your firm's competitors, you'll find that many of them treat copy as an adjunct to site development. Often the technical side—design, coding, and production—takes center stage. Pieces of copy are picked up from old material to fill the space left for it, or hastily written words are plugged in at the last minute. This guarantees a second-rate site no matter how much effort goes into it.

As writers of course believe and the research bears out, it's the words that matter most. So start with words, but be ready throughout the process to reframe for design and behind-the-scenes needs.

If you're starting a brand-new site, base it on "audience" and "goal." Plan the overall "architecture"—the sequence of pages, basically, and how each page will lead to the next and connect through hyperlinks. Some planners think of this structure as a plant with roots branching out and down in various directions.

Think about how you envision the site "now" and also down the line in the future, whether a month, six months, a year or more. That helps you to build a framework that easily accommodates growth and development.

Even for a blog, you may want a "stable" section of the site that remains basically unchanged. Consider the essentials:

Home Page: Represents full site content and leads to it: Headline, tagline, positioning statement, links to inside content

About Us: Your "story": Who are you? Why do you do what you do? Why are you good at it?

Services or Products: What needs you fill and how what you offer is unique, will make life better

Newsroom: About your company and the industry, media releases

Contact Us: E-mail, telephone, social media as appropriate

Additional useful pages can include Testimonials; Case Histories/Success Stories; FAQs; How to Donate (in the case of nonprofits); sections specific to your organization and industry; and, of course, blogs.

A plan on paper also shows you how the different parts of your site can link and reinforce each other. Even though many viewers may never visit the home page, it should represent and lead to the rest of the content.

Does using a blog format (officially an "online web log") lessen the importance of this kind of planning? Individuals and small businesses may be able to bypass heavy investment by going the blog route with online service sites (such as

WordPress, Wix and Google's Blogger) to create websites geared to interaction and easy updating. Especially if you don't have tech and design team backup, this can be a good approach. But just because a blog site may be easier to get online doesn't mean you can skip planning.

Translating Print Content and Style to Virtual Media

The rule for "body copy" everywhere on the site: never take a piece of print copy and plaster it on your website. The tone will be wrong and so will the writing style. Print pieces are typically much more diffuse and formal than good online writing, which must distill the subject and feel informal.

For example, here is some writing drawn from a business consultant's print brochure.

Executive On Call: Business Counseling When You Need It

Since 1999, Executive on Call has served a distinct niche in the Tanner Region, consulting to the CEOs of small and mid-sized businesses that need knowledgeable advice, a resource of best practices, and a sounding board to advance to the next level. Founder/CEO Ellen Black, who has successfully founded and operated three enterprises, draws on her own extensive experience and works with a team of specialists to help owners develop and align their business mission with strategic vision and goals.

Ellen helps clients reassess the constantly shifting marketplace, reevaluate their working approaches so they don't miss good opportunities, and recognize and strengthen their own resources so they can better focus on the future. Typically, results include a steady 10% annual growth rate.

In a print medium, this copy would come across as reasonably clear and down-to-earth. But online, it would feel empty and rhetorical. Someone looking for a consultant will probably not make it past the first sentence or two. Here are the reasons:

1. There's no instant engagement, an essential of online copy via the headline and/or lead.

2. It fails the speed test. Long, complex sentences, formal wording and a rambling, almost literary tone s-l-o-w it all down.

3. The writing is abstract and altogether lacks a "you" perspective.

4. The copy is dense and uninviting visually; it looks like reading it would be work.

5. The case for the company is not compelling. This is much more obvious on the web, which may be the best comparison-shopping tool ever devised. In former times, a client in search of a service would need to identify suitable resources, request material from each and screen suppliers' qualifications. Now, limitless sources are a click away.

How might the Executive on Call copy be recast for a home page? Here's one way.

Do you need business counseling *now*?

Here are three clues.

- You don't see chances to grow your business
- You feel the marketplace shifting under your feet
- You never have time to focus on reaching the future

If you're a Tanner Region entrepreneur and this hits home, talk to us. We'll show you how to rematch your business to the marketplace and *see a steady 10% growth rate.*

A common problem with online business writing is a dependence on overstatement, jargon, inflated wording, adverbs and adjectives. All these work against you on the Internet. Adopt the writer's axiom, "Show don't tell." Don't make claims—cite evidence.

What if what you can say is radically limited?

Here's some business management About Us copy that annoyed *New York Times* columnist Thomas Frank: "[The mission is to inspire clients] by leveraging our global senior-management experience to ensure optimal, yet realistic and practical solutions."

It was written by a successful consultant accused of being a long-term undercover Russian spy. The problem, Frank said, was that such language is just like that of mainstream American business culture—much of which is "nothing but pretense, a matter of posture and assertion, a grand confidence game with awful consequences."

Naturally, you don't want to go there. But how can you avoid writing such overblown, empty statements if in fact your work is hard to differentiate?

First, try to dig deeper and identify something that makes you unique. Can clients call you at 4:00 in the morning? Do you offer 20% off to first-time buyers? Teach clients how to do part of the work? Provide a community they can join? Before you can communicate your basic business value, you need to have one and know what it is.

Second, write with transparent simplicity. The statement might say,

> We're senior managers who've led global enterprises. Now we help *you* find quick, practical solutions to the problems facing today's CEO.

That may not say much but suggests a way to amplify the idea—the copy might go on to specify the kinds of problems the group helps with. But it's true that sometimes, when you cut the buzzwords, you discover that you're left with . . . nothing. Then, either figure out what you mean to say in simple, clear language, or find something else to talk about.

VIEW FROM THE FIELD: WRITING FOR THE WEB

Online space is different from print: You have seconds to grab people's attention, so you work at three things.

- First, accessibility: Use friendly, warm language; short sentences; and the direct second-person address—you.
- Two, a conversational feel: Personify the brand and the audience, empower the audience to be part of the conversation.
- Three, scannability: short sentences, heads, subheads, lots of white space, line breaking. Distill things into simple principles that are easily grasped.

Don't throw around all those superlatives. It's much more important to demonstrate why something is true. Web copy should also be actionable. Don't just tell readers something, give them the next step and lead them somewhere.

But fundamentally good writing hasn't changed. Web writing is like storytelling and that's not much different from the caveman days—it needs clear sentences, coherence, a structure, a point of view, resonance. Spontaneous-engaging-fun is hard to do but important to strive for. Whatever the subject, if you can clearly say something or even say it with a sense of wit, it's a breath of fresh air.

—Amanda McCormick, founder of Jellybeanboom.com;
social media consultant and web communications specialist

Guidelines for Online Writing

These general guidelines apply to most writing for the virtual world.

Stay short.

- Use simple one- and two-syllable words.
- Write simple, clear sentences without a lot of clauses, averaging 8 to 14 words long. Work in an occasional one-word sentence.
- Keep paragraphs between one to three sentences long, and make a point of keeping some paragraphs to one sentence.
- Keep pages short enough to read with minimal scrolling or at least put what you most want noticed near the top. Otherwise, viewers who don't scroll down past the original screen will miss it.

Stay positive. Keep the tone light and bright and upbeat, unless common sense dictates otherwise (if the company is a funeral home, for example).

Use "inverted pyramid style." Like journalists, put the most important information at the beginning of each page and each copy block. And put the most important words of each headline and sentence on the left. This may mean not using an anecdote to open, unless you're writing a personal blog or the story is very magnetic.

Look through the viewer's eyes. Write in terms of *you* as much as possible. Don't say, "Customers will save hours of time in their account keeping"; better to say, "You'll save hours of accounting time." Framing in the first person rather than the abstract third person will help you more easily achieve the personal, warm tone you want and will lead you to use wording that's more friendly and direct. Also opt for *we* rather than *they*.

Create information "chunks." Small chunks are easily absorbed and remembered. Cognitive psychology research claims that the brain can only remember seven or eight pieces of information at a time, whether words, numbers, sentences or bullet points. Unless you're writing for people who like a lot of long, dense information, break material down into short pieces.

Be specific and concrete. If your company focuses on telecommunications or recruitment, say so, rather than referring to "management services." If your filtration systems are designed for water in hot climates, say so. If you only serve customers in Delaware, say so.

Stick with action verbs. Don't water things down with *will be, can be, should be,* and a passive style. Use strong verbs and nouns to carry the ideas, not adjectives and adverbs that make meaningless claims (*most experienced, amazingly efficient, revolutionary, groundbreaking,* etc.).

> *The road to hell is paved with adverbs.*
>
> —Stephen King

Keep Writing Sayable

A conversational style is especially best for online writing, so test it out by reading it aloud. Be ready to take liberties with conventional English. You don't need formal "literate" statements. Fragments are fine if meaning is clear. You needn't (and shouldn't) say,

> If you're interested in finding out how we at GBH can customize our consulting services to increase your company's telecommunications efficiency, please call us at xxx-xxx-xxxx during business hours.

Better:

Want more efficient phone service? Let's talk. Right now. xxx-xxx-xxxx.

Remember the Scanners and Divers

Include your selected search terms in copy and headlines, and consciously think about what you want viewers to notice. Put the most important information at the beginning of headlines and sentences.

SUCCESS TIP

ON THE WEB, SENTENCE FRAGMENTS WORK

Speed-reading is your goal in writing website copy. Leading sites have steadily evolved to speak more through images (photos, illustrations, video, infographics) and less through words. Language gets tighter and tighter. When I wrote the first edition of this book just a few years ago, General Electric—whose website is considered one of the best-written corporate sites—presented its home page positioning statement this way:

GE IS IMAGINATION AT WORK. From jet engines to power generation, financial services to water processing, and medical imaging to media content, GE people worldwide are dedicated to turning imaginative ideas into leading products and services that help solve some of the world's toughest problems.

More recently, a similar statement appears on the "consumer" home page this way:

GE works on things that matter. The best people and the best technologies taking on the toughest challenges. Finding solutions in energy, health and home, transportation and finance. Building, powering, moving and curing the world. Not just imagining. Doing. GE works.

CREATING A HOME PAGE

The first imperative is to use your six-second time frame to assure visitors who land on your home page that they are in the right place. It helps if your "name" is specific—for example, Hats by Max. If you're entrenched in a less explicit business name, like Max's Head Cases, you need a tagline. Catchy is good. But straightforward is okay too, and often better. For example:

Catchy:

HATS BY MAX

From my hand to your head

Plain vanilla:

HATS BY MAX

Hand-crocheted hats with a high-fashion look

Pictures of the products reinforce the message. Of course, it's harder to telegraph the nature of less tangible services and products. Even if you devise a relevant visual, the words become more important. You need them to clearly identify what your organization is and does and who it serves. It sounds obvious, but a great many websites fail to do this. A tagline should drive straight to the heart of what your organization offers. Consider these:

UPWORTHY

Things That Matter. Pass 'Em On.

LULULEMON

Creating components for people to live longer, healthier, fun lives.

WALMART

We save people money so they can live better.

UBER

Moving people. Tap the button, get picked up in minutes.

A tagline can morph into a positioning statement (aka value proposition):

BASECAMP

Last year alone, Basecamp helped over 285,000 companies finish more than 2,000,000 projects.

Others choose to be opaque—here's an example not to follow:

ALCHEMY API

Alchemy API is democratizing breakthroughs in deep learning to power your unstructured data applications.

A positioning statement is always smart because even if a business is a household name, viewers may be unaware of its size and scope, or relevance to them. A good positioning statement on a website serves a similar function to an in-person "elevator speech": It instantly identifies the individual or organization as clearly and advantageously as possible. Aim for a statement that says the following:

1. What you do

2. Who you help

3. Your main competitive advantage or differentiator

You can start simply . . . .

J&L solves training problems for small businesses. Our psychologists and talent specialists create custom programs that bring key hires up to speed swiftly.

And then play with the ideas and language:

Are you investing too much time and money to train new staff? Our psychologists and talent managers bring your key hires up to speed—fast.

Note that there is a big difference between a positioning statement and the traditional "mission statement"—typically a bland, committee-made sum-up full of clichés and abstractions. If it's your site or you have the power, go for the concrete tagline that speaks to your target audience.

Subheads are important for both graphic and chunking reasons on every site page. Each subhead is a new chance to attract and engage the scanner. They also keep you organized. A number of writers create the subheads first, as a progressive series of statements. Keep them loud and clear. This method forces you to decide what's most important to cover and how to sequence it. Then you fill the copy in, via short, manageable chunks. This helps pull readers through, too.

Website headlines, both on the home page and inside pages, should aim for utmost clarity and be built into the graphics and site architecture. While it's good to consider creating lively headlines using journalism techniques (see Chapter 14), simple labels may serve your purpose well. Groupon, for example, on a particular day, said simply Recommended For You and featured a set of images showing monogrammed fleece sets, limo service, and a few more things superimposed on photos, all clickable. Novica, a site that sources Latin-American crafts, used three different rotating images labeled Ethically Sourced Fashions for Dreamers and Jet-Setters, Shop Now; Global Jewelry, Always Handmade, Always Unique, Shop Now; and At Nova, we live by one simple mantra, Spread Happiness: Learn More.

Use a call to action on all pages. "Buy today!" "Call us now at xxx-xxx-xxxx" or "To find out more ..." "For a peek behind the scenes . . . " Remember that visitors are not viewing your pages sequentially; don't leave them wondering where to go if they want to follow through—lead them. You can also refer them to other parts of your site—for example, "Check out more products you may like" or "Read what our clients say about us." Or lead them to your blog, offer them a newsletter, entice them to take a quiz and so on.

Include clear contact information on every page. You may reserve the opportunity to ask questions or make comments for the Contact Us page, but in line with the self-contained landing page premise, provide this information everywhere. And give visitors real ways to get in touch. It's becoming trendy to provide no e-mail addresses other than "info@" and phone numbers are often omitted. This frustrates people: Why not give them direct e-mail access to key staff members? In any case, using a name is by far preferable to "info." Nobody likes writing to a nonperson. Use a false name if you must—for example, write to Mary White at . . .

Customer service may be time-consuming and problem-prone, but keep in mind that many of the biggest Internet fortunes are built on acing customer service. Think Amazon, Zappos, Groupon and Uber for a start.

VIEW FROM THE FIELD: WHAT'S TOUGH ABOUT WEBSITE WRITING

How do you make web copy good? Get a spontaneous notion on paper, take a deep breath, and go back and do the crafting. Spontaneity is hard to achieve. We've edited some of our website copy 15 or 20 times and have been polishing some of it for 20 years. In an age of e-mail and messaging, the idea of stopping to rewrite tends to disappear.

Web writing is not to be taken lightly: You're writing for two audiences simultaneously: a human one and a robot audience. You can't ignore either one and have to combine the different information needs of both. It's tricky, because you're rewarded for originality but punished for doing the unexpected—because people have expectations about how to find information and get to links. This diminishes the opportunity to be wildly entertaining and creative with a capital *K*.

—Bob Killian, CEO of Killian Branding

Keep Navigation Simple

To make it as easy as you possibly can for people to find their way around your site, use crystal clear rather than subtle directions that are clever or simply attractive. Aim not to confuse someone who might misinterpret a graphic symbol, misunderstand your wording, doesn't speak the language well, or perhaps can't read tiny type. That's a lot of people to alienate!

Menu tabs must be short and snappy and obvious.

While creativity is always a plus, it's best not to fool too much with audience expectations. A page devoted to the services you offer, for example, should usually say "Services," unless there's a reason not to. If you're linking to an About Us page, viewers will know what you mean if you use About or Us, or Who We Are, but it may not pay to go farther afield. A solo entrepreneur, however, might use "Meet Jane," or something of the sort.

Keep Visuals Simple

Remember that your home page is often viewed on a smartphone or other tiny screen. Don't load it up with copy and unrelated visuals.

And avoid totally anything that makes the site slow to come up or delays the viewer's diving and scanning. For most sites this means:

- Keep design simple: no clutter, lots of white space, few colors, few typefaces.
- Don't use visuals that distract or interfere: Skip the music, flash, splash, intro pages, and most animation unless it's important to your story.
- Work to attract and guide the eye.
- Build clear navigation: unmistakable pathways to your content.
- Tighten copy: Edit your message down to the core and then distill it. A rule of thumb is to make online copy half the length of print.

If you want to demonstrate creativity beyond good design and writing, do so "inside" the site so your viewer has a choice about whether or not to go there. The About Us page is a good place to come up with an original approach such as telling your story. See Chapter 14 for ideas on that.

VIEW FROM THE FIELD: GRAPHIC GUIDELINES FOR WEBSITES

Legibility is king: This applies to all online media as well as websites. The most common mistakes: too many fonts, too many colors, too busy.

Clean, simple and well-organized home pages make it easy for users to get where they need to go, quickly. Understand that you cannot overwhelm or bully someone into reading every word on your website. In our attention-deficit world, effective headlines, meaningful graphics, and bite-size chunks of information go a long way.

Use bite-size pieces of information with links to the long-form version of the content. This quickly defines the nature of the content and acts as a trigger to pull a user into your website. (For two brilliant examples, see www.newyorker.com and www.good.is.)

Color: Don't use too many colors. We recommend a limited palette of two or three colors—a handful can do a lot to set a mood or tone. Typographer Robert Bringhurst once wrote, "Typography exists to honor content." This statement rings especially true for web design. The trick is to be objective and honest with yourself. Does bright red type on a camouflage background make it easier or harder for someone to read the content? Obviously, this is an extreme example, but the point is important. We have found light color, heavy type on a dark background works best for short ideas like headlines, while darker text on a lighter background works best for long passages.

A great resource is http://colorexplorer.com.

(Continued)

(Continued)

Typefaces: The more sophisticated and elegant websites use only one or two fonts—and use them well. Remember that what's legible on your 30-inch high-definition monitor might not be on a 14-inch laptop or mobile device. If in doubt, make the size of the body text bigger.

We generally try to match a client's brand style but favor legibility and try to find the closest match based on standardized web-safe font sets that work universally across Mac, PC and mobile devices. A terrific resource for testing font legibility is www.typetester.org.

These font families provide adequate cross-browser compatibility.

Sans serif family: Arial, Verdana, Geneva, Helvetica

Serif family: Georgia, Times New Roman, Times

Monospace family: Courier, Courier New

Also, Google offers a very broad array of free open-source typefaces that will likely provide a "close enough" match to your existing brand standard.

Never, ever use Comic Sans.

Images: Choose images that are relevant to the site's content. Don't steal them! If it's not in the public domain, or a photo you took yourself, or one that you purchased or have the photographer's express consent to use, it is not yours to use.

Scrolling: Avoiding the need to scroll on the home page used to be the rule, but many developers are abandoning simplicity for higher search engine ranking opportunities. Finding a good balance is very subjective.

Professional design goal: Our overarching goal with design is to communicate and build the client's brand in a simple and effective way. This is subjective based on a client's goals and initiatives.

—Christopher Sanna, partner and creative director of Atomic Wash Design Studio (www.atomicwash.com)

BRAINSTORMING CONTENT IDEAS

Do not hoard what seems good for a later place . . . something more will arise for later, something better.

—Annie Dillard, American author

Deliver Your Best

How do you attract "the right people" to your site or blog, keep them there to fulfill their needs (and yours), and bring them back?

There is remarkable agreement among Internet experts on what you need: compelling content. But there is no single answer to what that should be. You have to figure it out based on your goals and audience. With your written priority lists in hand, think about what each of your important audiences wants to know, worries about, finds interesting and will value—*in context of your own goals and information you can share.* There's no point in establishing expertise in motorcycle repair if you're selling cosmetics (at least, not as a central theme; it could make great blog material or help you humanize someone in a profile).

Commit to delivering your best possible ideas, information and advice to the readers you hope to capture. The Internet is an almost unimaginable source of free information. Don't stockpile your expertise; find ways to give it away generously. That's how to succeed on the Internet.

Build on your strengths or your company's. Realistically, many industries limit what can be used in a public forum. Attorneys and management consultants, for example, may not be able to showcase client case studies or demonstrate unique capabilities. Insurance brokers are limited by strict government regulation. A non-profit that helps abused women can't highlight individuals. Schools avoid showing actual students on the Internet.

So it's not always easy to use what might speak for you best. That's where creativity counts.

> *People do not buy goods and services. They buy relations, stories and magic.*
>
> —Seth Godin

Build Content on Strengths

As this chapter stresses, a good website means good content. Design and functionality should support content—they are not ends in themselves, though a great many websites behave as if they are.

The following checklist outlines some of your content choices. Use it as a planning aid if you're working on a new site or revamping one and to identify good opportunities for further development. Beyond these ideas, mine your own industry in depth to come up with ways to attract, engage, intrigue, sell, and help your audience. You want them not just to come but to come back.

Strength	*Content*
Successful track record	Show in • Statistics or data • Video • Images • Charts and graphs • Client testimonials (video or written) • Case studies about how clients were helped or problems solved • Infographics
Good visuals	If you have them and they're relevant, use them BIG.
Staff credentials and achievements	Cite in profiles and news items: awards, honors, publications, speaking engagements, impressive appointments
Staff expertise	Show in • Videos of speaker presentations • Podcasts • Articles, blogs, and white papers
Third-party recognition	Success stories written by other sources, client testimonials
News flow	Releases about the organization, products, leaders, activities, employees, and media coverage in a Media Room section
Thought leadership	Post in-depth papers contributing to the industry, such as • Research • Advice and insights • Trend forecasts
Community and good-cause engagement	Do good things and report on them • Company contributions, donations, leadership • Employee engagement
Good bloggers	Find one or more people to write them regularly—staff members, loyal customers, fans.
Fun and entertaining activities	Devise contests, quizzes, games, sharing opportunities.
Interactive possibilities	Find chances to include a Q&A, discussions, collaborative projects.
"Great man" or "great woman"	When CEO or other team member is a well-known or interesting person, make the most of it.
Giveaways	Such as • Items, including small, "fun" ones • Newsletter subscriptions • White papers • E-books • Free sample services or products
Stories	Know and tell the company story. Scout for inside storytellers—people who can blog about the product or aspects of your service or are able to frame the organization in an interesting way.

STRATEGIES THAT HELP WEBSITES SUCCEED

Take Account of Search Engine Optimization

Because people typically find websites or blogs through search engines, pitching to Google and their competitors has become a high art and a major rationale for SEO services that can be very expensive. Simply speaking, an optimized site is one that ranks high on search engine rankings so that it comes up at or near the top when you're looking for that category of product or service.

Visibility is a big factor for Internet success: a route by which small companies can gain big business and a way for large ones to outmaneuver the competition. Unless you're HTML proficient and understand SEO in depth, you'll likely need help with "front end" and "back end" development to write the coding. But a little knowledge and common sense go a long way.

Today, "long-tail" search terms work best: full five- to seven-word phrases, like "how to write employee e-mails" rather than "writing e-mail." A number of online tools are available (such as Wordtracker and WordStream) to help you select the best search terms. Input a set of search terms to see how many people are using each one and the level of competition. This lets you identify words or phrases that are popular for your category, which you can then narrow it down in some way—for example, according to the type of service, geographic location, key product ingredient or other factor.

"Original content" is the best way to rank well with search engines. While their formulas are very complex and change constantly, they value new material that makes a real informational contribution rather than a self-serving sales pitch. Not unlike people! Useful information can be offered in blogs, articles, research reports, FAQs, Q&A, white papers tips, conference reports and technical material related to your subject. Online newsrooms offer a good way to generate new material (see Chapter 14 for ways to create your own releases).

In considering your own subject, interpret it broadly.

The crocheted hat website might, for example, run material on the history of headwear, how a hat should fit, how these particular hats are made, where the yarn comes from and how that's made, how new styles are developed, an interview with the designer, how to buy a hat for someone else, how to match hats to different outfits, hats around the world.

An accountant's site could include a wide range of material on how to choose an accountant and work with one, keep records, interpret tax forms, understand accounting terminology, handle an audit and so forth. A firm serving large corporations can feature more complex advice on investments, changes in tax regulations and more.

My rule of thumb is build a site for a user not a spider.

—David Naylor, managing director of Bronco,
a digital agency (DavidNaylor.co.uk)

Audience profiling, as detailed in Chapter 2, is the best way to come up with good content. Make a construct of your ideal visitor. Talk to relevant people. Look closely at competitor sites and those in allied fields. Brainstorm the content possibilities—and don't forget you need to produce the material, consistently. Aim to become your audience's best resource.

Search engines also reward content change: This is where many businesses fall short. Unless a static brochure-style site serves your purposes, relentless development matters. It attracts both search engine robots and keeps your visitors coming back. It also helps achieve another SEO priority: "inbound links"—legitimate leads to your site from other sites.

Use your keywords and search terms. Experts advise optimizing for one key term throughout. Place it in your title tags, page descriptions, "metatags," headlines, subheads and body copy. Try to lead left in every case—that is, put the search words first. SEO is one of the subjects most frequently blogged about so it's easy to explore in-depth—but the viewpoints and explanations can be contradictory.

The one universal: Never distort your writing so it reads in an unnatural way. Readers come first, not search engines.

SUCCESS TIP

DO YOUR OWN USABILITY RESEARCH

Surprisingly, the premier group that researches website and other communication tools, Nielsen-Norman, reports that even one site reviewer gives you valuable input on how well your site is working and that six people is ideal. So recruit a few colleagues or acquaintances to explore your site. Watch them work with it, ask what they like and dislike, and pose questions. This simple technique gives you everything you need to improve usability for the price of a coffee.

Treat Company Websites as Cooperative Ventures

Because an organization's website is its most public and universally accessible face, it's typically where every function and operation meet—and often clash. So websites are inherently political. They are prone to whatever pressures various interests can bring to bear. Moreover, to maintain and develop the site, broad buy-in is needed.

So, every element of the organization should be involved in planning and setting guidelines. A steering committee can be created so the process is less unwieldy.

Despite the trouble, team thinking and buy-in is essential to both developing and maintaining a site. These principles apply to Intranet sites as well, of course— as do all the ideas in this chapter.

Think Global: Websites Go Everywhere

The Internet becomes more global every year, as millions in India, China, Latin America, the Arab world and elsewhere expand their access to it. At the same time, opportunities to buy from sites in their own languages are increasing, and it's natural for people to prefer doing so. Thus, if you want to reach an international audience through a website—or think you could benefit from doing so—consider nonnative English speakers in the early planning stage.

Graphics, navigation and writing are all big factors to consider when you're targeting an audience whose main language is not English or want to include such audiences. This is true even as online translation capabilities improve and are used. Writing must be crafted to translate easily.

To launch you on the right track, here are some basics. They should reinforce your commitment to simplicity.

Keep Graphics Simple and Uncluttered

Make navigation as clear and straightforward as you possibly can. Make all your headers unambiguous and don't get too clever; skip subtle graphic devices. Build in plenty of white space.

Keep Wording Especially Simple and Direct

Minimize slang, idioms, clichés and colloquial expressions. Use one- or two-syllable words. Try to avoid abstract words and words that can be misinterpreted. Contractions can confuse; "we have" is better than *we've*. Spell out even commonplace abbreviations like ASAP.

Keep Language Structure Especially Simple

Try to average 10 to 14 words per sentence. Avoid multiple clauses and "there is" and "that is" constructions. Also cut wordy phrasing with many prepositions—for example, rather than "in a position to" (better: *able*); "give a justification for" (better: *justify*). Keep paragraphs one to three sentences; use space between paragraphs and substantial margins.

Try to Be Aware of Cultural Differences

Observe basic differences in how various cultures cite dates, times, numbers, etc. But you must know another culture and its language really well to understand its idioms, attitudes, sensitivities and inside jokes.

If you're aiming to reach a particular language-speaking group, it's wise to have someone from inside the culture review your copy. Remember that a widely used language such as Spanish has many cultures, and there are real differences between a Spanish, Cuban and Argentine audience, for example.

When it's important for the message to reach a global audience effectively, you may want to consult with specialists and use good translation services.

Note that if you're writing for a global institution with facilities in other parts of the world, you're automatically writing for a multiple-language workforce and need to consider cross-cultural guidelines.

Moreover, writing to be understood by nonnative English speakers is similar to writing for the diverse audience that characterizes many U.S. workplaces and the country as a whole.

In general, drill down to the core of your content and be specific and concrete. People with basic English skills will not invest time in finding your important points, so don't bury them in material that doesn't matter or is there just to be clever.

Does writing for international readers mean you'll have to strip the color and make the message duller? Yes, that may be the case. Again, that's why you must really know your goals and priorities. A website aimed at a world audience is necessarily a balancing act.

Here are two resources to use if writing for international audiences and for translation are important to you. Both address print media as well as online.

Edmond H. Weiss, *The Elements of International English Style: A Guide to Writing Correspondence, Reports, Technical Documents, and Internet Pages for a Global Audience*

John R. Kohl, *The Global English Style Guide: Writing Clear, Translatable Documentation for a Global Market*

PRACTICE OPPORTUNITIES

I. "Reading" Websites

Pick a leading organization in the field you want to pursue. Review the organization's website closely and based on what you see, draw up a list of the site's goals and the specific audiences it's designed to reach. How well does it achieve its goals? Do you see missed opportunities to be more valued? Write your analysis as a blog.

II. Plan a Website

Decide on a website you want to produce for yourself, a company or a group. Identify its goals. Then list and prioritize the target audiences. Characterize them in as much detail as you can, referring to the audience criteria covered in Chapter 2 plus additional factors you think relevant to your goal. Also consider whether you want to reach a geographically focused audience or a regional, national or international one. Write a synopsis of your goals, an audience profile, a content list, and a graphic plan for the home page.

III. Group Project: Build a Website for a Good Cause

Plan a website for the charitable cause you invented for Practice Opportunity II in Chapter 10—Build a Project Proposal. Collaborate on draft copy for the home page, including all necessary tabs and heads. Share the result with another group and evaluate its website plan; provide a helpful written critique to the other group.

IV. Group Project: Evaluate and Compare

As a small group, select three firms in any field of interest and in detail, compare and evaluate their websites. Look critically at the overall site plan, home page, content, writing, design and visuals, and navigation. Are the site's overall goals clear? Can you define the targeted audiences? Do you see any missed opportunities? Use your evaluations to come up with a list of criteria for websites in general that the whole group agrees with.

Discuss: All groups share their criteria lists with the rest of the class. How are the lists the same? Different? Assemble one full list that the class concurs with.

V. Evaluate Foreign Language Sites

Do online research to identify websites of overseas organizations that use the language you studied in school or gained a basic knowledge of for some other reason. Pick three websites in that language. How easy are they to understand and use? What presents the biggest barriers? Which work better for you and why? Compile a written list, and share it with the class or in small groups; together, assemble a list of dos and don'ts for international websites that validates and extends the guidelines given here (or disagrees with them).

VI. Build Your Own

Write a home page for your own website. See it as an element of your next job search or for a business you'd like to operate. First, spell out (in writing) your goal, audience, selected tone and proposed content. Create a basic plan for the words, graphics and architecture of the site.

VII. Turn Print Copy Into Website Copy

Select a piece of marketing-style material from your own work or something you come across anywhere else—a brochure, flyer, newspaper article, and so on. Translate the writing into web-style writing, and format it to read well.

Chapter 12

Business Meets the Interactive World

Leveraging Internet Opportunities

LEARN HOW TO . . .

- Understand how business sees social media
- Use social media strategically
- Write blogs and comments
- Create online profiles
- Use micromedia for business

Have something to say, and say it as clearly as you can. That is the only secret.

—Matthew Arnold, 19th-century philosopher

"Content is king": That's the new mantra—I even have it on a coffee mug. But what is content?

Content is all the information an organization publishes and distributes electronically via websites, blogs, social media platforms and e-mail. Content connects businesses with customers and builds trust. It's the basis of "permission marketing," which means giving people what they want so they welcome what you send, and come to you for more. Older marketing techniques—print advertising, commercials, telemarketing—are far more expensive. And their impact is more scattershot, compared to the narrow audience targeting and tracking that's commonplace with digital channels. So no wonder organizations of every type want to seize the opportunities.

But here's the price: Websites, blogs and social media call for a humongous amount of writing. Content includes images of every kind, video, presentations and podcasts. Still, at heart, it's all about writing. And content doesn't attract readers unless it's good, relevant, valuable and new. Never before has there been such an appetite for good writing. And the media platforms keep expanding. New tools materialize and new technology shifts what's possible. It's like watching the tide come in, go out, and come back in on a new wave. So what can be usefully communicated about writing for this world?

Quite a lot, actually. There are three reasons.

First, as the most sophisticated social media users will tell you, the new platforms are basically different ways to distribute information and move people to thought or action. Only the speed is different. The tools may be new to the communication arsenal but the same principles frame their use.

Second, even though you may be a "native" user of interactive media and find it as natural as talking, you may not have thought about its use for strategic business or career purposes. This requires a different mind-set than using sites for pure social networking.

And third, if you do want to use online channels to promote your career in any way, whether as a job seeker, employee, consultant or business owner, you'll find that the field is crowded and competitive. So much good stuff is given away for free that it isn't easy to engage audiences with your message. It takes your best thinking and writing skills. And standards for thinking and writing have essentially not changed and will not change.

Because the e-media evolve so fast, use the guidelines in this chapter with extra imagination. A particular venue may have been outdated by a newbie when you read this, but the principles show you how to handle whatever may come.

HOW BUSINESS SEES SOCIAL MEDIA

Asked back in the 1930s why he robbed banks, Willie Sutton said, "Because that's where the money is." Today's smart businesses might say that they invest in online communication because that's where the people are.

If social media are a natural part of your life, step back for a minute to view this revolution in a broader context. Never before has there been a way to instantly connect with so many people at once, find a community or create a following. The possibilities are turning corporate communications and marketing upside down, not to mention politics, government, and information industries. But for many people in power positions, entrenched in traditional media, accepting the power of digital media has been a struggle.

Today, online communication is creating a culture in which trusted opinions come not from professional reviewers, critics and other authority figures but from peers and credible strangers. This makes selling a whole new game.

Businesses see the Internet as a chance to raise their profiles and build their brand, and also, a new way to listen to customers and engage in dialogues that help them improve their marketing and products. They use blogs and social media to announce new services and events and build communities around their product. Nonprofits add social media to the mix for communication, fund-raising and volunteer recruitment.

Organizations (and governments) have also learned that displeased consumers or ordinary citizens can now generate not just a complaint but a mass protest or boycott—without hiring a lawyer or spending a penny.

Corporate communicators used to talk about generating good media relations so when a crisis arose, the company had a solid base with which to manage public opinion. Today, companies find that a sturdy social media network must be in place not only to proactively influence the public but as a defense mechanism so they are ready to respond to problems.

Beyond all this, the big draw of digital tools for savvy organizations is their popularity. People of all ages are embracing digital media in their everyday work and personal life. And businesspeople know that social channels are key to how Millennials relate to the world. Social media represent current or future customers, potential recruits, an increasingly influential public, new donors and much more. Even business leaders who dislike social media are finding that they must go there because that's where the people are, and the money, too.

The online world is transforming business communications. But the basic communication tool kit has not changed. Writing remains the most important ingredient of success.

When you're competing with the whole world, your best strategies are good planning and good writing. All the skills you build for traditional media and e-mail will work for you here, with some adaptation.

USING ONLINE MEDIA STRATEGICALLY

It's important to remember that while social media are incredibly effective for distribution and engagement, it's just another tool in your marketing and communications tool bag. I get excited about new technologies because the possibilities for engaging supporters increase exponentially. But what always matters most is having a powerful story that you can share in an authentic way.

—James Wu, senior strategist at
SY Partners, formerly with Acumen Fund

1. Adopt a Business Mind-Set for Your Own Blogging and Social Media Interaction

They're your best tools for future jobs, professional connections and reputation building. Use them thoughtfully and strategically.

One corollary is to start your reputation management now. Every time you pursue an opportunity, assume the person who can bestow it will check out everything that he can find about you—and by you—online. And it will all be found—you cannot protect your privacy when you post blogs, text, pictures, video, tweets or whatever. Police what other people are saying about you or posting, too.

Another corollary: Never use online channels for negative commentary. Personal opinions are fine, and of course you can critique a product or company, but don't personalize it: you'll create enemies *and* undermine your own credibility. Beware of using social media power to embarrass or poke fun at anyone, too: It carries consequences.

2. Build in the Interaction

Social media by definition is the opposite of traditional one-way communication. Aim not to give lectures or perform in a vacuum. Expect, feed and encourage audience participation. Don't just ask for reader opinions—work at presenting ideas or information in ways that entice a response. Ask thoughtful questions, request opinions and input, share an idea that's a bit edgy or controversial. And follow up with responses so the conversation doesn't fade away sooner than it might.

3. Foster Relationships

Just like in the face-to-face world, building online relationships takes time. Don't expect to post a comment or blog and become an overnight sensation. The online world is already heavily populated.

Notice how children make friends or join a social circle: They'll watch a group from the sidelines for a while, feeling things out by observing the interaction and rules of the game. Then they'll "kibbitz" a little—make comments about the action. Eventually they feel comfortable asking to join the play.

Research the relevant blogs, groups and content communities and dig in. See what people talk about and what concerns them. Contribute thoughtful comments. Ask questions, start conversations, follow what others say and continue to contribute. Absorb the culture and you'll start to see what it values, where the gaps are, what you might contribute.

4. Create a Plan

Some experienced users believe that new media have no real rules yet and that it's best to just plunge in and find out what works. The drawback—trial and error is expensive. Better: Think strategically, like a business.

Who do you want to build relationships with and why? Do you want to expand your social or professional circles? Find people with similar interests, or potential customers? Interest prospective employers? Sell something? Be recognized for your good ideas and opinions?

You can choose to see your blogs or Facebook posts as purely personal, in which case you could define the goal as, "to keep up with friends." That's fine and so is seeing a blog or social posts as contributions to the universe of knowledge or a narrower sphere of professional or personal interests. In fact, the Internet is fueled by generosity. Writing about something you're passionate about without expecting a return on the investment suits that spirit.

But if you view your online life professionally—in terms of business and career—define what you want to achieve and the audience you want to reach. It will lead you to choose what you write about and where you post it strategically, rather than randomly. Online media can be intensely time-consuming, so knowing how to invest your energy matters.

5. Choose Your Media

Based on your current goals, choose to be active on sites that align with them: social networking sites, professional networking sites like LinkedIn and the European XING, a host of focused sites for industries and specialists, and/or microblog sites like Twitter. The lines are of course blurry since business and individuals alike use all of these sites, as well as Pinterest, Instagram, Second Life, and many more. You can have separate accounts on such sites but don't consider a personal one totally private, whatever the settings options.

VIEW FROM THE FIELD: HOW TO LAUNCH A STRATEGIC SM CAMPAIGN

People start at the wrong end, with the tools—it's like asking how do I use this hammer or screwdriver? They jump on the tools instead of what they're trying to accomplish. Before leaping into social media, conduct a social media marketing audit. Know your objective and who you want to connect with. Then ask, where do these people participate? First listen—people don't listen enough.

Start there; learn what this community you're building or joining is looking for. Next think about what you want to share and how and whether the content is in sharable form so you can go viral. If you can identify information gaps and fill those, you'll quickly and naturally gain a standing in that community and a following. It's good to work to a theme; chunk your content down. If your resources are limited, limit your scope so you can make a solid effort.

—Arthur Germain, principal and chief
brandteller of Communication Strategy Group

You might scout for sites and discussion groups of like-minded people, look for competitors' sites to see what they're saying and doing, and identify sites your target market frequents. If you're a graphic designer who wants to share ideas and problems, for example, you could join an online community of design professionals, assess your competition and find collaborators, and/or build a presence among potential buyers—business owners, communicators or editors.

Beyond showing you how to invest your time, using social media strategically lets you mesh it with all your other marketing efforts and build your personal brand so that the whole adds up to more than the parts.

6. Provide Solid Substance

There is no "content" without "substance." On the Internet, faking it doesn't make it. Offer something genuinely useful. Where does substance come from? Canvass your own resources. What do you know that's worth sharing?

If you can write a how-to piece about anything at all, you probably have a great blog or article subject or source of tweets. If you've identified a problem that bedevils many of your clients, customers or colleagues and can offer even a partial solution, write about it. If something piques your interest and you want to know more, do some research, report on it and invite reader input. If you have a story to tell that will make people laugh, or feel good, or think, write it.

People particularly look for leads to valuable material they don't run across themselves. With so much out there, it takes many eyes to find the gems. So sharing discoveries ("curating") is an excellent way to build your own online presence, whether you're blogging or tweeting.

7. Soft Sell the Commercial

When your purpose is to promote a product or service, or yourself, never make it blatant. Suppose you're an accountant blogging about an unusual tax loophole. Devoting a big chunk of content to your firm and its greatness would turn off most readers—and what's more, it isn't necessary.

Your material should establish your expertise and authority. All you need beyond that is a clear tagline identifying who you are; how to reach you; and, perhaps, the kind of clients your business serves and/or its range of services.

There are also times when your new product, or a solution to a problem, is what you're writing about. This is fine as long as it's audience relevant, but don't let empty hype creep in. Give content with value. With so much to choose from, online readers steer clear of everything that seems self-serving.

SUCCESS TIP

THE SOCIAL MEDIA ADVANTAGE

Social media know-how is valued by most employers today, so putting these skills up front in your résumé and for interviews is smart. *But* employers need people who are prepared to use media in context of marketing, public relations and branding, not as an end in itself. There's a trend to move away from hiring social media specialists. If you can offer a broad perspective on using social media to accomplish business goals, based on your education or work experience, do so. Research how the organization is currently using social media against its goals and what you would recommend *if asked*; don't take the initiative on this.

8. Respond to People Who Connect With You

It's smart to thank people who follow you, favorite a tweet, comment on your blog or share your content. To build a role in a community or connect with someone, keep the conversation going. Here's how Chris Brogan, one of the most popular social media presences and a business consultant, e-mailed me when I signed up for a newsletter:

Subject: So Glad You Signed Up

Hi Natalie—I wanted to thank you again for signing up to my newsletter. I'm sending this out to just help you get the lay of the land, and to check a few things.

He goes on to say I can ask him not to use my first name if I prefer; that he will personally answer every communication; that he has more free material; and, ultimately, that I can take his courses at a discount. And he'll check back to see how I like the newsletter in nine days.

The close: *Thanks for signing up. It means the world to me!—Chris*

There's no fancy design, just a plain vanilla e-mail—but impressive.

BLOGGING: HOW TO GENERATE IDEAS, WRITE FOR THE MEDIUM, ENGAGE READERS

> *One of the exciting things about the Internet is that anyone with a PC and a modem can publish whatever content they can create.*
>
> —Bill Gates, in a 1996 essay

In the olden days, to reach a substantial audience with information and ideas you'd write an article. The process could take a year—to research, pitch, interact with an editor, draft, revise and so on.

While some publishing still works that way—notably newsstand magazines and many professional journals—today anyone can be a published author. There's no gatekeeper or editor to block your voice or demand that you meet her standards.

In 10 minutes, you can write and post a blog (or an article) on someone else's site or a discussion forum. If you want your own blog site, it is easy to set up at little or no cost. Then you become your own publisher as well.

There's a catch: To succeed, you must perform most of the editorial functions yourself—choose a good topic; angle it right for the audience; and write, edit, and proofread. That's a lot of responsibility!

And it takes real time, considering that you typically need to blog at least once every week to keep people steadily engaged. If you're blogging for yourself, consider how much time you're able to commit. If you're working for a larger entity, scout for resources beyond your own to multiply what you can handle.

There are many ways to go about blogging. For example:

1. Present yourself as a person with a unique viewpoint, whose ideas, opinions and responses to experience are worth reading about because they're interesting, insightful, inspiring, entertaining, and so on.

2. Offer valuable information and insights about a specific subject or field based on your own knowledge or access.

3. Write about something that provokes your curiosity and start a conversation.

4. Relay someone else's ideas or information, and add your own commentary.

Widely read bloggers typically do all this and more. But creating an online personality can take talent plus trial-and-error experience. The best starting point and one you can count on is to provide useful information.

Generating Conversation

To sustain a blog, you need to constantly generate subjects to write about. Start, of course, by inventorying what you can share, and divide your expertise into narrow pieces.

Take an accountant, for example. She could break her expertise down into a great many absorbable pieces, such as how to prepare for an audit, choose an accountant or work with one, take advantage of tax loopholes, revamp a financial system and so on. Each of these subjects can be further broken down—for example, organizing your papers for an audit, what to say to the auditor, what not to say, and should you bring your accountant with you?

She could also blog about

- how a movie presented an outdated view of the profession,
- how she solved a problem that readers experience,
- a conference that covered the impact of new tax laws,
- a challenge the profession is facing,
- a professional view of a relevant court case or issue in the news,
- common mistakes people make on their tax returns, and
- how to evaluate your accountant's service.

And/or, if she chooses, she can write about a passionate hobby, an interesting experience or an inspiring book. In fact, many bloggers-for-business deliberately choose to concentrate on a hobby or pastime, rather than the work itself, because of the relationship-building factor.

If a company seeks to cultivate clients in its local area, for example, it may showcase employees' off-hour activities rather than sticking to business. Some large multinationals encourage employees to blog about personal passions because this provides humanizing connections.

So, choose subject matter that relates to your goals in a broad way.

Notice that most of the ideas on the accountant's subject list translate to many professions. If you're a business student right now and define that as your profession, you can come up with a similar list of knowledge areas and viewpoints worth sharing—for example, the impact of a brand new tax law that you learned about, an interesting celebrity lecture, an observation on effective teaching methods and so on.

In your work as a student, you may look at cutting-edge research, interesting statistics, trends, big-picture thinking and insights on current problems or legislation that will affect businesspeople. Or you may engage in debates or conversations about ethical issues. People in the workforce rarely have time to keep up with such subjects and might like to read about them.

And, of course, you can choose to blog about your passionate hobby, fitness program, travel, experience living on $50 per week, whatever. Never think your own present world is not a potential gold mine for sharing and conversation with people even beyond your peers. It just takes some thinking.

If you need help with that thinking, the Internet is crammed with information, ideas and advice on developing content. Here's a fun resource to generate ideas when you're out of steam: Portent (www.portent.com/tools/title-maker). Enter your general subject and the generator instantly comes up with promising titles. I entered "business writing," and Portent suggested: What Mom Never told You About Business Writing; Why Business Writing Should Be 1 of the 7 Deadly Sins; 20 Ways Business Writing Can Find You the Love of Your Life; How Better Business Writing Changes How We Think About Death. And, the titles come with funny comments on why they work.

A similar resource is offered by Hubspot (www.hubspot.com/blog-topic-generator). Here, "business writing" brought me The Worst Advice We've Ever Heard About Business Writing; 10 Signs You Should Invest in Writing; and Why We Love Communication Problems (And You Should Too!)

VIEW FROM THE FIELD: HOW A PUBLIC RELATIONS PROFESSIONAL BLOGS

When I write a blog, I write it as if I'm talking to somebody. I want readers to open up, trust me, feel they can have a conversation with me. Unlike an article, a blog is not structured and analytical, it's looser and more conversational. I'd say you should blog the way you speak. But make sure the blog represents you in a positive way. Try to avoid using slang. Also, make sure there are no grammatical or spelling errors.

I write about what I'm involved in, like running...business situations...things I find funny, an unusual experience. I make it personal. You're trying to build a relationship with the people in your community, really get to know them, and hope it leads to business. Eventually it does.

—Hilary JM Topper, president and CEO of HJMT Communications

Whatever you write about, remember your audience and aim to come across as the person you are. You can't build relationships by sounding like a research journal. Some excellent bloggers invent another persona because they find this frees them psychologically to be more original or forceful.

If you're blogging for professional purposes, remember that consistency helps. People like knowing what they'll find if they return to a site repeatedly. It may be ineffective to present as a motorcycle repair expert one week and an insurance salesman the next, because you're bound to disappoint one audience or the other.

The challenge is to figure out how to keep mining your general subject so you have something fresh to say regularly.

SUCCESS TIP

DIFFERENT RULES WHEN YOU BLOG FOR YOUR COMPANY

When you blog or handle social media for an employer, the "be yourself" advice applies less or not at all. As a voice for the company, you must use a style and choose subject matter that reflect the organization's culture. You must understand company goals and challenges and be familiar with its overall marketing strategies. Welcome opportunities to work closely with people in marketing and PR because blogs and social media don't work well in a vacuum.

Writing Tips for Blogs

The Internet compels us to streamline our ideas and shorten our discussions.

—Frank J. Pietrucha, "Homage to Simplicity"
in *Communication World,* International
Association of Business Communicators

If you're writing a "me" blog—and your real subject is your opinions, ideas, experience and/or reactions to life around you—you're working in a creative realm. There are few guidelines for how to be an interesting person. Should your natural writing style work beautifully for this medium and you draw good responses, go for it.

The tips in this chapter are geared more to informational blogging—posts that share concrete advice on a subject of choice—because this is a more practical kind of writing for most people. It's also a good career-building strategy that helps establish professional authority.

But whichever way you go, remember the old question: If a tree falls in the forest and nobody hears it, is there a sound? The corollary—if you can't articulate an idea in a way that other people understand, does the idea really exist?

The point: Many of the tips also apply to personal-expression-type blogs and can help your writing work better. They also apply to writing articles for both print and online media, meaning more formal, carefully structured pieces in the tradition of journalism.

First things first: Create your written plan. State the goals in detail, including, for example, to connect with potential customers, improve company image, back up job applications and attract readers to your website. And profile the audience, as described in Chapter 2. Brainstorm at least 20 headlines for subjects you believe will interest your audience. This prevents you from scratching your head every few days and failing to post new material.

Start posts with strong headlines. Think carefully about how to engage your target audience. You need a strong descriptive headline that tells viewers instantly what's in it for them. Here are a few I saw and liked recently.

What to Do When You're Shtickless: How to Add Humor to Presentations

How the U.S. Army Uses Social Media

New Twitter Analytics Tool Helps You Decide Whom to Follow

Tips to Topple Procrastination

Why a Bad Memory's Not Such a Bad Thing

You may or may not be drawn to read these pieces. But if you have any interest at all in the subject, the headline is, well, a head start. For the writer, creating a headline that targets the reader is often a very good way to frame and organize content.

Numbers are especially effective for blog headlines and articles and give you an almost automatic way to organize what follows. Some examples:

The 5 Biggest Reasons People Get Depressed

8 Incredibly Simple Ways to Get More People to Read Your Content

Six Ways to Change People's Minds—and Make Them Like It

17 Quick Wins to Boost Your Social Media Marketing Right Away

Focusing on people's "pain"—what they fear or worry about—is also a great technique for choosing subjects and waving that headline flag:

Want to Foil "Shrinkage"? Here's Nine Easy Ways

How to Turn Workplace Obstacles Into Miraculous Wins

Three Ways to Turn a Monster Boss Into a Booster

How to Say "No" to a Contractor and Keep the Door Open

Secrets of an IRS Insider: How to Prevent an Audit

Notice that many of these sample headlines tend toward some drama or exaggeration and are heavy on the adjectives. For blogs, this tone works better than understatement. Questions are good—and so is hinting that you will share "secrets," or something new or surprising.

But don't shortchange your readers: Give them what you promise—practical advice they can put to work or ideas to stimulate their thinking.

Research on what works on the Internet is overwhelmingly available. For headlines, the general advice is to write up to 65 characters, including spaces. And use your keywords as early as you can.

Craft an engaging lead. Once you've hooked your readers with the headline, keep them with you by starting strong. One way is to start with a question. Or connect the reader directly to the problem you're more or less solving for them. For example, a lead for the piece on "Three Ways to Turn a Monster Boss Into a Booster" might read,

Do you have a critical, carping boss? Nothing makes life more miserable than a supervisor who's always waiting to pounce on your mistakes. If you assume that grin and bear it is your only option, it ain't necessarily so. Here are three approaches that can turn the situation around almost overnight.

Another good tack is to use an anecdote, your own or someone else's, to make an instant connection. For example, "How to Say No to a Contractor—and Keep the Door Open" could lead,

Have you ever rejected a supplier or contractor, and then found out you made a mistake because the guy you did hire screwed up?

It happened to me last week. The job seemed simple enough . . .

But keep the stories short. Many blog readers are impatient and want to get to the crux quickly.

Write clearly and to the point. Once you've pulled readers in, keep them with you by crafting well-written material that makes sense, sticks to the point and moves quickly. If you've promised six tips, deliver them. Some ways to write tight:

1. Use the short, basic, unpretentious words as much as you can plus lively verbs. Keep your average sentence short: 12 to 18 words.

2. Keep paragraphs short: generally one to three sentences. Use some single-sentence paragraphs.

3. Write simple sentences that make meaning clear and trim structures that require words ending in *-ing, is,* and *are* phrasing and lots of words like *to* and *of.*

4. Build in subheads both for your own sake and readers'. Writing a set of sequential subheads first is an approach that works very well for writing blogs. Bullets and numbered lists are useful.

5. Use transitions to clarify how sentences and paragraphs connect to support comprehension and make yours more convincing.

6. Decide on length. Just recently, general advice was to write shortish blogs, in the 350- to 600-word range. But research shows that across most industries, long posts pull many more readers. Some studies document that blogs 2,500 words or longer generate many more shares than shorter ones. Are they read from beginning to end? Maybe not, though in-depth treatment of a subject does lead people to save such posts as well as share them. Still, some of the most popular bloggers choose to write short. Therefore, choose the length you're comfortable with and that makes sense for your subject and time constraints.

7. Consider graphic impact. Including meaningful images, video, or infographics, the research proves, vastly increases a post's chances of being opened and shared. For all material, build in plenty of white space, and avoid very wide columns that discourage reading.

8. Edit, edit, edit. Cut every unnecessary idea and word. Say things as tightly and simply as you can. Skip the empty hyperbole, jargon, and buzzwords. Use the say-it-aloud test. In other words, apply all the techniques described in Part I.

9. Proof, proof, proof. I bet that if you look at your favorite blogs, you'll find virtually no grammatical or spelling errors. If you want to get respect, be correct—but don't sound stiff and formal.

10. Link, link, link. Enrich what you offer by linking to other online material, yours or other people's, that offer more dimensions of a subject or support your point. Demonstrating that you know what's out there besides your own viewpoint makes you more credible. But don't weigh your post down with so many links that readers are distracted.

VIEW FROM THE FIELD: CHOOSING YOUR SOCIAL MEDIA WORDS

Think twice before you speak once—that's incredibly important. Does it fit with your message, your image? Try to keep the message consistent, and stay in context of your online persona.

Your writing must be clear and concise so people don't misconstrue what you say—they'll read into it and interpret, which is a big problem online. So write unambiguously. Keep away from sarcasm; many people don't get it. Never write when you're angry or impassioned. No vulgarity: It damages your credibility completely.

Use terminology that promotes your expertise and makes your message searchable by interjecting keywords, like for SEO. I keep a list of the top words I want to include handy. Also, you can check out what you write with a word cloud [e.g., via www.wordle.net] so you can look at a visual of your message and see what words you used the most.

—Bill Corbett, president of Corbett Public Relations

Techniques to Engage Readers

It sounds contradictory, but pay attention to all these guidelines and sound spontaneous. A warm, friendly, easy-flowing style engages readers. But just as with websites, spontaneity can take work.

To get the right tone, practice the tools of informality. Sentence fragments are fine as long as meaning is clear. Starting sentences with *and* and *but* and *because* works well; forget the elementary school grammar lessons. Contractions are better than formal versions—such as *can't* rather than *cannot*. Try for a conversational tone. And frame what you write with *you* wording and thinking. For example:

Is Blogging For You?

Answering Three Simple Questions Tells You

Here's how to decide whether to make blogging part of your life.

First ask yourself, **"What's in it for me?"** What will you gain professionally, or how can your business benefit? Be specific. Strategic blogging has accomplished miracles for many people, and maybe it will for you, too.

Your second question: **"What's in it for them?"**—meaning the readers you want to write for. Figure out what you know that's worth sharing—it's probably a lot more than you think. Try writing a list of subject ideas and see if that inspires you.

And third, consider **"How much time can I give it?"** No question, it takes time to produce blogs that are useful, interesting and well written. So besides answering the practical questions, think about whether blogging would be fun or satisfying. Whether it could lead you in new directions. And whether it could help you build new relationships.

If you do want to plunge ahead, **here's a starting point** I know works....

Seek to involve readers directly **by planning interactive elements from the outset.** Posing questions is a good technique and gives you an excellent way to end a blog post. The blog about handling monster bosses might, for example, conclude:

What about you? Have you worked for a critical boss and tried a technique for improving the relationship? Did it make things better? Or worse? Share your experience!

As you dig into social media and connect with the communities you relate to, add bloggers you like to your personal list and check them out regularly. And review their posts analytically: What works well? What can you learn? Most professional writers have a shortlist (or a long list) of other writers they admire not because they want to imitate them but because they find their work inspirational.

Posting Good Comments

Posting good comments can open many doors for you.

It's a good way to introduce yourself to a community. And it's a strategy that, more and more, attracts the interest of employers.

To do it well, have something real to contribute. You might begin by connecting immediately with what you're responding to; preferably say something positive, then move into what you want to add to the conversation. For example:

Thanks for your suggestions on how to avoid an audit—you've created a great checklist for entrepreneurs to use when preparing their taxes. I'd like to add one more idea, which came to me the hard way, in the course of being audited.

If actually you disagree with all or some of the blogger's post, still begin politely; it will make you more credible.

Thanks for your suggestions on how to avoid an audit. It's a useful checklist for entrepreneurs and I agree with most of the points. However, I've learned something the hard way—through being audited—that gives me a better way to avoid questions on paperwork.

Then present your experience, idea or comment concisely—a paragraph is often enough. Between 100 and 300 words is "average." But again, know your audience and the medium. If you're contributing to a political blog that boasts a well-informed readership and comments run 1,200 words, then write on—provided you have the substance.

A plus: Commenting on what other people in your field say links you directly to your business competitors, who are part of the community that interests you. Here too, the Internet is shifting how we look at relationships. Today smart people in every profession share far more information than people were accustomed to a decade ago, and they benefit through collaborations and referrals.

VIEW FROM THE FIELD: HOW TO GENERATE AN ONLINE CONVERSATION

Search by keywords for people who are interested in what you're interested in, read them, see what they think, go in with a how-can-I-help-you attitude. A community is about a purpose, a shared passion, maybe a vision of a better future or something everyone can believe in and get on board with. Once you see what the culture is like, add value. Start conversations. Ask curiosity-based questions, which are often better conversation starters than statements. A question can relate to the topic or culture of the group, it can pique people's interest and beg for a response. It can help promote your interests, too.

For example, I asked on LinkedIn, "What comes up when you Google your name or brand?" A few people responded in ways that made it clear they were open to help that I was able to give without selling. I've asked, "What impact has SEO had on your business?" This is a much-misunderstood subject and the question opened up revealing dialogues. I've also asked, "What is the worst or funniest experience you've had on a website?" I heard from angry, frustrated people, and it helped my own knowledge base—and ability to deal with clients.

—Jerry Allocca, founder of CORE Interactive
(www.coreinteractive.com); author of *Connected Culture*

As with all Internet communication, be careful not to come across as self-interested or grinding a personal ax of any kind. If you're commenting on the "avoid an audit" example and you're a CPA, identify yourself as such in the signature or in the body of the post; say at most something like, "As a CPA of seven years' experience, I'd like to point out..."

If your comment looks like a self-promoting commercial, people will probably never read it at all.

THE ONLINE PROFILE: YOU ARE WHAT YOU WRITE

Presenting your credentials well online can make a big difference in how you're perceived by employers, clients, prospects, collaborators and everyone else. This is a relatively new challenge, so there are no set guidelines for writing a good profile—which is quite different from a résumé. If you scan self-descriptions even of well-known individuals, you'll find a very wide range in content, style and level of detail. Many are minimalist.

If you stand to gain by making professional connections, then online profiles, particularly for LinkedIn, are worth a lot. For one thing, almost universally, employers will check out your profile and take it seriously as part of your job application (so beware of contradicting your "official résumé"). LinkedIn has evolved into a premier international venue for industry networking, recruitment, business development and personal branding.

When you share updates, tweets and articles on LinkedIn, or people look for you, your profile backs you up. So make a good first impression. Start with a good headshot. Use a job title if you're employed (the organization might be offended if you present yourself as independent) or a headline that sums up who you are and what you do. You have 180 characters for this.

Employers and other site users expect to find more insight into your personality and way of looking at things than your official résumé affords. A good summary aligns with your overall social media strategy. And like a résumé, it should tilt toward the future—where you want to go—using your past as the platform.

As always when communicating, review your goal: to support your general networking? Job hunting? Prospecting for clients, customers, or people to work with? Will you use the profile to back up your in-person contacts or e-mail approaches? An online profile gives you a chance to reverse the old equation: Instead of hunting for promising contacts, you may succeed in drawing them to you.

Where to start? Your own background gives you the best clues. Explore what energizes you, motivates you, gives you the biggest rewards, and makes you happiest and proudest.

VIEW FROM THE FIELD: PUT YOUR PROFILE TO WORK

My core message to clients is that an Internet presence gives small businesses and individuals the same tools that once would have been the playground of very large companies.

One important way to use the power behind it is to flesh out your online profile: The more you can keep it pointing at your expertise and intelligence and can get recognized as an expert at what you do, someone who is a knowledgeable information resource, the better. So make a concerted effort to update your status. Link to blogs you've written, note if you're giving a speech or win an award, or tweet—everything counts.

—Adrian Miller, CEO of Adrian Miller
Sales Training; founder of Adrian's Network

Here are some concrete ideas to draw on.

Frame it in *I.* First person helps you share who you are with more genuine feeling and warmth and feels more authentic than talking about yourself in the third person. If you think it's more professional to use the third person for LinkedIn and other business networking sites, try writing it in first person anyway, then translate it into *he* or *she*. It will pick up more life that way. Scout the profiles of people who interest you to see how they present themselves.

Write with a clear sense of what you want. Take account of both immediate and long-range goals—perhaps who you want to work for, the kind of people you'd like to connect with, what you want to learn. Your content, focus and style will help you achieve your goals if you are clear on them yourself. Notice how good profiles make what the people want very explicit.

Position yourself quickly with a strong summary. If you have a career job, start with what it is and what you do—your employer expects this. But this is also the place to tell your story in a human way—see Chapter 13 for ideas on how to develop that story. Go way beyond résumé-speak and talk about why you chose your work or what you like about it, for starters.

Here's one example:

As a customer service trainer, I love showing managers how to improve customers' experience and turn them into raving fans. Drawing on all my background as . . .

Show your passion, or at least enthusiasm, for your work (or the work you plan to do). You don't necessarily have to say, "I love what I do," but you can build in a bit of *why* you love it and what led you to it, and why it's satisfying. You can also try statements that start out with "I help . . . " or "I plan to help . . . "

People respond to passion in other people. Given a choice, we'll always opt for the enthusiastic, dedicated individual. They're more rewarding to deal with and we see them as winners—and want them on our side.

If you're not yet embarked on the career you're preparing for, you might focus on how who you are connects with what you're preparing to do:

A marketing career found me when I was in college—even though I'd begun life as a chemistry major.

I've always been the person people come to when they can't settle an argument.

Find the achievement in what you do—the things you're most proud of. Get past the jargon and vague generalizations we all find so easy to write and convey a sense of what you've actually done, what it means, and what your capabilities are. (See the résumé section of Chapter 7.)

If your brainstorming suggests some particular evidence of why you're good at your work, like an anecdote about an achievement or a glamorous credential, work it in.

Keep the overall profile simple and focused. But add personal elements to spice it up. If you're a Big Brother or Big Sister, for example, or an enthusiastic member of an amateur theater troupe, or raise money for the local arts council, many readers will relate. But be cautious about including any that might prove a turnoff to some people, like a specific religious or political affiliation.

Here's how a few people who are popular bloggers and/or are quoted in this book introduce themselves on LinkedIn:

Ivan Walsh
Finance Technical Writer, Ireland
   I help people write, publish, distribute and extend information assets.
   My skill sets cover technical documentation, content strategy, information architecture, and web publishing activities.
   In the past 20 years I've worked in the UK, United States and Asia with Fortune 500s and small startups.

Drop me a line if you'd like to talk. Maybe I can help; if not, I might be able to link you up with someone.

Arthur Germain

Brand Storyteller (Brandteller); B2B Marketer; Builder, Promoter of Branded Thought Leadership

I help technology, manufacturing, professional services and media firms develop and deliver brand stories that can be remembered, repeated and rewarded. I leverage 25+ years of corporate communications, public relations agency, plus business and technology editorial experience to help clients feel confident as they sharpen their brand stories. This delivers measurable results that build stronger market recognition and contribute directly to increased sales.

Amanda McCormick

Copywriter, Social Media Pro, Web Maven, Digital Educator

I work with organizations and individuals to help them use the web and social media to tell their stories with passion and impact. I've overseen web development projects both large and small. A specialty is implementing WordPress in creative ways as a content management system.

USING TWITTER'S MICRO MAGIC

When you work with 140 characters, it's hard to believe that you're using a highly effective business communication tool, let alone one that fosters political revolutions—but of course, you are. And by now most of us refrain from telling people what we're eating for lunch (except for famous chefs, whose lunch is riveting to followers).

You can tweet to solve problems, get help or advice, let people know where you are and much more. Often it feels like you're throwing information out into the world without expecting results. We all know stories about happy surprises: a reporter who won a plum assignment from an editor who noticed he was vacationing in a hot spot, a company that fixed a problem because it received a complaint tweet, somebody who landed a dream job because an executive read his good tweets, etc.

Rather than using Twitter in a random way, however, make it part of your strategic campaign to promote your goals. It's an extraordinary chance to establish yourself as a subject expert, connect with people who have similar professional or personal interests and reach people you'd ordinarily have no hope of accessing. It's also a principal means by which to channel people to more substantial social media efforts, like your blog or website.

All you have to do is be relevant, useful and interesting! The fact is that audiences expect from micromedia very much the same things as they want from all media: substance and relevance.

Asked to explain his goal in tweeting, social media commenter Steve Rubel stated, "To share my passion with the community and solicit ideas all with the intent of moving me toward my long-term goal of revolutionizing marketing communications through technology."

Your own goal may be more modest than that, but identifying it empowers you to identify good subjects and target audiences. You can be a firsthand source of information or ideas and at other times, by monitoring your universe for interesting things other people are saying, link to or retweet that information.

Always write well. People will help you get the word out by favoriting or retweeting your message if it has value, makes them look on top of things, or is interesting or funny. Including images increases the number of retweets exponentially.

Twitter gives you a formidable way to keep in contact with employers after an interview, build your acquaintance with someone you met at a meeting, introduce yourself to someone you want to know and keep your presence alive in the minds of clients or prospects—assuming, of course, they actively use the medium.

VIEW FROM THE FIELD: DIGITAL ATTACK—WHAT TO DO?

Your most unhappy customers are your greatest source of learning.

—Bill Gates

Thanks to its public nature, social media carries risks for businesses as well as individuals. Complaints, criticism and personal attacks can be damaging, even if they don't go viral.

A company's social staff should use keywords to scan Twitter sites constantly to identify problems before they escalate. Because social media specialists are today's front line for customer relations, they should be trained to handle irate people.

Organizations need . . .

A. A good social media policy. Here are a few of the rules to consider:

1. Members of the public should know they are expected to interact in a civil manner. Social staff should have explicit guidelines on what they are authorized to do and when to consult management.

2. Social media specialists should enjoy an open door to senior executives so problems can be resolved quickly.

3. Supervisors should be told not to friend employees and vice versa—this avoids troublesome situations.

4. Employees should know they do not have the right to post negative comments about the company.

B. Clear procedures for handling complaints:

1. Response to every complaint should be handled individually and be fast—ideally within two hours—to prevent serious consequences.

2. Negative comments should not be removed. This angers people.

3. A friendly, neutral tone should be employed. If the complaint is not justified, engage, correct, and educate.

4. If the complaint is justified . . .

A reasonable, articulate person with a valid point about your company's shortcomings is your biggest challenge. Reach out to say thanks for the input, you'll look into it and will be in touch. Take the customer offline if you can—ask her to e-mail you so the conversation isn't public. If she refuses, then handle it online. Resolve the issue: It may be necessary to consult executives on what to say, whether to apologize. Then, ideally, the problem that created the complaint should be fixed!

The good news is that if you've been providing good content, your community will rally round and respond to unfair or ignorant comments so that you don't have to do it.

—Phaedra Barlas, social media strategist

Some Twitter Writing Tips

- Use fewer than the allotted 140 characters—120 at most—to facilitate retweeting.
- Abbreviations are okay *if you're sure your audience will understand them.* If you aim to connect with HR managers, for example, don't assume they will understand texting shortcuts. Find a different, tighter way to say what you mean.
- Adopt an active tone. Use simple direct sentences—avoid *-ing, -ize,* and similar kinds of words as well as cluttered constructions that need *is* and *are.* Good active verbs go a long way.
- Use short, basic words and only those that are essential to the message. Cut every unnecessary word and phrase.

- Make sure the finished message doesn't get so telegraphic that it's hard to understand.
- Ask for what you want. Saying "please retweet," for example, hugely increases the likelihood that people will.
- Check online sources (like Twitter itself) for up-to-date guidance on using the medium's conventions effectively.

Two Don'ts

- Don't send first drafts—review your message and work on simplicity, clarity and wording. All the editing guidelines in Chapters 4 and 5 apply. This super-condensed format is a good test of your editing skills.
- Don't blatantly self-promote in your tweets. A general guideline is to tout your own article, blog, book or service once out of every four or five tweets.

Your Twitter Profile

A snappy, concise profile is well worth your time. Give yourself a good title if you wish and use either a carefully honed paragraph, or a telegraphic style. For comparison with LinkedIn, here are a few examples of the same people cited in the previous section.

Arthur Germain

Arthur Germain is Principal & Chief Brandteller, Communication Strategy Group (www.GoCSG.com); I'm a brand storyteller, helping companies share insights.

Ivan Walsh

I work with small business owners. How can I help?

Other Channels?

Obviously, only a few of the current social channels can be covered here—and in any case you don't want to and shouldn't use them all. There's not enough time in the universe. How should you choose? Consider whether the platform is peopled by individuals you want to meet based on their industries, occupations, age, companies and other factors important to you. If you create a product with a strong visual aspect, a site like Pinterest makes sense. Some channels offer features that add special value: Participating in Google+, for example, directly helps with search engine optimization because Google, the most important search engine, favors it.

Remember to integrate your social media channels with each other and with whatever traditional print media you use. Repetition is good in this flicker-fast world so posting the same items on multiple channels, multiple times, is productive. Many experienced social media users repeat the same tweet four or five times, because different people read it at different times. If you're promoting a blog post or article, you might promote it half a dozen times with different headlines or information nuggets.

Add your most important social media platforms to your e-mail signature. Maximize your time through sites that aggregate your social media output so your new material is widely distributed.

Social media and blogging give you the power to brand yourself, once solely the prerogative of giant enterprises. Why do this? Because you can determine what you want to be known for and how you want to be seen. Then you can use all the tools of digital and traditional media to present a consistent, thoughtful, strategic "you"—a you that can make the most of opportunities and accomplish what you want.

Of course, this is a lifetime enterprise. Your goals will change and so will the tools of communication. Plan to stay flexible and learn to use new channels that make sense for you as they materialize.

Exercise your writing skills and you'll be equipped with the most important constant.

PRACTICE OPPORTUNITIES

I. Create and Post a Comment

Identify at least three bloggers who write about a subject that interests you. Read at least five posts for each one. Write a paragraph or more saying what you think works for you as a reader, as specifically as you can, and also describe anything that doesn't work for you. Then choose a post inviting input and write a comment. Exchange the draft with a partner, make changes based on the input according to your judgment, and post your comment.

II. Plan and Write a Blog

This series of activities can be done in pairs so each student receives ongoing feedback during the project's course.

1. Find a subject that relates to your current expertise or interest and that will contribute in some way to your professional image or career.

2. In writing, plan a blog, considering your goal and audience. Also do online research to locate bloggers in your area of interest and review those that would compete with you.

3. Brainstorm content ideas and make a list of at least 20 topics for suitable blogs.

4. Write the first blog explaining your purpose, who you are, what you'll be writing about as you think appropriate—or just plunge right in and focus on a relevant subject.

5. Plan a program, in writing, to promote your blog and find readers you want.

6. Based on the plan, write promotional messages enticing people to subscribe to your blog suitable for e-mail, Twitter and so on.

III. Group Debate: An Ethical Issue

Is it appropriate for people to blog in someone else's name? Tweet? Should authorship be explicit? Is it legitimate for CEOs and politicians to use staff members or outside PR people to blog in the CEO's name? To tweet? Divide into groups of about five: Half the groups prepare to argue that hiring other people for this work is ethical, and the second set of groups will argue against. Hold one debate or more. Evaluate results by comparing people's opinions before the debate with their opinions after the debate. The winning team is the one that changes the most minds.

IV. Tweet Practice

In a series of 10 tweets, distill the most useful information in this chapter as if you're sharing it with friends.

V. Build an Online Profile

If you have a LinkedIn profile, review and update it, taking into account the advice in this book. If you don't have one, create it now. Start by writing down your goals and describing the characteristics, interests and needs of your intended audiences.

VI. Q&A Practice

Identify an affinity group new to you on LinkedIn or another site and review the Q&A. What self-interest can you identify for various contributors? What questions provoked discussion, and which did not? Can you draw useful generalizations from this?

  Can you offer answers to any of the questions? Do so.

   Then think of five good questions to ask that would stir a conversation and give you something helpful—an idea, information, solution to a problem, a connection and so on.

VII. Plan a Social Media Program

In the same groups, look at the website you created for a charitable cause in Chapter 10. Plot out a comprehensive social media strategy for that charity. In context of goals and audience, what tools would you use, and how? How would you integrate with traditional marketing strategies (e.g., brochures, newsletters, marketing materials, mass-media campaigns, press releases) and cross-promote?

VIII. Plan a Reputation Management Program

Some tools you may want to use:
Tweet Eraser, TweetDelee, Delete

RESOURCES FOR ADVICE ON SOCIAL MEDIA AND THE INTERNET

The best way to keep up with the fast-changing world of social media is . . . online. Here are some resources and a few personal favorites.

Website or Blog	*Address*	*Description*
For good general advice and to stay abreast of online trends:		
Mashable	mashable.com	Portal to a wide mix of social media news and information
Copyblogger	www.copyblogger.com	Online copywriting and content marketing strategies
HubSpot	blog.hubspot.com	"Inbound Internet Marketing Blog"
Mediabistro	www.mediabistro.com	Media news, blogs, job listings
Jeff Bullas	www.jeffbullas.com	Good in-depth blogging advice and ideas
Shel Holtz	http://holtz.com/blog	Social media commentary and advice from an established voice

(Continued)

(Continued)

Website or Blog	Address	Description
Buffer	https://blog.bufferapp.com	Helpful information on content, building traffic, and relevant research
For graphic presentation tools:		
Before & After	www.bamagazine.com	How to use design tools and sharpen your eye
Canva	https://www.canva.com	An easy-to-use design tool with templates for non-designers
Gimp	www.gimp.org	A free image manipulation program resembling Photoshop
Easel.ly	www.easel.ly.com	Templates for creating infographics
Infogr.am	https://infogr.am	Helps you create charts and graphs
For tech support, writing and SEO help:		
Internet Marketing Ninjas	internetmarketingninjas.com/seo-tools/free-optimization	Free on-page optimization tool
The Readability Test Tool	http://read-able.com	Tells you how readable your website copy is
Emotional Marketing Value Headline Analyzer	aminstitute.com/headline	Tells you how emotionally appealing your headline is
BuzzSumo	buzzsumo.com	Analyzes what blog content performs best in a particular niche
Keyword Planner	https://adwords.google.com/KeywordPlanner	Helps you figure out best keywords
SavePublishing	savepublishing.com	Finds tweets on your website pages
For finding stories and facts:		
Digg	http://digg.com	What's happening on the Internet
Medium	https://medium.com	What's happening in the world
Contently	https://contently.com	Helps you tell great stories
Quora	www.quora.com	A super Q&A forum

PART VI

WRITING FOR ORAL PRESENTATION, VIDEO AND PUBLIC RELATIONS PURPOSES

Chapter 13

PRESENT YOURSELF

Write Well to Speak Well

He who fails to plan is planning to fail.

—Winston Churchill

The oldest tool of human communication is the newest: storytelling. Today, stories are seen as the lifeblood of advertising, public relations, branding and marketing as well as journalism. It makes perfect sense that this ancient art is probably the best way to reach other people so they see what we see, feel what we feel, and connect on a subrational level.

How to create stories is a big topic on its own. Fortunately, a certain kind of story is the most effective for business communication: the personal why-I-do-this and how-I-got-here kind.

The personal story works for individuals, of course, but it is also the best tool for organizations. The most memorable stories about companies, and nonprofits too, are the founder narratives—from Florence Nightingale to Mark Zuckerberg.

Developing your own story will benefit you immediately, because it will serve you well in job interviews and self-presentation. Knowing your story centers your own sense of who you are, where you want to go and how to get there. And in bigger picture terms, you'll have tools to deploy on behalf of organizations you work for or lead.

How do you find a story to tell about yourself? It's there, guaranteed, but you may have to dig.

FINDING YOUR PERSONAL STORY

Here's your goal: To tell a story that communicates who you are. Try scanning your own history for an experience that turned out to be a pivotal point—either an aha moment, or a more sustained life situation. A small incident or a big one may have illuminated a life-changing truth and shifted the way you look at things. How you interpreted what happened is often more important than the event itself. What did you learn? How did that influence your life path, what you want to accomplish, the life you want to live?

Try Ginny Pulos's approach.

VIEW FROM THE FIELD:
A STRUCTURE FOR FINDING YOUR STORY

Storytelling is the most underutilized persuasion skill in business. A great business story is about you, your company, or someone you work with intimately. It must be brief, true and engage emotions with twists and turns—and end on a high note.

To help people mine their stories, I use this process: First, write a list of the major events in your life—birth, death, graduation, marriage, divorce, winning a race, your triumphs and pitfalls. Next, write a few words about each situation and what happened; then, your age at the time; and finally, what you learned from it—how that event changed your life.

You need never share this list but must choose one story idea to write out fully: What did it sound like? Taste like? What were you wearing? How did you feel? What did you see? Use all the senses. Paint pictures for people. And, this is key: Write in present tense, like "Picture this. I'm walking down Main Street and it's 2001. The sky is crisp and clear. I hear . . . ." When you've got it right, introduce your story directly: "This is a story about overcoming failure." At the end, say something like, "That's how I learned to turn failure into . . . "

(Continued)

(Continued)

Edit to no more than 850 to 900 words; aim for five minutes or less orally. You'll save time and words if you act the story out a bit. For example, tilt one shoulder forward if you're talking for one person, the other shoulder for the second person, so you don't have to keep saying, "I said," "she said."

Now you have a great story for many occasions, by heightening one aspect for one audience and muting it for another. And, you can make it much shorter (what I call a vignette), to the 30, 60, or 90 seconds you need to for networking events. Or you can expand the story over lunch or a long flight. Once you've done the entire process, you'll have unlocked a powerful skill set.

One final piece of advice: Stories work best when you risk revealing who you truly are because it's a key way others come to trust you, your ideas, your character. You'll not only gain the confidence that gets you the job, you'll be able to bring that power to your business and the relationships you build there, make self-introductions at meetings, and persuade clients and colleagues which path or pitch will add to their success.

—Ginny Pulos, founder & president of Ginny Pulos Communications, Inc. (www.ginnypulos.com). Specialist in presentation and persuasion skills, media training, team building and storytelling as a leadership tool

Here are a few more situations to start you thinking.

- Losing a job—through a mistake you made, personal interaction or company layoff
- Witnessing an injustice, or experiencing one
- Losing something you worked hard for
- Getting your first good grade (or bad grade)
- Scoring the winning goal—or failing to and being booed
- Having someone express confidence in you or question your value
- Learning something eye-opening from a specific person
- Feeling friendless and having someone reach out to you, or vice versa
- Receiving a gift or piece of advice that took you in a new direction
- Handling an unusual amount of responsibility at an early age
- Losing someone important to you
- Recovering from a major setback of any kind
- Leaving home, family and friends to forge a new path
- Deliberately choosing a harder road

A good story idea is one that makes a reader or listener want to know what happened, what you did about it and how you changed. Perhaps you were led to see past the obvious, dedicate yourself to standing up for others, reassess your life goals, practice patience, redress injustice in the world, or commit to being your best self. Think about how the experience relates to your immediate goal.

Do some of these ideas echo your memory of writing a college entrance essay? Probably, because it's true that there are just so many themes in the world. That doesn't make your story less unique if you make it specific and individualized.

If you are established in your career, working for an organization or running your own business, draw on additional possibilities, such as how you

- decided on your career path, or got your idea;
- found your inspiration or sense of mission;
- dealt with losing an opportunity you worked for;
- handled a difficult project that came without a blueprint;
- took an unorthodox route to a goal;
- persevered through a series of setbacks;
- managed a team enterprise with problem members; and
- created success for other people.

Here's a surefire tactic: *Ask yourself* **why** *you want to succeed in the particular field, win the opportunity, pursue a goal, take a new direction. Probe for* **why** *you care so much about what you're doing or what you want, the ultimate reason*: Do you want to build bridges because you grew up next to one? Do you want to design robots because someone gave you a kit for your seventh birthday? Do you want to help people because someone helped you? Do you love empowering people to reach *their* goals?

Dig deep into your memory and experience. The answer to one of these questions may surprise you and provide the seed of a unique story.

SUCCESS TIP

ANOTHER WAY TO IDENTIFY YOUR STORY

Think about a story or anecdote anywhere in your experience that feels important, or you like to tell, or that periodically occurs to you. Then ask yourself, How does that story relate to what I'm doing or want to do? Chances are high that it does. You're tapping into your instincts. From there, think it through, and you may be able to illuminate your own motivations, personality, or aspirations.

DEVELOPING YOUR PERSONAL STORY

Your story idea must be crafted in writing. This is true of nearly all oral presentation, though of course, you must ultimately write for speaking rather than reading.

Here are some guidelines for developing effective stories.

Build on experiences most people relate to. The ideas listed as starting points are based on experiences most people have shared: not in the same form, probably, but something in their own lives may generate similar feelings. Almost everyone has lost a job, or a person; handled a challenge over his head; felt lost and alone; experienced failure or a moment of triumph, and so on.

Center on how you overcame challenges. That's the essence of the stories we love from Hollywood, fiction books and biographies. Suspense is built in—how will "the hero" (that's you!) overcome those obstacles? How will she change? How does the experience motivate her? What's the big lesson? How does it relate to your audience?

Find a strong lead. You can start in the middle, at the point of crisis, then go back to cover how-I-got-there, and what you did to emerge successfully. Or tell it sequentially from the beginning. But don't wait so long to introduce a challenge that you bore your audience.

Be specific and concrete. A story may lead to an abstract kind of conclusion—like "I learned to always give people a second chance"—but how you got there must be spelled out and feel real. Use simple, unassuming language that works orally, even if you're writing the story to be read: short words, short sentences, conversational tone.

Writing well means never having to say, "I guess you had to be there."

—Jeff Mallett, Internet developer of Yahoo and other dot-coms

"Show don't tell." That's the mantra for novelists, playwrights, choreographers and artists. The more you can bring people into an experience, the more you engage both their emotional and rational sides. Work with the language to recreate the experience so they see, hear and touch what it was like to be there. Use graphic words and present tense to impart immediacy.

Communicate how you felt during the experience. Rather than saying something directly, like "I was shocked," it's better to use imagery to accomplish this. An unexpected job loss, for example, might be described this way:

It's like I'm sauntering through a beautiful safe garden smelling the roses. I feel the solid ground under my feet, I'm casual and confident, know where I'm going . . . and suddenly a trapdoor opens under my feet. Whoosh! I'm in a dark, tight, silent cave. Alone. All I hear is my own voice: Why did it happen? What did I do wrong? Or you might draw on common cultural ground—a book, film, television show:

Suddenly I'm Alice in Wonderland—falling dizzy into a whole new world with a landscape I never saw, never imagined. I just want to go back where I was but can't figure out how to find the path.

To explore using metaphors, think about what the experience felt like—and what else that experience reminds you of or can be compared to. Use your imagination to connect two things that are ordinarily thought of separately. (Remember Forrest Gump's "Life is like a box of chocolates"?)

You can pick up on such metaphors at the close of your story when sharing where you are now and how you feel about it:

"So that's how I found the path and left the cave. Now I live in the light, everyday. Now I know how to . . . and can help you . . . "

WHAT YOU CAN DO WITH METAPHORS

Using metaphors and other comparisons brings a story (and a lot of other writing) to life and spurs the reader's imagination. Don't aim to use complicated words and pretentious sentences. Check out how Ernest Hemingway—a great journalist as well as novelist—uses metaphor power in this novel excerpt. The "life" described has no relation to common experience for most of us, but the language makes us share it through our senses.

Dying was nothing and he had no picture of it nor fear of it in his mind. But living was a field of grain blowing in the wind on the side of a hill. Living was a hawk in the sky. Living was an earthen jar of water in the dust of the threshing with the grain flailed out and the chaff blowing. Living was a horse between your legs and a carbine under one leg and a hill and a valley and a stream with trees along it and the far side of the valley and the hills beyond.

—From *For Whom the Bell Tolls*

End happily. Avoid stories that don't help you look good in the end. Certainly, depict how you started from a dark place, but you must eventually come out on top in a meaningful way. This upbeat approach can be surprisingly hard for some people, depending on cultural or family traditions. Be sure not to use story power to undermine your own image and how you are remembered!

Adapt for the version you need. How long should a story be? "Just right," like Goldilock's porridge. Basically it depends on the audience and occasion. You can turn a story into a 20-second elevator speech, a one page About Us for a website, or a half hour inspirational speech if invited. Take the trouble to write a long version first in order to think through your material thoroughly. Then work to trim and intensify it with sharper language.

Always plan to adapt your story to the goal at hand. Ask yourself this: Will this particular audience relate to it? How can I adapt the story so it does? Does it clearly connect to what I aim to accomplish, what I want to result from the situation? If you want people to fund your invention, there's no point telling them how you became a champion basketball player even though you're only 5'4"—unless what you learned relates to the product you want to make or you show how the experience helped make you a committed, resourceful, reliable business partner.

Say what you mean, and mean what you say.

—General George S. Patton

Try out the story on friends or colleagues for clues on how to strengthen it. For in-person purposes, practice, practice, practice. You want to deliver it with conviction and energy.

THE "ELEVATOR SPEECH": WHY YOU NEED IT, HOW TO WRITE IT

If you're not familiar with the term *elevator speech,* also known as *elevator pitch,* it means "what to say to someone you want to connect with when you're in the same elevator and you have about 15 to 20 seconds till he gets out."

It's the statement you make at a meeting when asked to introduce yourself—or any event where you meet new people and exchange business cards. Professionals of every kind who are networking, job hunting or looking for new customers tend to obsess about their elevator speeches. A good one crystallizes the speaker's marketing message and is a key element for developing new business.

If you're not yet working in a career position, do you need an elevator speech? Definitely. It's never too soon to connect with your industry of choice—and your peers. If you're studying for a degree, consider yourself a professional now, refer to yourself that way, and use the professional's tools.

Like a speech or presentation, this brief pitch about yourself is, of course, spoken—but first it must be written. Planning to wing even a mini-speech won't do you justice. In earlier times it was assumed that a typical building had 50 floors and you had 60 seconds. But elevators, not to mention the world, move much faster now, and most advisers would say 20 seconds is pushing it.

Everything you've learned about writing in terms of goal and audience applies to crafting an elevator speech. Getting your statement brief enough is tough. In some training approaches, participants must deliver their mini-speeches while holding a lit match and finish before getting burned.

So the challenge is to distill what makes you special, what differentiates you, in that sliver of time. Communicators call this the value proposition or core value statement, and it usually applies to how an organization self-defines to distinguish itself from the competition. Try to see things from the audience viewpoint—what about you or what you offer could be relevant or interesting enough to hold listeners for 15 to 20 seconds and make them want to know more? It boils down to WIIFM—the tried and true what's-in-it-for-me factor.

It often works to start with your name and what you do, mentioning the company if you work for one. Then explain how you help, what problems you solve, and how what you do can benefit your listener. Here are a few paired examples to demonstrate what works:

1. "I'm a CPA, and for 15 years I've been practicing with Atlanta's largest accounting firm, ABC & D. We handle taxes and financial planning."

2. "I'm a CPA, and I help single women plan their finances so they save on taxes and can count on a secure future."

3. "I'm a communications consultant and I do public relations, advertising, and crisis communications for Fortune 500 companies."

4. "I work with companies that are in trouble with their customers or the public, and show them how to solve their problems with good communication."

5. "I'm a personal trainer and work mostly with middle-aged women."

6. "I'm a personal trainer, and I specialize in helping older women who think they're out of shape get fit and healthy and look great."

Notice the main differences between versions 1 and 2 in each case: The first versions, focused on process and generalities, are not likely to spark interest. The second versions are calculated to pique the interest of possible clients and provoke questions—and they are far more specific. Granted, in each case the speaker may not be talking to a prospect. But the other person may know people who need the service or may immediately remember the message should someone they know need it.

In each example, the speaker tailors the message to the audience. If the CPA also works with business people, for example, he adapts his introduction appropriately.

IF YOU'RE A NEW CAREER BUILDER

If you're just starting out in your career field, or moving into a new one, don't feel shy about identifying yourself as a professional. Your serious intent entitles you to feel part of the industry. Just as writers are told to present themselves as writers even if they've not yet published anything, you're an accountant or consultant or marketing specialist as soon as you have a few years of academics or training under your belt.

This is true if you're between jobs as well as when you're switching careers. If you're earning a living at something else until you complete a degree or get a career break, it's still legitimate to present yourself as what you want to be.

If this feels uncomfortable, identify yourself as a management consultant, or whatever, in training.

You can use your elevator speech to advantage if you're at an interim or preliminary stage and the setting is hospitable. It's also fine to ask for something. Here are two examples:

> "Hi, I'm Margaret James. I'm finishing my master's in public relations this spring and plan a career helping nonprofits communicate better. I'd love to contribute right now as an intern, and I'm looking for an opportunity. Can you suggest anyone for me to talk to?"

> "Hi, I'm Jerry Jones. I'm a business management major headed for a career in retail marketing. I'd really appreciate some insights into the field from people working in it now. Can you suggest anyone?"

Once you have your basic message written, read it aloud and revise it— repeatedly— until it sounds natural and conversational. It must be easy to remember and comfortable to say. This dictates short words and very short sentences.

VIEW FROM THE FIELD: A SALES TRAINER'S TAKE ON THE ELEVATOR SPEECH

Here's what I taught people when I worked for a sales institute—and still teach people I work with. I have seen this approach work for so many people.

1. **Communication begins with listening.** Whether you have the opportunity to share your elevator speech in a brief introduction on the elevator or in the context of a conversation that will last more than a couple of minutes, begin by asking a question or two that helps you get to know the other person. When you start by listening to someone, you earn the right to be listened to.

2. **Differentiate yourself from your competition.** We're all accustomed to sales people who quickly dive into all the wonderful things their product or service can do for us and why they're better than everyone else—so much so that we become numb to it. Instead, formulate a brief description of what you do in a way that differentiates you without being self-promoting.

3. **Make it about them.** When you talk about features, it's all about you. Don't take it personally, but your listeners don't care about you—they care about their own issues, challenges and objectives. Get into their world and talk about how you solve the problems they may be experiencing. If you are able to ask good questions first, you may have a better idea of which problems to include.

So the elevator speech components are name, company, framing statement (very brief description of what you do), and two or three problems you solve (ideally tailored to the audience). If you do it right, they will want to learn more.

For example, my elevator speech for my current position is:

I'm Catherine Gates with WorkMatters. We help people close the gap between faith and work. People come to our programs because they're struggling with chaos and uncertainty—they feel overwhelmed by a lack of balance and the demands of the workplace today. They want to figure out how their faith fits in. Our programs help them find peace, courage and workable solutions.

CRAFTING PRESENTATIONS AND SPEECHES

When I get ready to talk to people, I spend two thirds of the time thinking what they want to hear and one third thinking about what I want to say.

—Abraham Lincoln

Creating and delivering presentations, whether two minutes or a half hour long, probably doesn't seem like an everyday need for you, but

1. When they do come along, they are usually make or break opportunities to impress superiors or peers—or fail to do so

2. Many smaller occasions call for the same skills, ranging from introducing yourself, pitching an idea or product, persuading a group, or sharing knowledge

3. You may find chances to shine in support mode by helping executives or team members prepare a speech or present an idea, result or request more effectively

4. You may see an opportunity to change the world, even if minutely, or one person's viewpoint, by being equipped to present on something you care about deeply

In virtually every industry, the ability to present well is a highly valued skill. In business and communications, it is indispensible.

Many parts of this book apply to presentations, from basic writing techniques to how to set goals, analyze audiences, edit, and tell stories. For an easy to use structure, see Marla Seiden's Presentation Planning Worksheet. Also check out the resources at the end of the chapter.

A PRESENTATION PLANNING WORKSHEET

Preparing

If you don't prepare, you prepare to fail!

Develop the right presentation for the target audience, and practice, practice, practice so you can deliver it with passion.

Profile your audience: Demographics; WIIFM? What do they want to know? Already know or believe? Need to know?

Clarify your general purpose: Demonstrate, inform, entertain, persuade, motivate, inspire (can be one or all)?

Define your specific purpose: Call to action—How do you want the audience to think, respond? Do you want them to improve their understanding, or change an attitude or behavior?

Crystallize your message in 20 words or less . . .

Examples:

First quarter earnings are down and we need everyone to pitch in toward recovery.

Learn six simple presentation techniques to advance your career.

Donate to our anti-hunger campaign and helps us save hundreds of children.

Exercise 90 minutes per week and reduce the risk of . . . 35%.

Writing the Lead

Grab attention in less than 30 seconds.

For example, use a story, rhetorical question, provocative statement, quote, statistic or visual.

Developing the Body

Create a series of main points (three often works), each with supporting evidence in this pattern:

Main Point 1: Appropriate support (can include examples, stories, statistics, anecdotes, and visuals).

Transitions: Link all elements to establish a logical flow with wording such as:

first; next; before; now; after we do that; here's an example; on the other hand . . .

Language: Be clear and concise.

Use:

Short sentences, short words

Sound bites—memorable phrases such as, "Ask not what your country can do for you; ask what you can do for your country."

Vivid images that paint pictures

Avoid:

Jargon and clichés

Concluding

Summarize: Tell them what you told them; restate the benefits.
Explain action they should take.
End on a high note: memorable quote, compelling statement, or story.

—Marla Seiden, president of
Seiden Communications, Inc.
(www.seidencommunications.com);
presentation skills and PR specialist

WRITING TIPS FOR SPOKEN MEDIA

Here's how to create simple, clear language that works orally:

- Use short sentences throughout but vary their length (short, a little longer, short, etc.).
- Use short, basic one-syllable words (like the Bible, Gettysburg Address, Winston Churchill speeches).
- Edit out ALL unnecessary words and phrases.

- Build in pauses to emphasize important points.
- Say *we* and *us,* not *I* and *me.*
- Say *YOU* often.
- Take the trouble to create a great engaging lead that relates to the audience (e.g., startling statistic, story, quote, vision of the future).
- Use transitions to ensure and underline logical flow and carry listeners along (e.g., "Our goal was to . . . " "We began by . . . " "Then we looked at . . . " "We also considered . . . " "So we decided . . . " "But we were surprised by . . . " "Here's what we concluded . . . ").
- Repeat your main message periodically—absorbing information and ideas orally is hard for people.

Rhetoric in the traditional sense is a highly polished art with a resource of devices to draw on. Many of these techniques have Latin names, because oratory was highly valued by early Romans and well practiced. Here are a few examples. Despite their formal sound, these devices can be readily used to create effective and contemporary oral presentations.

- Rhetorical questions: a familiar device to vary pace and spark interest ("Why does this seem inevitable?")
- Alliteration: a phrase or sentence with repeat initial consonants ("the market's dreary downward dive . . . ")
- Anaphora: repetition of a word or phrase ("We believe that . . . " "We believe that . . . " "And in the end, we believe that . . . ")
- Oxymoron: a two-word paradox ("happily miserable")
- Onomatopoeia: words that sound like what they mean (splash, plop, whiz)
- Metaphors, similes, analogies: Graphic comparisons of all types
- The rule of three, which resonates with us in many contexts: three main points, three examples, three-part statements ("We came, we saw, we conquered." "We set out to identify the problem, find the solution, and tell the world.") There is a Latin name for this, but it's so long, you don't want to know it.

Studying rhetoric to any degree will improve all your writing. Train yourself to listen analytically to speeches, political and otherwise, and observe how good presentations achieve their impact.

Of course, don't focus on the trees and lose the forest (metaphor). Deliver your messages in a big-picture context. Whether people look to you for a helpful perspective, a better way to do something, or general inspiration, make your message matter to them. Nearly always your audience wants you to help them improve their lives in some way. Give people a vision of a better future, even in a small way, and your message is more compelling.

And always, make it sayable. Most experts advise writing a speech out in full, timing it, and practicing from that script exhaustively. Notice every stumble and unnatural phrasing and rewrite to fix them. You can drill down to a set of talking points for on-site reference, but always remember that connecting with the audience is your first imperative.

SUCCESS TIP

HOW MANY WORDS DO YOU NEED?

On average, 130 words take one minute to speak—unless you're from the northeastern United States or another place where people speak faster or a slow-speaking place. So a two-minute speech is 260 words, a 10-minute speech is about 1,300 words, and so on. Time your own speaking pace: If you find you speak fast, work at slowing down so people can absorb what you say more easily. Plan a long speech based on word count—for example, in the case of a 30-minute speech, 260 words/two-minute lead, 1,950 words/15 minutes is the "middle," 390 words/three-minute conclusion.

Think about imaginative ways to keep people engaged: A live demonstration is a great technique in some cases, or a staged attention getter. Steve Jobs, for example, introduced the MacBook Air laptop to a huge audience by pulling one out of a flat yellow mailing envelope. Sometimes you can build in suspense. Or design one or more audience interaction pieces to wake people up.

Always keep an eye on your audience. If attention wanes, change the pace, speed up the section, or move on to something else. You need not tell people everything you know about a subject and if you leave material out, few will suspect.

Delivery techniques are beyond our scope, but here's the nano version: Breathe deeply and steadily; stand with good posture and hands at your sides when not gesturing; make eye contact with specific people for three to five seconds each; maintain your energy and enthusiasm; and throughout, reflect your total conviction in your own message.

Audiences will forgive a great deal if you share something of value that you clearly believe in. But don't risk an impromptu performance when the stakes are high: rehearse. You might video yourself or at least sound-record your full presentation and review that critically, then do it again. And/or practice with an audience, just one is enough. Always time what you plan to say, too, so you don't undercut your message by jamming up important points or skipping your close. Almost always, it works best to say less, but say it well.

Be sincere; be brief; be seated.

—Franklin D. Roosevelt on speechmaking

HOW TO PREPARE YOUR OWN SPEAKING NOTES

If you need to deliver a speech word for word because the occasion calls for it or you must not forget a thing, here's a simple trick for preparing your script.

Type it up to reflect how you'd read it with natural pauses. Start a new line at each pause. Take, for example, this excerpt from a memorable speech by President John F. Kennedy:

And so, my fellow Americans:

ask not what your country can do for you—

ask what you can do for your country.

My fellow citizens of the world:

ask not what America will do for you,

but what together we can do for the freedom of man.

Finally,

whether you are citizens of America

or citizens of the world,

ask of us the same high standards of strength and sacrifice

which we ask of you.

This method allows you to deliver the message much more powerfully. It also enables you to look up frequently and maintain almost steady eye contact with the audience. And if you use this approach, you won't need to hold long lines of copy in your head as you speak and will feel much more relaxed. Help an executive use this method and you'll be appreciated.

P.S. What rhetorical devices can you spot in this short excerpt?

CREATING AND USING POWERPOINT WELL

PowerPoint and similar programs have evolved into two different uses:

1. As a presentation aid, for which it was designed

2. As basic vehicles of communication in the business world. For which it was not designed

Unfortunately, PowerPoint, Prezi and the rest are rarely well used in either capacity, which has led to a lot of impassioned criticism. But realistically, PowerPoint is a core tool in many business programs and use proliferates. So creating a good slide deck is a valuable skill. Good writing strategies are the key.

PowerPoint for Presentation

Too many presenters allow this medium to become the message. They shape their content based on a predetermined format rather than developing a solid presentation that uses PowerPoint as an adjunct tool.

PowerPoint is best seen as a way to add visual dimension to a speech and/or keep it clearly organized. In general, it should not distract the audience from focusing on the speaker.

VIEW FROM THE FIELD: POWERPOINT PRO AND CON

PowerPoint conveys information very well—but it's horrible at persuasion. So knowing your objective is the first step. If you're doing a data dump, it can be very effective. But if you want to persuade and move an audience or change the way they think, it's actually counterproductive. Writing a speech is about constructing the arguments and synthesizing the ideas—a valuable process. PowerPoint can be like creating a cheat sheet rather than doing the hard work—like building a lean-to instead of a house, where the data points are second to the arguments.

—Dan Gerstein, founder and CEO of
Gotham Ghostwriters; political adviser, analyst, and commentator

The way to present well with PowerPoint is to plan and write your presentation as a speech. As covered in the preceding section, a speech needs an engaging opener; a central focus; a clearly presented sequence of ideas and facts (not too many of either, though); a strong close; and, preferably, planned audience interaction at given points.

What role does that give PowerPoint? Use it as a visual backdrop to do the following:

- Interpret the meaning of information—relevant images and photographs as well as easily understood tables, charts and graphs that leverage the medium's ability to show change over time or helpful comparisons. Embed video clips to liven things up if relevant.
- Provide cues to keep yourself on track when speaking and guide the audience through. Slides can be as simple as a headline: "What we learned from this research" or "Moving into the future" or "Questions." Steve Jobs of Apple was famous for using a few simple words with splashy, imaginative graphics.
- Reinforce important points you want the audience to focus on. Visual learning is very effective, provided the material is simple and easily absorbed. Some advice recommends using slides solely to reinforce points you want the audience to remember.
- Provide ready-made handouts—which gives you a chance to circulate your contact information if you want people to find you later. (But never supply handouts before or during the presentation because they will distract people from focusing on you.)

As you develop the content, note any ideas that arise for using the visual dimension to enhance and support your message. *But it's best to complete every step of your speech, from idea to messages to support points and organization, before planning the visuals.*

Aim for simplicity in slide content and language—note Guy Kawasaki's famous advice. Pay close attention to transitions between slides and keep them visually consistent.

In giving presentations, use the 10/20/30 rule.... Use only 10 slides, take 20 minutes maximum, and use at least 30-point fonts.

—Guy Kawasaki,
media expert

PowerPoint for Business Communications

PowerPoint has become the communication tool of choice in many business environments. It's used extensively to share information and guide discussion at meetings, both in person and increasingly, through virtual media. It also is employed as the medium of record.

Such uses can present major challenges. If you spend all your time and energy turning information into visuals that fit a limited format, the message can easily get lost and the information distorted. If you use bulleted lists heavily, they're only shorthand and just don't work for some kinds of information where context and connections matter.

If all or part of your purpose is to distribute printouts, then you can cram a lot of data onto your slides. They may be readable when printed out and distributed, but that doesn't mean people will understand them.

Don't plunge immediately into slide making. Instead, decide what you want to communicate. Take the time to understand the topic or problem in depth and your main message points. Figure out how things relate and connect. Then plan your slides, keeping them simple, and once they're created, check how well you can explain each one.

The result may differ somewhat from the PowerPoint that people are used to seeing. However, you are apt to get positive reactions even though viewers may not know why they liked the presentation.

Also, you'll be far better equipped to answer questions and expand on your points than if you'd concentrated on turning out a batch of data-jammed slides.

VIEW FROM THE FIELD: HOW TO WORK WITH POWERPOINT

I always start by profiling my audience, understanding their core needs and expectations. And if I want things from the audience, what are they?

My next step is to go with pen and paper. A lot of people start with a blank computer screen and the tools, PowerPoint or whatever they're using, but I believe that's limiting in building a story line and coming up with content organically.

So I develop a storyboard, thinking about it like a filmmaker—what's the overall plot line? The key messages or takeaways? What are the scenes that will build up to deliver that? I think about the logic of the ideas and how to translate them into visual representations. When that's well developed on paper, I go to the computer screen, and that's where some principles of slide design become more relevant.

I think audiences do one of two things: read what's on the slide or listen to your words. You want them to listen, which means using fewer words and more images to depict complex content graphically.

When I've written the presentation's initial draft, I spend most of my time preparing to deliver it—I present to a colleague or stand in front of the mirror. This leads me to simplify the slide content even more. If you learn your message, you rely less on the slides to remember your notes, and the audience focuses on you. The final step is to refine the content, which usually means simplifying, stripping what's unnecessary so the key messages speak louder than the detail.

Keep in mind that PowerPoint is not always the right tool, as opposed to spoken word alone or a written memo or video. People might not perceive there's an option, but I think they're actually hungry for innovation. They want to be communicated to in a way that suggests they are unique and understood, and that you're not just defaulting to what you've done with other audiences. I think people are hungry to move away from death by PowerPoint. But deal with expectations early on.

When you're preparing slides to distribute as a handout, the concepts are the same in that you want the audience to listen to you, so put less on the page and know your story really well. But if you're handing out a presentation without delivering context and it must stand alone, it's different. Then you're writing more of a document in slide format and people need time to sit down and read it. If it's then used for presentation, you must translate it to simplify content and deliver more verbally.

—Clint Nohavec, director of SwitchPoint

HOW TO PLAN AND USE EFFECTIVE VIDEOS

With new technology that makes it easy to produce and disseminate video, the medium is everywhere. It's becoming more and more important as an adjunct to websites, blogs, social media résumés and many other venues. You can now easily create a six-second video with an app like Vine to use on your blog or website and share online.

Whether your video is six seconds long or 30 minutes, it's best to know your story before you shoot. It's popular to assume that production values no longer count. In fact, some PR agencies have found, literally, that video shot by the mailroom clerk draws more viewers than expensively produced "traditional" video.

People often do seem to find unfocused video with shaky movement more "authentic" than the carefully created kind, at least on YouTube.

But generally, such video needs to be short or immensely entertaining, lest we lose patience with it. More important: When you're using video for business purposes, be cautious. No matter where you show it, your clips speak for the organization. Huge numbers of viewers don't necessarily provide a benefit you want.

Whether you're a job seeker using video to introduce yourself on your social media résumé, a consultant interested in making your website more personal and engaging, a company president using it on the home page to explain the firm's mission or apologize for a disaster, or a CFO using video to review company financials for distribution to a worldwide audience, in every case, you need a clear idea of your goal and your audience. And for a substantial video you need a script.

This applies even if the whole video consists of you as seen by an unmoving camera. At the very least, see video as a speech. And a speech needs a good lead, informational middle and an effective end. It needs to be smoothly and convincingly delivered, so you must know exactly what you will say and rehearse. You can't read the script on camera, but you can use written cues.

Or if you're a confident speaker, just as for a speech, you can use talking points to wing it. The advantage of video versus a live performance is that you can do the "bad" parts over and edit the best takes together.

If you're creating a more ambitious video, you need a storyboard to represent the main points and how they connect. This can be done simply, as described for PowerPoint. In addition to video clips, you can include stills and graphics. This takes planning. You'll need to marshal what's available to work with and decide what else you can feasibly add to the mix.

Another way to plan is to create a two-column script with a line down the middle. The visuals go on the left side, which reminds you of their dominant role in this medium, and the words go on the right. For example:

Visuals	*V/O (Voice-Over)*
C/U (close-up) of JB	Hi. I'm John Brown, and I'd like to show you how my team won this year's debating conference in Miami.
WS (wide shot) of team giving presentation	We took a long road getting there and learned a lot. Here's how we got ready.
Stills/team practicing	Live sound
Cutaways of notes, papers, faces C/U of Ellen	I can't believe how much work it took. Every day we spent three hours . . .

The core concept is that with video, you don't just script words: You also must script the visuals, in tandem. You need something on the screen for every second of voice-over. Of course, you'll have to edit everything together neatly, but these days, if you have the time, the software is there and the skills can be learned.

Unless you're creating the kind of simple, straight-on video where the camera stays on you and you talk through it, perhaps demonstrating something, words and images must be juggled to tell the story. Video specialists aim to use few words and let what's on the screen say as much as possible. For informational material, the narration is used to bridge between scenes and ideas and explain what can't be translated into visuals.

However, those few words must be carefully chosen. Try for very accessible language—short, sayable sentences with good rhythm. Fragments work fine, since in spoken language, formal sentences can actually sound unnatural and jarring. *Don't fill the script with wall-to-wall words. Silence is the videographer's version of white space.* It allows viewers to focus on the images and hear the ambient sound—for example, the team members rehearsing—or absorb the music if there is any. Music is one more dimension for effective video. Music can underscore emotions and unify the presentation.

The very smallest camcorders, or even your smartphone, can work amazingly well for many purposes, thanks to the digital revolution and fast-improving technology. But they carry some important limitations.

One is sound quality. With tiny machines, this has lagged far behind the level achieved for visual recording, and research says that people have far less patience for bad audio than for bad picture. Especially if you're selling something, or delivering any message that people don't need or doesn't entertain, *pay attention to the sound quality.* You may need to use auxiliary equipment for this. And you may need to use a camera that allows you to plug in a mike.

A second limitation is lighting. If you watch a professional video crew at a shoot, you'll notice that excruciating time is spent setting up the lights. It's the critical factor in getting good, real-looking, interesting pictures. You are unlikely to have a lighting specialist, but know that simple front-on lighting gives you a flat (and unflattering) image. Worse, though, is backlighting—where the source comes from behind the subject. This obliterates all detail and produces, at worst, a silhouette. So (1) watch for where you position your subject and the angle you shoot from, in relation to the light, and (2) consider a supplementary light when your video matters.

A third limitation is the shakiness of tiny cameras. This is easily solved by attaching a suitably sized tripod.

A content caveat—try to not rely solely on what the industry calls "talking heads" to deliver your message. Use imagination to come up with visual ideas so the camera doesn't just stay focused on one person. When you can't do this or don't have the resources, keep it short. That generally means less than two minutes.

Another way to use video is to assemble your "show" from still images, drawings, and other existing materials. This can be done without shooting any new footage at all. Create movement by panning across an image, or zooming from the full image to a detail, or vice versa. Assemble the images carefully using special effects like fade-out and fade-in. If you have a trove of material to work with, this can be a very effective technique—especially if you add music or narration.

Planning, shooting, and editing video takes hands-on practice. So if you want to use it, spend some time experimenting and see what works.

Ideas For Using Video

Some of these ideas are best suited to substantial organizations that have video support—always nice if you can get it. But many can be done by nonprofessionals. An increasing number of ready-made templates that can be customized to your business message are available online. Stock video can be purchased from stock photography companies for short clips.

Consider video for:

- How-to demonstrations of a product or process
- Behind-the-scenes looks of your company at work
- Interviews with specialists on your staff, the CEO, a local guru
- A "meet the staff" short video for your website
- Interviews with staff members to show others in the organization who they are and what they're interested in (great tactic to promote esprit de corps in large companies)
- Customer testimonials
- Case histories of how a client problem was solved
- Employee involvement in volunteer activities
- Commercials or public service announcements (PSAs)

If you do invest in good video production, recycle the results imaginatively to recover the cost. Depending on the nature of your video and the components you can draw from it, use it on the website landing page, About Us page, or product or service pages; for presentations, meetings, e-mails, internal communications, and more—and of course, YouTube, but only if completely appropriate.

TRANSLATING VERBAL IDEAS INTO VISUALS

Like oral storytelling, the use of images to communicate predates written language. Think caveman drawings. Today, we're returning to the power of visuals in the form of photos, illustrations, charts, graphs, videos and much more. It's always been obvious that a picture is worth—well, not maybe a thousand words—but clearly, images make communication more effective, entertaining and memorable.

In "the old days," graphics were limited by expense and practicality. New reproduction processes have brought the costs of print graphics way down, but it's the Internet that has really revolutionized the possible. It costs virtually nothing but time to create simple visuals for online or print media. Free or inexpensive photographs are easily available with a little research. Even (some) clip art is better than it used to be and more easily customized. The only limits are your imagination and skill with technology that's ever easier to use.

Groups that research media effectiveness circulate startling statistics about how much more successful blogs, tweets, and even e-mails are when visuals are built in. Posts are far more likely to be opened, and material from tweets to white papers are much more often shared.

How can you come up with good visuals to support blogs, PowerPoint, reports or promotional materials? If you're a "word person," it's ideal to have a graphic-design colleague to work with. But today you can be your own art director, as well as your own editor and publisher, by adapting your mind-set.

To come up with an image, whatever the subject and medium, first clarify:

What you want to communicate

How you want the audience to respond

What you have to work with

Then think about the kind of visual that will work best for your purpose. In addition to photographs, illustrations, icons and maybe animated GIFs, remember that your toolbox includes typeface choices, color, and layout. The guiding principle always: Simplicity works.

Here are a few tactics to help you translate your ideas into visual form.

Consider what would make complex data and information more absorbable. A graph that changes to show a trend? A table or pie chart that makes the proportions visible for a survey or budget?

Review your content for theme. Is it a concept like "streamlining" or "improving," for example? Look for a graphic that conveys that concept.

Illustrate a point with contrasts. If you're talking about the impact of poor agricultural technique on land, for example, show a field that demonstrates the result and perhaps a contrasting field where better techniques were used.

Think about what the central idea resembles or feels like. A post that talks about how hard it is to meet self-imposed deadlines might be visualized as a person pushing a rock up a hill; a group of kids scrambling after a moving target; a trapeze artist reaching for a bar or set of hands; or three coffee cups and a pile of crumpled papers.

Use image resource sites. Then look for a suitable illustration, photo, icon or vector (primitive-style abstract illustration) to illustrate your concept. The Internet offers a huge array of image resources. Some are free and cleared for use, like Flickr and Wikimedia Commons. Paid but affordable resources include Google Images, Shutterstock, Veer, and GraphicRiver. Some will customize images at reasonable price. Depending on the site you can look up a subject, like "giraffe," or a concept—like lateness, decision making, confusion, profitability, communication—and find hundreds of possibilities. (Yes, it's time-consuming.)

Scout image sites and work backward. Spend some time browsing one or more of these sites, and save images that suggest visual ideas that resonate with your current project or may apply to a future one.

Limit yourself to one image style throughout a presentation. It rarely works to mix cartoons, photos and vectors.

Once you have a good image candidate for your e-book, slide or blog, juggle it against your headline words so they work to reinforce each other and make your message more fun. For example, choose the trapeze image for the blog about deadlines and write, "Reaching Those Deadlines: 10 Ways to Make Sure You Don't Miss." Use a photo of kids running with one of them moving in the opposite direction and write, "Deadlines: How to Keep Moving in the Right Direction." Or use the uphill rock image: "Meeting Deadlines: Why So Hard? Five Ways to Lighten the Load."

A sophisticated kind of visualization is the infographic, which integrates an idea, theme, or set of facts into a substantial, visually driven document. See Chapter 9 for more on this.

PRACTICE OPPORTUNITIES

I. Write Your Elevator Speech

Create your own 15- to 20-second elevator speech based on the ideas in this chapter. Write and practice it so you can deliver it without referring to notes. Present it to the class and collect feedback; then revise it.

II. Group Activity: Develop Guidelines for Elevator Speeches

Together, listen to all the elevator speeches and pay attention to language, memorability, general impact and delivery style. When all have been presented, collaborate as a class, or in smaller groups, to develop a set of guidelines for effective elevator speeches based on the practical experience.

III. Analyze a Speech

Find a speech you like by a politician, a historical figure, a business leader, or someone you personally admire. Print it out and mark it up to identify the rhetorical devices and other tactics used, as described in this chapter or additional reading. Write a review 400 words or longer summarizing what you see as the most important takeaways about writing for oral delivery, illustrated by the specific speech you chose.

IV. A. Plan a PowerPoint Slide Deck

Drawing on methods suggested in this chapter, create a storyboard for a presentation your group will deliver to raise funds for a good cause you select—either an existing one or one you make up. Use either a paper and pen or computer, but fully develop your plan and content and describe the visuals.

IV. B. Present the Plan

Each group presents the plan to the class—which represents the management team—to request funding to further develop the ideas and create the actual presentation. Each class member evaluates the plans and votes on which to fund. Group discussion of what worked best.

V. Graphic Interpretation/Nonprofit

Pick a cause you personally believe in and come up with a practical visual idea to express the severity of the problem or need in a way that will connect with a specific audience.

VI. Graphic Interpretation/Corporate

Read the annual report of a company that interests you, or Warren Buffet's most recent one for Berkshire, and develop a set of visual ideas to support the facts and ideas for a slide show of 5 to 10 slides.

VII. Group Project: Plan a Video

Your subject: How to write a good proposal. Review the guidelines in Chapter 10 and decide on the most important points to make. Then use a simple storyboard or the two-column script approach to plan the audio and visual segments, together. Pretend you have a substantial budget. Brainstorm at each step about what visuals can be created or drawn upon to explain, illustrate and engage (e.g., still photos, documents, original footage). Write the script, including a strong lead and close, and minimize the words.

VIII. Group Discussion

Create a set of guiding principles for deciding when video, PowerPoint, or a speech without visuals is the best vehicle.

RESOURCES

Speechwriting

10 Steps to Writing A Vital Speech, by Fletcher Dean: Excellent readable and doable ideas from a top speech ghostwriter

On Speaking Well: How to Give a Speech With Style, Substance, and Clarity by Peggy Noonan: Personal advice and ideas from a great political speechwriter

How to Write & Give a Speech, by Joan Detz: A practical and down-to-earth how-to

Resonance, by Nancy Duarte: Very slick presentation mapping out the elements of specific great speeches

Americanrhetoric.com: Online speech bank with hundreds of speeches relating to current events, movies, historical figures, etc.

Cicero Speechwriting Awards, vsotd.com: Presents best speeches of the year

The Genard Method, www.genardmethod.com/blog-detail/author,3: Gary Genard's blog on "performance-based public speaking"

In-Person Training

Public speaking is best learned "live," with constructive criticism and practice. Consider Toastmaster International (http://www.toastmasters.org), where many business leaders started. Courses are also available at professional education programs in colleges and universities. Trainers are often people with theatrical, voice, or media experience. Learning to use your voice and feel comfortable in front of audiences is a terrific investment for virtually everyone.

PowerPoint Style Presentations

TED.com: Great examples of presentation techniques by specialists of every kind, many with good use of visuals

Slide.ology by Nancy Duarte and www.duarte.com

Presentation Zen by Garr Reynolds and www.presentationzen.com

Video

For helpful advice, try the websites of journalism schools.

Many colleges offer hands-on video training courses in their continuing and professional education departments.

Chapter 14

PUTTING JOURNALISM AND PUBLIC RELATIONS TECHNIQUES TO WORK FOR YOU

Professional Strategies, Techniques and Tips

LEARN HOW TO . . .

- Deliver your message in news releases
- Use energizing headlines and subheads
- Pitch editors
- Prepare talking points
- Use research and interviewing techniques

Don't tell me the moon is shining; show me the glint of light on broken glass.

—Anton Chekhov

REACHING YOUR AUDIENCES WITH THE "NEW" MEDIA RELEASES

They used to be called "press releases," "media releases" or "news releases" and often still are. But these labels are pretty narrow considering that today's readership is much broader than editors of traditional media and good subject matter goes far beyond "news." I'll just say "releases."

Most organizations and public relations agencies still prioritize this skill. Good media coverage remains invaluable, just as in the "old" days when print dominated. Then the goal was to pique editors' interest so they would cover a story or event, giving the subject free space—so much cheaper than paying to advertise in publications, television and radio.

The digital revolution hasn't killed the release—far from it. But it does transform the playing field and the players. The World Wide Web gives anyone with Internet access the chance to reach consumers, clients, the public, the media, or other audiences directly. And, of course, it gives all those audiences the ability to select what they want to know. Today, both those with something to say and those who want to read about it need not depend on the *media* to *mediate*: that is, filter the news and decide what's important and worth reporting.

This infinitely expands anyone's potential to sell, market, publicize. And it expands the pool of release writers. Getting word out is no longer just the province of PR professionals and big business. The opportunity is open to small businesses, professionals, and specialists of every kind, and ignoring that opportunity may mean losing to the competition.

In short, release-writing skills probably belong in your toolkit now or in the not-so-distant future. They give you power. Just like big established companies, small enterprises and individuals can post a release on a website, distribute it by e-mail or use an online service at little expense. Releases give you a stellar chance to establish relevance, relationships and expertise—and sell a product or service.

Further, the once-separate domains of PR, marketing, advertising, branding, customer service and social media are integrating fast. In today's world they're all **content.** For a small enterprise, melding outreach efforts is a no-brainer. Issuing releases can help develop a business—and releases contribute nicely to search engine success. An online media room is an essential part of many websites these days.

The not so good news is that while creating a release is far from rocket science, the field is intensely competitive. Today's professional communicators must produce really good releases and so must a nonprofessional. Here's how.

New Goals, New Audiences

In the old days, when editors and reporters were the targets, the general goal was to interest them in covering a story or event. "Newsworthy" was the mantra. PR people tried for "hard news" subjects that were important or could be made to look that way. They included just enough information to reel the reporter in.

Today traditional media is still with us, and many editors still scout releases for leads. Additionally, the Internet harbors an exploding array of publications, news sources, bloggers and video outlets—nearly all hungry for content. Everyone is looking for good material and releases are important sources.

And millions of people look for and read news releases themselves, online. They want news, ideas, events and insights that interest them. They may regularly tune in to a brand or pastime they're passionate about—like Nike or the NFL—or search for a release by subject: the same way we find how-to material or opinions about a movie or restaurant or plumber.

People don't much care about the difference between delivery channels and formats: blog, video, release, whatever. They want information.

So the potential audience for releases is vast. As in all communication, the most effective releases are written to accomplish specific goals with specific audiences.

Today's Perspective

If I was down to my last dollar, I would spend it on public relations.

—Bill Gates

Once upon a time, releases were typically written more or less as announcements and rigidly formatted. Editors were expected to follow up for more information. Now, it's usually better to supply a complete ready-to-use story and not restrict it to format limitations.

A ready-to-use piece is much more likely to be picked up by all but the most major print or online channels. A release you post yourself must be informative, relevant and engaging. As with every other mode of written communication, accept that no one is breathlessly waiting for your news. You must take the trouble to interest people.

Ideas about appropriate subject matter are changing, too. While "news" is still important, "feature" material is at least as important—and badly needed. Think about all those outlets trying to keep their followers happy and loyal in the face of so many reading choices.

So when you write a release, rather than trying to think like a PR person, think like a journalist. Do the planning that goes into a good story: Identify a good subject, figure out what to include, dig for what you don't know and find a strong angle. Edit carefully. It's not so different than writing for other media, especially blogs, so the ideas presented in Chapter 12 apply here—and vice versa.

Here's how to use the basic planning structure detailed in Chapter 2.

First, be very clear on both your immediate goals—who you want to reach and what you want them to do.

Beyond accomplishing immediate goals, releases should contribute to long-range ones. For example:

- Build a positive image for the public, the staff, media, investors and other stakeholders.
- Establish expertise and authority.
- Build the brand to support sales and promote goodwill.
- Establish good relations with the media and public to insulate the organization from attack or criticism.
- Raise money (usually the imperative for nonprofits).

Review or brainstorm your basic communication goals, which should directly relate to the organization's business goals. It's essential to *know your core message*: Who are you? What do you do and why? What problem do you solve? Why should people care? This message should underlie all your communication.

When and How to Write Releases

Each company or nonprofit has its own identity, personality and attributes, all resources to mine for leads. The basic questions apply: What's happening? What's being done? What's changing? Why does it matter?

Some common reasons to produce a release:

Events:

- Publicize in advance to attract people and/or media to them.
- Publicize after the fact to reach wider audiences.

Share news:

- Staff achievements and recognition
- Organization milestones
- Good deeds—scholarship awards, charity drives, participation in a good cause, grants to organizations or individuals
- News such as results of an initiative, financial performance, celebrity involvement, important hires, new products, acquisitions, new communication channels, new locations, contest winners—and bad news, as early as possible

Thought leadership: Share new ideas, facts, solutions and opinions through:

- White papers and position papers
- Blogs
- Survey and research results
- Solutions to customer problems

Share "inside" information:

- How a product or service was developed
- Technical specs of new products
- New direction or strategy
- First-alert news

Invite people to ask questions and participate in . . .

- Contests and competitions
- Surveys
- Sharing photos or ideas

An announcement-type release may just need to be well written, complete and correct. But non-"spot-news" releases must be engaging and relevant to capture your intended audience.

VIEW FROM THE FIELD: HOW TO CREATE ENGAGING RELEASES FOR TODAY'S AUDIENCES

I look at releases in two categories. One is the "milestone momentum" release about an achievement, an award, a designation—they're important because it shows a pulse: that something is going on. Also an organization's online media center may be the only place where visitors see fresh content.

The second category is the thought leadership release, which take a point of view. These releases are targeted less to journalists than to the audience you're trying to reach—the end users. Unless you're Apple, whose new product announcements can be earth shattering, you need to find your angle: some specific interesting thing people will gravitate toward.

The approach I like is to tell a story—to be journalistic. I try to learn as much as I can about the client and product, what's most important. Often the sales team knows this—they may tell me, for example, "This system is about being able to recover data after a disaster." You can weave that nugget and lead with tips, guidance, or best practice—things people actually find useful.

Don't bury the lead! Big publicly traded companies may need to put out a high volume of releases with just the dull facts but often miss opportunities to shine—when a new product is put out, for example—by burying it in industry jargon and acronyms. Small start-ups can level the playing field by promoting benefits. Nonprofits can use releases as a rallying cry and create messages that convey emotion.

Try to target releases so people know the event or product is for them: for example, "Business owners and executives are encouraged to attend . . . " This helps for Google searches, too. And look for chances to embed or link to video or an infographic, and use good images to illustrate a complex idea.

—Arthur Germain, principal and chief brandteller for
Communication Strategy Group, a brand storytelling agency

Example of a Storytelling Release

Here's the beginning of a release Communications Strategy Group recently developed for a client, ICC—Information Control Company—an IT service provider.

COLUMBUS, Ohio, July 9, 2014/PRNewswire—Most employees are not fully engaged in their work and this spells trouble for businesses already under greater pressure than ever before to grow, according to Steven Glaser, CEO of ICC. Part of the challenge is that the makeup of today's workforce is shifting—to a younger demographic with different work styles, business requirements and skill sets.

To guide HR professionals and others involved in hiring and managing enterprise workforces, ICC, the business and IT solutions company that correctly predicted the 2014 Oscars and designs collaboration solutions for today's workforce, has outlined Four Ways Businesses Must Engage Employees Today to Remain Relevant to the Workforce of Tomorrow.

"Engaged employees—especially Millennials—are the future of business. But they are not engaged," says Glaser. "This has to change. Without them there will not be anyone to replace Baby Boomers who are beginning to retire en masse."

The release goes on to cite Gallup statistics on employee engagement, four ways to work more successfully with Millennials, and ways to get more information.

How to Make Releases Interesting

The most damning revelation you can make about yourself is that you do not know what is interesting and what is not.

—Kurt Vonnegut, novelist

To persuade an editor to read your release, assume you have six seconds. So make a relevant or interesting point quickly. Many writers focus so hard on correct formatting that they forget the new cardinal sin: being non-newsworthy and/or boring—especially in the headline and lead.

In teaching new PR professionals from other countries, I find this point hard to get across. PR practices differ from place to place and many non-Westerners see the release as an "official" one-way statement from a government or company. But in truth, there are no captive audiences anywhere: Every reader must be earned.

Here are some ways to be interesting.

Target specific media, understand *their* goals and audience, then tailor to their needs. A local newspaper prefers a local angle; a national one needs broad appeal. Television needs strong visuals. Both TV and radio like good interview prospects. Magazines each have their own personality and mission, and you can figure that out by reviewing a few issues. A blogger may welcome special access—an advance copy of your new gizmo to use and report on, a technical specialist to interview. To generate a ton of ideas, study your target media and figure out what *they* want to give *their* audiences.

Find a human angle. Who made the discovery or founded the nonprofit or company—is there an intriguing backstory? What's special about the new CEO as a person? Show how someone used your product or service and benefited. Did the new device change someone's life? People are interested in people. Reporters look for someone to personify the story and so should you.

Tell people what's new and why it's important to them. Will it save them time, money? Improve their lives in some way? Solve a problem? Case histories work well. Events will attract readers if you make it clear why they're relevant. Post-event releases can work if you report on what actually happened that was worth knowing, preferably with visuals.

Include great quotes. Never waste valuable release space on dull quotes you make up or generic ones that carry no emotion or conviction. Don't use them to communicate information you could provide yourself. The right quotes liven things up with a personal viewpoint or emotion.

Give the facts *perspective*. Facts, data, and specs are not in themselves interesting except to the most technical readers. People aren't hungry for more information— we want to know what things *mean*. Find a big picture to present. Does your product or service or event relate to a trend? Will it affect people's lives? Change their thinking?

Connect to what's hot. Monitor the news for events that make your product matter. If it's hurricane season, people are primed to learn about your tree inspection service. If cold weather is coming, promote your heated earmuffs. Most editors still look for seasonal material that ties to holidays, graduation, arrival of spring, and so on.

Connect to a social cause or charitable initiative you support. If people care about an organization or good cause, they will respect your contributions to it. An individual can also use this approach: for example, offer a local charity a free computer checkup, or donate time to teach elderly people to use social media. Ideally, reach out to causes that align with what you do.

Supply visuals. Publications *love* images, both for print or online, and you multiply your chances of getting noticed both by the media and online readers if your release comes with photographs, video clips, charts and graphs, and/or infographics. This does not mean clip art and random unrelated material, both of which irritate people.

Create news worth knowing. Sponsor a survey and share the results. You can run a small inexpensive survey yourself on social media or through a service like SurveyMonkey. Or invent an award to present to leaders in your field, or an event. If you sell books, for example, or support a nonprofit that promotes literacy, sponsor a book donation event for a cash-strapped library.

If you work with more than a few people, build a news pipeline inside your organization. It can be amazingly hard to find out what's happening in your work community. Those with PR responsibility for a unit or company typically spend time educating other people on what to share and give them a super-easy way to do it.

Assembling a Release

Here are the standard elements of a traditional release.

Organization name or logo

Contact info: A person, preferably available 24/7 with numbers to call and e-mail

Place and release date

Headline: About 50 to 70 characters that say what your subject is, concisely and accurately

Subhead: Optional—can be longer than headline and provide intriguing details or say why the subject matters

Lead: Your first paragraph—designed to engage your target audience

Second paragraph: Adds any necessary detail about who, what, when, where, why (the traditional 5 Ws)

Third paragraph: Sums up the story's import—why readers should care (editors call this the "nut graf")

Fourth paragraph: Relevant quote from a significant involved person

Call to action: What you want the reader to do

Boilerplate: A pithy description of the organization that positions it

Cover all this in one page—or one and a half at most. Do you need to follow this format slavishly? No. You might change the order of the elements, as long as you create a logical flow, and use more or fewer paragraphs depending on your content. The option of distributing releases online, coupled with the newer story-telling focus, means you can further loosen up on presentation. It's often more important for the lead to hook the reader rather than stick to the 5 Ws. In an e-release, contact information can be positioned at the end.

But if you're specifically pitching the media, be rather conservative about upending the format. Editors are used to scanning information in a familiar way.

If you're delivering online, consider linking directly to images, video, your website or blog, and other resources—but don't overload with links that pull readers away from your main message.

And be aware of search engine optimization (SEO) when you distribute releases online—figure out the best phrases to use and be sure they're included. Ideally, use them up front in the headline and lead, and work them in right at the beginning of each.

Be sure your story or announcement delivers the heart of your message and answers the obvious questions, even though concisely. Try the talking points method later in this chapter to help plan the release, and check that the important points are covered before sending and are logically sequenced.

SUCCESS TIP

HOW TO BEST REACH THE MEDIA

A 2014 survey by Business Wire, a press release distribution service, came up with surprising results: of the 300+ reporters surveyed, 69% preferred receiving story pitches via e-mail alerts, 22% preferred press releases, and social media was cited by only 1.1%. Corporate websites and online newsrooms continue to be top destinations for company-specific information. However, 74% said they use social media for research—Facebook, Twitter and LinkedIn about equally. (At the same time, it is important to know that PR people leverage social media contact to connect with reporters and editors.)

What Works, What Doesn't: An Example

Here are two releases promoting the same event to editors.

Version 1

MaryJo Bullet
777-222-4444 (9 to 5)
777-222-5555 (24/7 cell)

School Schedules Beach Cleanup for April 10th

April 1, 20xx—On April 10th, 20xx, from 10:00 a.m. to noon, kindergarten students from John B. Whiting Elementary School in the North Point community will participate in a cleanup of Pitter Beach, it has been announced by Emma Jones, director of Whiting's Coordinating Council of Community Outreach, and Jack Smith, executive director of the Council for Marine Education.

During the course of the morning, the students will rake the sand, enjoy a play activity, and eat lunch.

Dr. Jones says, "We are pleased to introduce our youngest students to the responsibilities of citizenship and a formal appreciation of the marine environment. The day should prove an excellent educational opportunity and enhance our curriculum."

Several local businesses are contributing support . . . etc.

Version 2

Kindergartners to Clean Up Pitter Beach on April 10

Whiting's smallest students will collect debris, build sand castles, and meet marine creatures face to face

Armed with pint-size rakes and pails, three dozen five-year-olds will converge on Pitter Beach April 10th to clean the debris left behind by a rough winter. Called the First Spring Sweep, the morning event is organized by John B. Whiting Elementary School and the Council for Marine Education.

"The children are so thrilled to be given real responsibility," said Charmaine Fox, who teaches one of the classes. "They've been studying the ocean for months and can't wait to do their part to make our local beach beautiful."

In addition to a garbage weigh-in and a sand castle contest, the schedule includes a special surprise: Dr. Mark Rice, a marine biologist, will participate and introduce the children to a crab, a lobster, a sea turtle and other ocean friends.

Local business have contributed . . . etc.

MEMBERS OF THE MEDIA ARE INVITED!

Children may be interviewed.

The schedule:

10:00 a.m. to 11:00 a.m.	Cleaning up in teams of five
11:00 a.m.:	Weighing the collected debris
11:15 to noon:	Building sand castles
Noon:	Picnicking and learning about sea animals with Dr. Rice

If you were a newspaper editor, which release would lure you to cover the cleanup? If you agree that Version 2 is more effective, consider some of the reasons:

Version 1 uses:

- A matter of fact recital that doesn't mention much of interest, or buries it
- A dull headline
- A lead wasted on boring unnecessary detail
- An uninspiring quote that sounds manufactured

Version 2 uses:

- A headline and subhead that create a graphic image of the activities
- A lead that makes the most of the event's cuteness appeal
- A genuine-sounding quote that underscores the event's interest
- A direct invitation plus a schedule, which highlights the fun stuff and alerts reporters and video teams to great visual potential and when to show up

It's true that you need to get your 5 Ws across in a release—but not in the first sentence and not at the expense of making whatever you're covering sound interesting. The example may seem obvious, but at least 75% of the releases I see, whatever the subject, look more like Version 1 than 2.

SUCCESS TIP

DIG FOR WHAT'S INTERESTING

If you think the beach cleanup specifics in Version 2 gave the writer an unfair advantage, and Writer #1 wasn't informed, here's the question: Whose fault is that? When you write a release for your company or anyone else—*or write almost anything*—the first command is to inform yourself: Dig to discover what's important and interesting. Most people won't tell you because they don't know! It's often up to the writer to figure it out. Further, the best PR specialists help shape events to provide better publicity potential—and improve the events.

Format, Style and Language Tips

What is the inverted pyramid? Do you need it?

Traditional release writing starts with what matters most and works down to what matters least. This allowed editors and press operators to cut from the bottom as needed without losing the article's sense. It's a good idea in releases and most writing. Readers' interest tails off, so this style ensures that the most important material is delivered.

The right writing style?

You're ideally wearing the reporter's hat, so sound objective, neutral and nonpromotional. Make your case with facts and solid ideas. *Do not treat this as an advertisement or opportunity to self-promote.* Write in the third person, except for quotes. Write as simply and clearly as you can with short words, sentences, paragraphs. No acronyms, jargon, clichés, and minimal adverbs and adjectives.

How long?

Aim generally for one to one and a half pages, typed single-spaced in a 10- to 12-point serif font. Writing block style—skipping a line between paragraphs rather than indenting—makes for better readability. Some online distributors charge more for posting releases that run long—for example, over 495 words—so take that into account.

Do visuals count?

Yes, yes, yes. Embed photos, charts, graphs, infographics—whatever helps tell your story in ways that work with and beyond words.

Will readers forgive spelling mistakes and other carelessness?

No, no, no. You shoot your credibility. Review, edit, proof. This must be your writing at its best and most correct.

ASSEMBLING A PERSONAL PITCH

Often you need to create a shorter pitch than a release, either to deliver by e-mail or via a telephone conversation. Aim for brief and concise: 150 words are usually more than enough—your goal is to spark interest, not deliver all the information. Bullet points may work. Aim to let the reporter know why you're contacting her, how your subject relates to her audience, and how to follow up.

Use the subject line space for a headline—and make it good, because the pitch won't be read otherwise. It's best to know who you're writing to and why he's the right person to pitch. PR specialists work to build relationships with editors and bloggers. Following them on Twitter or LinkedIn is a good way to know what interests them and develop a connection.

Personalize the message by introducing yourself and reference any connection. For example:

Subject: Alert: Kindergartners Cleaning up Pitter Beach Next Monday

Hi Joe,

We meet periodically when you cover Northpoint school board meetings—I handle communications for the district.

On April 10th at 10:00 a.m., 45 adorable kindergartners will wield their pint-size rakes and clean the winter debris from Pitter Beach. The highlights:

- Raking it all up
- Weighing the garbage
- Building sand castles
- Meeting marine animals face to face with a marine biologist

Great seasonal story with cute photo ops! You're invited! And welcome to talk to the kids. Would you like details and the morning's schedule?

Best,
MaryJo

When you don't know the person—if you're introducing yourself to a blogger, for example, who might review your product—say something more like,

Subject: PITCH: Launching new package openers for the kitchen.

Hi Jennifer—I'm a big fan of your blog and read it regularly. I especially liked your report on new cooking tools last week. I expect you're working on the Christmas gadget roundup and want to offer you a KitchenBreaker: it's a brand new package opener for people with weak hands, a great gift for . . .

It's important to familiarize yourself with the blogger's work and let her know that. Saying something nice that is specific goes a long way. A telephone pitch can be delivered along similar lines. Introduce yourself very concisely and present the gist of your pitch. If you're talking to the right person you needn't explain why she should be interested, but be sure you provide a clear picture of the event, product or idea as soon as possible. Take care to verse yourself thoroughly in the subject so you can carry on a good conversation if you have the chance. Try the talking points method explained in this chapter.

SUCCESS TIP

HOW TO PITCH BLOGGERS

The Internet gifts us with millions of bloggers who may lack formal journalism training but may be nonetheless highly influential in their niches. Collectively they represent an unprecedented chance to reach a specific audience with your idea, product or service.

Pitch them as you would professional editors—here too, start by researching their interests, subject matter and tone. Take trouble to understand how they define their readers and what they aim to give them. Additionally:

Join the conversation. Connect by commenting on their blogs and perhaps retweeting them. If you offer sincere compliments on their content and enthusiastic input, it will be noticed. If you can act as a resource and contribute useful information, do so.

Write in line with the blog world's informality. A friendly, breezy, conversational tone works best when you communicate with most bloggers. Be as concise as you can. Take time to make your subject lines catchy, funny or creative.

Personalize your communication. Mass pitches do not work here. Don't try to interest hundreds of bloggers—identify those with the most influence and invest your time into knowing how to relate what you want with what they need.

USING MAGNETIC HEADLINES AND SUBHEADS

Here is a classic piece of advice: See headlines as flags to wave at people who are whooshing by on a train. You have a second or two to attract their attention, so what words will accomplish that?

Whatever medium you write for, the first challenge is to gain reader attention. Headlines are an essential way to accomplish this. In e-mail, the subject line is your headline and determines whether people read the message or not. The same is true for releases, reports, white papers, proposals, articles, blogs, marketing materials, websites and more.

The guiding rule: Use what is most exciting and worthy of attention to turn scanners into readers.

For releases, similarly to an article or blog post, make headlines

- brief (about 50 to 70 characters),
- specific and accurate (capsulize the material honestly),
- curiosity-provoking (to pull people into the material), and
- connected to target readers (take account of the basic universal question, what's in it for me?).

Journalists learn to build headlines on action verbs to convey that something is happening—static information is of scant interest in the news world. For example:

House Sales Zoom in First Quarter and Economists Cheer

Is less snooze-worthy than:

First Quarter House Sale Figures Are Higher, Say Economists

The latter headline sounds passive and dull. Here's an even worse one:

First Quarter House Sales

This one isn't a headline at all; it's just a topic heading or label. Such headings dominate the pages of most reports and other long-form documents. Don't they need interest-provoking headlines? Yes, they do! Use your headline writing skills to say something real—deliver a message—in all your writing. Good headlines bring many writing formats to life and set you on track to keep what follows on target.

But you can take liberties with the action verb rule as long as you trouble to instill an active feeling. A report headline, like a release or article, might say

First Quarter Report: House Sales Way, Way Up!

What about keywords and search terms? Know the ones that best match up with how your target audiences will find you, because that guides you to develop the right material. And use the words in the release and headline as practical. But don't make SEO the priority. It's more important to come up with graphic headlines that grab people, as long as you play fair and deliver what you promise.

Every headline can't be brilliant, but think through what you have to work with. For example, is there an element of surprise?

The Economists Goofed: House Sales Fly Higher for First Quarter

Is there an "inside information" or "first to tell you" angle?

Early-Bird Word on House Sales: Our Survey Shows Unexpected Jump

Can you connect with readers on an emotional level?

Home Sale Streak Brings Hope to Anxious Sellers

With the advent of blogging, headline writing has drawn new attention because everyone wants his posts to stand out and be read. Various studies show what strategies succeed best online.

Here are some approaches you'll find familiar.

10 Ways to . . .

The Secret of . . .

What No One Knows About . . .

Six Strategies for . . .

Do You Know the 7 Signs of . . .

What No One Told You About . . .

Good News for . . .

Notice the focus on *benefits*. If what you're writing about may make the reader richer, happier, healthier, more successful, more efficient, less shy, etc., etc., flaunt it in the headline of your release or blog. But keep the promise.

The headline considered by many mavens to be the all time best:

How to Win Friends and Influence People

Who doesn't want to know both things? Dale Carnegie built a whole empire on that book title.

In contrast, here's the worst headline I've seen recently from a respected online news publication whose editors should know better:

Charter Schools Emerge as Proof of the Strategy of Putting a Priority On Student Achievement

Why so bad? It's hard to understand, passive, boring, and doesn't say much if anything . . . for starters. And notice all those prepositions.

Subheads can be used to amplify a headline and add value when the format allows. They give you another tool to attract attention and particularize a release or a story. For example:

Surprise! *House Sales Soar in First Quarter*

Reversing 2-Year Trend: *Existing homes sold 25% faster than same time last year. Why did economists miscalculate?*

Or, an alternative subhead to the same headline,

First-Time Buyers Account for 15% Rise in Numbers: *While purchases by retirees produce 10% increase*

Subheads are also extremely useful for sparking up long-form documents. Ditch the labels—

Fall technology rollout

And deliver a real message that when possible, is benefits oriented:

New Accounting Software Debuts This Fall: *Expense account invoices to process 40% faster*

A technical note: Headlines can be written either upper–lower case throughout as they are in this section, or you might prefer to just capitalize the first word, which some people feel looks more "modern." Subheads are best written lower case except for the first word.

And make friends with an online or print thesaurus when writing headlines and subheads. Notice the word variation in the foregoing headline examples. Don't expect to hold synonyms in your head—15 seconds' work will yield a lot more compelling choices than occur to you on your own.

TALKING POINTS: HOW TO CREATE AND USE THEM FOR MANY SITUATIONS

Another very helpful tool from the PR arsenal is the talking point document: a one-page rundown of the most critical points to remember when you face a challenging situation—on behalf of your organization or yourself. Don't bring this with you into a meeting, interview or other situation. The idea is to absorb it before the event. Its purpose is (1) to prepare you to field every question that you (and your team) can imagine and (2) to supply you with the points most worth introducing as opportunity allows.

A talking points sheet crystallizes the story you want to communicate in your terms and for organizations, is a way to align the stakeholders. Preparing these guides is a mainstay tactic in the corporate, political and government arenas—and a highly effective way to get ready for job interviews. Here's how to do them.

VIEW FROM THE FIELD: HOW TO CREATE TALKING POINTS

In professional communications, talking points—usually a few brief sentences to address a key topic for your organization—are the basis for every public conversation about policy and important issues within the organization. They ensure that everyone is on the same page and in agreement, because the points have been debated and vetted by company experts, including the legal department, if necessary.

Talking points are a key tool in preparing for an in-person presentation that may be controversial or hostile. As in government and politics, big companies depend hugely on talking points, especially when events open them to criticism. The approach is not often used by smaller businesses but offers an easy way for them to implement tactics and for individuals to present themselves optimally in interviews and public situations.

Compose talking points by asking the most logical questions you can ask about the subject matter—as many as you can—and then come up with good, clear, concise answers. Put yourself in the mind of the interested parties and think about the questions they are likely to raise. Act like an investigative reporter familiar with the subject and think of what he or she would ask, and write the answers. Remember that in the logic of an investigative interview, one question leads to another, a follow-up question. Often, the logic is the logic of "if–then" questions.

Begin by anticipating the questions that worry you most, especially the one you dread—it's the most important. Find out anything you need to know to develop an answer to that question. Other questions—and their answers—grow out of that process and help bolster your key message. Combined, they result in a balanced communication.

When positioning is involved, frame the answers the way you want them perceived. The entire project should be based on a communications strategy with objectives, goals and tactics. You want to persuade and influence but with accurate, factual, and verified data so no one can poke a hole in it.

Thus, an approach often used to tell a positive story about your organization, product or service is to take the offense. Draft your key messages in a conversational voice, prioritize these "selling points," and be sure to include them in your interview with your "defensive" talking points. Beware of the unintended interpretation of a statement. Be sure that what you say could not be misinterpreted in a pejorative way.

(Continued)

(Continued)

If you're going into a job interview, create talking points to present and position yourself so you share your strengths, the value you'll bring to the organization, and the reason you should be hired. Limit yourself to a one-page sheet with a sentence or two at the most for each point: just enough words to remind you of the point you want to make more fully in person. Do the same if you're selling something or introducing yourself with an elevator speech. Just as for press briefings, the talking points become a type of script.

Don't underestimate the time it takes to come up with thoughtful questions and phrase good answers.

—Ken Koprowski, communications consultant, writer and professor

GATHERING GOOD INFORMATION: RESEARCH AND INTERVIEW TECHNIQUES

Nothing beats solid substance in everything you write: good information, well-thought-out ideas, evidence for your claims or arguments. Fortunately, today it's easier to do research than ever before.

Basic Research Techniques

When I recently threw out a few tons of old papers, I came across a fat packet I'd saved for years—hundreds of print and online resources and directions for using them. Today, just as for most professionals I know, my research starts with Google and Wikipedia. Endless specialized resources and search engines still exist, of course, and you should know those that relate to your field. Some valuable ones are listed next. But realistically, you'll probably use the new basics frequently and they work well, with an important caveat: You must evaluate what you find:

1. **Don't trust popular "secondary" sources quoted on Wikipedia or by media.** The bigger the audience aimed at, the less accurate the citations are likely to be. Popular media is likely to jazz up information—on surveys and research, for example—and assume people won't know the difference. Therefore . . .

2. **Chase down the original source the material was based on.** You may often find it inaccurately quoted by the secondary source. If you're suspicious of the original source, look for corroboration elsewhere.

3. **Evaluate credibility.** Look at the writer's position in the field, how other professionals regard the person, what the person has accomplished. In the science world, some recent high-profile cases revealed that some respected researchers' work was faked; so be skeptical, even of peer-reviewed journals. Look also at the dates when the material was issued.

Some resources to know about: Free unless otherwise noted

Additional general search engines—Bing.com, Ask.com

Statista.com: Statistics "portal" to government, organizations, market researchers, specialized publications (basic account is free)

RefDesk.com: Library desk-like index to web-based resources notably including newspapers from the United States and around the world

Encylopedia.com: Includes pictures, facts and video

Dictionary.com, which defines and also answers grammar questions

LibrarySpot.com: Endless leads to more information sources

Infoplease.com: Research and reference help

CIA World Factbook (www.cia.gov/library/publications/the-world-factbook): In-depth data on the countries of the world

Quora.com: Personalized information feed and Q&A sharing on a ton of topics

Hoovers.com: Business information (by subscription)

How to Ask Good Questions

Interviewing is a critical skill for reporters, PR professionals and businesspeople in every field. Beyond its preeminence for PR and journalism purposes, interviewing skills work wonders when you interact with specialists from designers to consultants, insurance agents to engineers.

Asking good questions enables you to make the most of learning opportunities and draw the best help from a mentor or a supervisor. And when you're the boss, it's your job to integrate diverse expertise and functions, plus make good matches when hiring. Knowing how to frame the right questions is an unsung but powerful leadership asset.

The following structure for creating questions and asking them is based on journalism strategies but adapts to many situations and contexts. Consider that you often need to ask good questions of yourself!

Steps to Good Interviewing

Before the Interview or Conversation

1. **Do some homework.** Ask your subject for materials to read, or find material on the Internet. Look for the natural keywords and phrases common to the subject and if you don't know what they mean, Google them, so you can be an intelligent listener.

2. **Brainstorm the questions**, based on what you've read and what you want or need to know. Make them open-ended, not answerable with a yes or no. Many questions work in myriad scenarios—see the following Success Tip box. Also devise sharp customized questions particular to the subject, your needs, and the individual's know-how. *Most specialists love to expound on their subject to an interested audience and enjoy questions that make them stop and think.*

SUCCESS TIP

ASK A GOOD QUESTION . . .

And you'll get a good answer. Here are some of my favorites for eliciting information from specialists, from businesspeople to scientists.

- What's the goal? How will this work solve a problem, contribute, etc.?
- Can you give me an example of that?
- What's most important to understand about this?
- Why does it matter?
- How did you figure it out? How do you know that?
- What will change if the problem is solved, product produced, people understand more, etc.?
- What do you believe will happen next? Or what are the next steps?

- How do you see the future as it relates to X?
- What surprised you?

If you're interested in drawing a personal response rather than just the cold plain facts, try a question or two like these late in the exchange:

- "How does it feel to have accomplished X?"
- "What is your vision of the future?"
- "Where will you go from here?"

To be sure you didn't miss anything:

- "What do you wish I had asked you?"
- "What do you wish people knew or understood better?"

Shuffle your questions into a logical, natural order so that each leads to the next. Take account of the time frame. If it's short, key in on your most critical questions. I once interviewed Hillary Clinton by telephone. Knowing I'd have about 45 seconds, I spent an hour fixing on the best three questions to draw the quote I needed for my article. It's okay to bring your list to a face-to-face session (not to job interviews), but look at them sparingly.

When interview time arrives:

4. **Take a minute to establish a trustful comfortable atmosphere.** Show interest and enthusiasm! A bored tone of voice elicits a bored and uninspired answer. If you can offer a preview of what you write before publication—to correct errors, not rewrite—say so. Reporters never agree to this but might offer approval rights of direct quotes.

   In face-to-face interviews, it helps to share *carefully monitored* information about yourself to create a conversational tone. Aim to maintain eye contact rather than staring at your screen or notepad.

5. **Explain what you want to know and why,** as appropriate. Share the parameters of your interest—for example, that you plan to focus on how Product Y was created (so he doesn't worry you'll ask about the current IRS audit of company books and focuses on what you need). Tell him how you'll use the information, too.

6. **Begin with a big-picture question so you don't limit the conversation to your existing knowledge:** "What's important about this decision?" or "I was especially interested to hear what you think about . . . " Or "What's most important for me (or the stockholders, etc.) to know?" But be sure to show you've done your homework.

7. **Follow the conversation.** A good interview or fact-finding mission succeeds best as a conversation. Be an active listener, mindful that unless you're face-to-face or using a visual communication system, the person can't see your expression or gestures. So cue with your most interested expression and vocal signals as you feel is personally appropriate—*Aha! Hmm!* Listen and frame follow-up questions based on the interaction.

8. **Try not to interrupt a specialist** unless he's becoming irrelevant. The best information comes from people when they follow their own enthusiasm and feel interested in the interaction, as opposed to

lecturing a novice who asks basic boring questions and distracts them from the point.

9. **But clarify as necessary:** Can you explain that another way? Do you have an example? I hear you saying X—do I understand correctly? Or be direct: Can you clarify that? But nearly always, an interviewee will repeat the same point on his own, using different language, so you catch up on what you missed later.

10. **When the conversation starts to wind down,** scan your question list to see if anything important remains uncovered or you still don't understand something that matters and need to ask about it. If you have any personal or "bombshell" questions, leave them for last. Though if you're interviewing the CEO or a client, better to skip them altogether.

About note-taking: It's best not to trust your memory, so use what works for the situation. If you type or scribble notes on the spot, review them ASAP while the person's voice is fresh in your mind. If you record, you'll need to transcribe, but it's good backup. Some reporters like to video record interviews so they can refresh their memories of expressions and gestures.

WRITING ARTICLES

Articles for publications, whether print or online, can be seen as relatively formal, in-depth treatments of a subject. They are valuable for establishing authority and credibility in most professions. While article writing is beyond this book's scope, most of the techniques are covered in various chapters: storytelling, blogging and news release tools all apply.

Here is one journalist's view of how to integrate information into articles people want to read.

VIEW FROM THE FIELD: A JOURNALIST'S ADVICE ON HOW TO TELL YOUR STORY

The challenge in my work is to integrate diverse kinds of information and explain everything clearly. It must be engaging, so we ask, what part of the story is most interesting? The test results? History? Related news? Writers must be aware of the range of tools and choose the most appropriate.

Figure out what you would tell your husband or daughter—the "Hey, Martha" moment. For the lead, ask, how do I begin the conversation? What would pique my own interest? That's your beginning point, but know your audience—what they care about, their values.

And know yourself how good a guide you are to what's interesting and your own biases and prejudices. Consult other people so you have different perspectives on what's interesting. For example, we know that some kinds of shopping advice may be very interesting for women but less so for men. Appeal to different demographics with a broad spectrum.

Write with clear, declarative sentences so language doesn't get in the way of a message. Headlines and captions must be interesting and work with the message but not repeat the information. Avoid jargon wherever possible and if something won't be familiar to readers, interpret it for them.

To bring things alive for readers we'll illuminate interesting points with information nuggets. And for investigative articles, like one on financial traps coming out of the recession that caused people to lose their houses, we'll use personal stories about people who were hurt or helped. We also dig into the research for a broader context and to find something people don't know.

Never skew information to make your point. Everything is helped by transparency and credibility; find the other side.

—Robert Tiernan, managing editor of
Consumer Reports; former editor at *Newsday*

PRACTICE OPPORTUNITIES

I. Headline Writing

Rewrite the headline and subhead for the kindergarten beach event five different ways. You may make up additional information and event features, but keep it realistic.

II. Write a News Release

Pick a major project that you accomplished at work or school or participated in for a good cause. Select a target place to "send" it: for example, an industry or campus publication, a blog, your own website. Write a complete draft with all the elements in place and format it for delivery.

III. Write a Pitch to a Blogger

Pick a blog you read regularly, or find a blogger who covers a subject that particularly interests you. Think of something you can contribute—a substantial comment—on a least one post, and write it. Then compose a pitch proposing that the blogger cover an angle or idea or event you suggest. Try following through and report back to the class!

IV. Group Project: Define Good Headlines

In small groups, collaborate to collect five good headlines and five bad headlines in a variety of media. Analyze the features of the ones that worked—and those that didn't. Create an annotated list, specifying the characteristics of good headlines and what to avoid, with examples. One group (perhaps for extra credit) can aggregate the lists to serve as a complete reference resource for everyone.

V. Interview Practice and Release Writing

In pairs, randomly designated: Pretend you've been assigned by a local or campus magazine—or for a class publication—to write a story about the other person. Research your partner for background and leads, and plan the interview, framing good questions. Aim to discover what's interesting about the person—find an angle.

Conduct the interview.

Write a complete release about the person based on what you found out.

The releases can be collected and given as a complete package to each member of the class.

VI. Group Discussion: The Interview Experience

Share: What surprised you in the preceding set of activities? What was hard or easy? What did you learn about interviewing? What did you learn from being interviewed? What did reading all the releases show you about how to write an effective one?

VII. Class Debate

Consider: Are all people interesting if we dig deep enough? Ask the right questions? Persist? Support your opinion with anecdotal evidence from your own experience.

VIII. Compose Talking Points

Find a help wanted post that represents your dream job. Prepare talking points for that job interview. Look at the situation from the other person's perspective and write down every question you think the interviewer will ask, should ask, and may ask—especially the tough ones that you worry about. Write down your best answers, briefly—one or two sentences each. Absorb the ideas on your talking point sheet and practice how to answer the questions in person.

IX. Role-Play Interviewing

In pairs: Exchange the job posts you each chose in Activity VII. One person assumes the role of the human resources manager who will conduct the job interview, and makes up a good series of questions to ask the candidate. The candidate should prepare for the interview with his talking points and during the interview, find opportunities to introduce those answers if the questions didn't come up. Reverse roles and repeat.

SELECTED RESOURCES

The New Rules of Marketing & PR: How to Use Social Media, Online Video, Mobile Applications, Blogs, News Releases & Viral Marketing to Reach Buyers Directly, by David Meerman Scott. An up-to-date approach to dealing with the media and using PR tactics.

The Micro-Script Rues—It's not what people hear. It's what they repeat, by Bill Schley. How to create the perfect pitch to communicate an organization's core value in eight words or less. Fun and useful for website copywriting, marketing materials and many other purposes.

Blogs on Public Relations

PR Squared (www.pr-squared.com): "Conversations about social media and marketing" with a PR slant

Richard Edelman's 6.a.m. (www.edelman.com/p/6-a-m): PR trends, issues and insights from a leading pro, the CEO of Edelman

PR Newser (www.mediabistro.com/prnewser): "Your daily PR Release"—lively reporting on events, ideas and faux pas in the PR realm

The Bad Pitch blog (badpitch.blogspot.com): A fun way to see what doesn't work

PR News Blog (www.prnewsonline.com/prnewsblog): Commentary by people in the industry

PR in Your Pajamas (http://prinyourpajamas.com): "Practical Publicity for Entrepreneurs." Useful how-to advice

CommPro (www.commpro.biz): "Your destination for answers." Brings together commentary, news and analysis in PR, marketing, advertising investor relations, corporate communications and social media

In Conclusion

I hope you feel this book has fulfilled its promise—to help you become a more confident, capable and effective writer who enjoys writing more.

Apply the strategies with imagination and they will work in every medium, even those not yet invented. Whatever the delivery system and no matter its speed, the essentials of good communication won't change. Most important: Good writing rests on understanding your own goals and other people's viewpoints, motivations and values.

Use this book's thinking process to help you know what to say, and the technical tools that show you how to say it. Draw on the techniques presented throughout to monitor your own writing so you can keep improving.

Good writing gives you a way to stand out in todays's intensively competitive career place. Every bit of trouble you take to write well wins rewards. Keep practicing your skills because. . .

When your writing succeeds, you succeed.

Index

ABOUT THE AUTHOR

Natalie Canavor is a business writer, author and communications consultant. A former journalist, magazine editor and public relations professional, she has orginated programs throughout her career to help people write better. Today she presents practical workshops on writing-for-results to business and professional audiences and serves as an NYU adjunct professor. Her courses include corporate communications writing and message strategizing, as well as advanced writing seminars for the master's program in public relations and corporate communication.

Natalie also develops print and online projects for commercial clients. Her byline has appeared on hundreds of features and columns in the *New York Times, Newsday, Long Island Business News*, *Communication World* and a range of business and technical publications. For six years, she wrote a column on better writing for the International Association of Business Communicators, read by 15,000 professionals worldwide. Currently she writes and edits the magazine *Impact* for Ben-Gurion University of the Negev.

As a national magazine editor, she created a series of successful start-ups including *Today's Filmmaker, Videography,* and *Technical Photography*. As an organizational communicator, Natalie built a 14-person PR department for New York State's largest educational agency and counseled agency management on communication strategy; directed print, video, and e-media; and created communications-skills training programs for school leaders.

Natalie is also the author of *Business Writing for Dummies* and coauthor of a popular book for businesspeople, *The Truth About the New Rules of Business Writing*. Her work has earned dozens of national and international awards for feature articles, video scripts, websites and publications. She served two terms as president of an International Association of Business Communicators (IABC) chapter, which recognized her as Communicator of the Year, and was a founding officer of IABC's Heritage Region. Natalie is also a member of the Author's Guild and the American Society of Journalists and Authors.